JONATHAN EDWARDS

It has often been claimed that Jonathan Edwards (1703–58) was America's greatest philosopher and theologian. From literary criticism of his sermons to philosophical assessments of his metaphysics, there has been a burgeoning industry in Edwardsian studies, but there has been no one place where an exploration of the theology and philosophy of Edwards has been brought together.

2003 marks the tercentenary date of the birth of Jonathan Edwards. This book draws together specially commissioned contributions from distinguished philosophers and theologians from the USA and UK, to present new analytic philosophical and theological thinking on Edwards in a way that reflects Edwards's own concerns as well as those current in the academy.

For Angela and Claire

Jonathan Edwards

Philosophical Theologian

Edited by

PAUL HELM
University of London, UK

OLIVER D. CRISP
University of St Andrews, UK

 Routledge
Taylor & Francis Group

LONDON AND NEW YORK

First published 2003 by Ashgate Publishing

Reissued 2018 by Routledge
2 Park Square, Milton Park, Abingdon, Oxon OX14 4RN
711 Third Avenue, New York, NY 10017, USA

Routledge is an imprint of the Taylor & Francis Group, an informa business

Publisher's Note
The publisher has gone to great lengths to ensure the quality of this reprint but points out that some imperfections in the original copies may be apparent.

Disclaimer
The publisher has made every effort to trace copyright holders and welcomes correspondence from those they have been unable to contact.

Typeset in Times Roman by Bournemouth Colour Press, Parkstone, Dorset.

A Library of Congress record exists under LC control number: 2002042676

ISBN 13: 978-1-138-71135-8 (hbk)
ISBN 13: 978-1-138-71134-1 (pbk)
ISBN 13: 978-1-315-19985-6 (ebk)

Contents

Notes on the Contributors   vii
Introduction   ix

1   Jonathan Edwards on Hell   1
    Jonathan L. Kvanvig

2   Jonathan Edwards and the Doctrine of Hell   13
    William J. Wainwright

3   Edwards on Free Will   27
    Hugh J. McCann

4   A Forensic Dilemma: John Locke and Jonathan Edwards on Personal
    Identity   45
    Paul Helm

5   How 'Occasional' was Edwards's Occasionalism?   61
    Oliver D. Crisp

6   The Master Argument of *The Nature of True Virtue*   79
    Philip L. Quinn

7   Does Jonathan Edwards Use a Dispositional Ontology? A Response
    to Sang Hyun Lee   99
    Stephen R. Holmes

8   'One Alone Cannot be Excellent': Edwards on Divine Simplicity   115
    Amy Plantinga Pauw

9   Jonathan Edwards, John Henry Newman and non-Christian Religions   127
    Gerald R. McDermott

10   Salvation as Divinization: Jonathan Edwards, Gregory Palamas and
    the Theological Uses of Neoplatonism   139
    Michael J. McClymond

Index   161

Notes on the Contributors

Oliver D. Crisp is a Teaching Fellow in Theology at St Mary's College, University of St Andrews, UK.

Paul Helm is Professor Emeritus of the History and Philosophy of Religion, King's College, University of London, UK.

Stephen R. Holmes is Lecturer in Christian Doctrine, King's College, University of London, UK.

Jonathan L. Kvanvig is Professor of Philosophy, University of Missouri, Missouri, USA.

Hugh J. McCann is Professor of Philosophy, Texas A&M University, Texas, USA.

Michael J. McClymond is Assistant Professor of Theology, St Louis University, St Louis, USA.

Gerald R. McDermott is Associate Professor of Religion, Roanoke College, Virginia, USA.

Amy Plantinga Pauw is Henry P. Mobley, Jr Professor of Doctrinal Theology, Louisville Presbyterian Seminary, Kentucky, USA.

Philip L. Quinn is John A. O'Brien Professor of Philosophy, University of Notre Dame, Indiana, USA.

William J. Wainwright is Distinguished Professor of Philosophy, University of Wisconsin, Milwaukee, USA.

Introduction

It has often been claimed that Jonathan Edwards (1703–58) was America's greatest philosopher and theologian. Whether this is true or not, he was certainly a thinker of the first rank whose work continues to generate interest today. From literary criticism of his sermons to philosophical assessments of his metaphysics, there has been a burgeoning industry in Edwardsian studies since Perry Miller's seminal work, over half a century ago.[1] The two disciplines most central to Edwards's thought, theology and philosophy, have been well represented in this Edwardsian renaissance. In recent years there have been several book-length treatments of Edwards's thought, from a range of theologians, some of whom are represented in the present work.[2] A welcome development in the same period has been a greater interest shown in Edwards (at least a greater published interest), from analytic philosophers.[3] But there has not been one volume where central theological and philosophical concerns in Edwards's thought have been brought together in a way that reflects the confluence of scholars working in both these traditions. This volume is just such a contribution.

The Rehabilitation of Jonathan Edwards

Edwards lived at the beginning of the Enlightenment, a time of great intellectual ferment and political upheaval. And he was a man of his times in more than one respect. In his lifetime he was successively a college tutor, a Congregationalist minister, a revival preacher, a missionary and the President of Princeton. He wrote on 'natural' philosophy (natural science), philosophy, theology and apologetics, and left a considerable body of sermons. But he was not engaged in simply passing on a tradition. He was concerned to demonstrate the reasonableness and veracity of the Christian faith and of Reformed theology to his early Enlightenment contemporaries. To this end, he was not afraid to use all the intellectual tools he could find, since he believed that 'all truth is God's truth'.

It is this concatenation of different interests and the way in which he sought to recast traditional theological problems that has given rise to a number of misrepresentations of Edwards's intellectual project. There has been an enduring, popular picture of the 'evangelical Edwards', which is sometimes in danger of reducing the canon of Edwards's works to the *Religious Affections, David Brainerd's Diary* and some popular sermons. Then there have been those who took up Edwards's mantle in the late eighteenth and nineteenth centuries, but gradually moved away from his own thinking, in the development of the so-called 'New England' and, latterly, 'New Haven' schools of theology. As the seriousness of Edwards's Calvinism and severity and rigour of his approach to theological issues fell out of favour during this period, Edwards was seen by many as a figure of tragedy, one whose early philosophical and scientific promise was thwarted by his conversion and adherence to an antique and distasteful theological tradition. It was because his philosophy was thought to be harnessed to what was regarded as an unpalatable theological programme that during this period (and, indeed, until relatively recently) his philosophy was not taken as seriously as it might have been. But theologically, too, Edwards was out of fashion. By the early twentieth century German theology had swept away the theological conservatism that Edwards had staked his reputation on. His high view of Scripture, and the implications this had for every theological *locus*, was considered quite unacceptable.

It was Perry Miller who rehabilitated Edwards in the academy, but at the cost of distorting central concerns in his thought. Miller was not primarily concerned with Edwards the philosopher or theologian, but with Edwards as a transmitter of ideas, and as an American cultural icon. According to Miller's reading of Edwards, his Calvinism was not the message, but the medium. Edwards's work was not an attempt to make plain the way in which God glorifies himself in the history of the work of redemption; it was an immense cryptogram that had to be seen through, to the real meaning beyond. That real meaning, according to Miller, was Newtonian physics and empiricist philosophy, which sought to redraw how the world should be seen. Edwards was a man born out of time, whose contributions were so prescient of the modern age that the present day is only just beginning to catch up with him.

Miller's work is itself a fascinating example of the reconstruction of the past in the image of the present. As the English historian E. H. Carr once remarked, 'The historian is part of history. The point in the procession at which he finds himself determines his angle of vision over the past.'[4] The work that followed Miller's presentation was as much an attempt at redressing the balance in favour of the stated concerns of Edwards as it was a development out of Miller's restatement of the Edwardsian project as he saw it.

However, Miller was also a guiding light of the Yale critical edition of Edwards's works. And this legacy has been, and continues to be, a most fruitful one, for several reasons. Chief among these is the nature of the *corpus* of material Edwards left at his death. His sudden demise as a result of complications arising from a smallpox vaccination left his literary executors a considerable task. The principal problem was that the unpublished work was so diffuse, spread out over numerous notebooks, sermons and treatises, that it was impossible to publish everything in a form that would be acceptable to public tastes. It is perhaps this single issue that has raised more chimeras and false trails in Edwardsian literature than any other. For while the vast majority of Edwards's texts sat moulding in New England (and Scottish) libraries in the nineteenth and early twentieth centuries, battles raged about

Edwards's orthodoxy, and what secrets these manuscripts contained. The Yale edition of Edwards's works has in recent years begun to address this problem by making accessible a large portion of the unpublished works, like his *Miscellanies*, a semi-public inventory of essays and comments on theological issues. But also, the Yale edition of Edwards's works has brought serious commentary on Edwards's thought back to the fore. Editorial introductions by scholars like Paul Ramsey, John E. Smith, Wallace Anderson and Thomas Schafer, to name four, have added considerably to the sum of knowledge about Edwards's work.[5]

In the same period, theological reassessments have continued apace, many influenced by Sang Lee's characterization of Edwards's philosophical theology as a dynamic ontology of disposition and habit, rather than one in terms of substance and attribute.[6] Philosophical interest has been less abundant, but in the last twenty years there have appeared a number of articles and essays dealing with Edwards's theistic metaphysics and religious epistemology.[7] Today, Edwards is once again recognized as a force to be reckoned with, and a philosopher and theologian of creativity and acumen.

The Philosophy of Jonathan Edwards

Recent philosophical reflection on Edwards has usually involved taking issue with one or other aspect of his metaphysics, although there has been some interest in other areas of his thought, such as his use of philosophical analysis in the elucidation of Christian doctrine, his ethics and his epistemology (in this last regard, see for example Alvin Plantinga's *Warranted Christian Belief*). In the philosophical essays that follow, three of these areas, metaphysics, philosophical theology and ethics, are represented.

One of the reasons for a renewed philosophical interest in Edwards is the rise in the number of Anglo-American philosophers writing about matters pertaining to traditional theological subjects. These philosophers have tended to look to classical problems in theology and their exponents as providing the raw materials for an assessment of the coherence and rationality of Christian theology. One such recent line of argument has centred on the doctrine of hell. There has been a lively debate in the journals and in several monographs about the coherence of hell and its place in the scheme of Christian theology.[8] Jonathan L. Kvanvig has written the standard contemporary philosophical assessment of this doctrine, including a critique of Edwards's account of hell. Edwards wrote a great deal about hell, and took what, to many modern ears, sounds like an extremely strong line on the doctrine. Indeed, this has been one of the reasons for neglecting his theology. (Note the oft-anthologized sermon by Edwards, 'Sinners in the Hands of an Angry God'.)

The central strand to Kvanvig's argument depends upon the notion that there is an ontological gap between God and his creatures. God is of a different ontological kind than his creation (since he is necessary, eternal, and so on), and has a different moral status. Edwards claims that it is plausible that different kinds of things have a different moral worth, such that killing an ant carries a different moral payload from killing a human child. The difference between the divine moral status and the creaturely is far greater than between one creature and another, since God is of a different ontological kind from his creatures. He is a perfect being; creatures are not. It is this difference in status between God and his creatures that Kvanvig takes up in his criticism of Edwards's argument for a traditional concept of hell.

William Wainwright has also taken up this issue in the literature, in partial defence of Edwards.[9] He maintains that Edwards succeeds in showing that the punishment of the wicked is a necessary condition of God's exercising and manifesting his attributes and communicating himself to creatures. In addition, Edwards also provides good reasons for believing that 'all sin, as it is against God, is infinitely heinous and has infinite demerit'. Edwards's premises support the conclusion that all sin is infinitely heinous when considered objectively. But they do not entail that the guilt of all *sinners* is infinite and that they therefore deserve infinite punishment. Wainwright concludes by considering Edwards's response to the charge that God acts unfairly in punishing some while sparing others who are equally undeserving. He argues that the success of any response depends upon which model of the divine–human relationship one privileges, and that the model Edwards uses, that of the parent–child, leads him into difficulties.

As well as providing a point of reference in contemporary philosophical discussions of central Christian doctrines, Edwards's metaphysical concerns continue to draw attention in contemporary philosophy. This is particularly the case with his treatment of free will. Until recently, Edwards's philosophical reputation rested almost entirely upon his treatise on this subject. His treatment of free will is primarily directed against what he calls 'Arminianism', which he opposes. Edwards saw in Arminianism an attack upon the absolute sovereignty of God, which he felt compelled to defend. Edwards also complained that the Arminian concept of freedom violates sufficient reason, by making human actions utterly contingent, unexplained brute facts. His solution to the problem is to defend a version of compatibilism, the view that freedom is compatible with actions being determined (in this case, by God).

But this view faces familiar complaints: that it destroys moral authenticity, makes God the author of sin, and delivers each creature to a fate which is undeserved. In his essay, Hugh McCann argues that while Edwards's complaints against Arminianism are in the main well founded, his solution is mistaken. An older view, put forward by both Augustine and Aquinas, insisted on uncompromised free will, but also on an all-embracing providence, holding that as primary cause God is active in all that takes place within creation. The key to defending this view is to develop an account of the relationship between God's will and those of creatures that gives creative control to God, while preserving what is essential to genuine moral freedom. McCann argues that this can be done, and that only such a solution can satisfy both sides of the Calvinist–Arminian dispute.

Paul Helm takes up an important theme in Edwards's treatise, *Original Sin*, that is, the question of identity across time. In a comparison with John Locke, the English empiricist philosopher whose work so influenced the young Edwards, Helm seeks to draw out the implications of Edwards's and Locke's respective positions for the imputation of sin. He finds that Edwards's metaphysical commitments ensure that his doctrine about the persistence through time of an individual, and the imputation of sin to an individual, lead Edwards into considerable problems, from which he is unable to remove himself.

Also dealing with Edwards's metaphysical views on imputation and persistence through time, Oliver Crisp takes up the question of Edwards's doctrine of theological occasionalism. This is the view that God continuously re-creates things out of nothing at each moment of their existence, coupled with a causal thesis that God is the sole cause of all things, so that there are no other causal agents apart from God. Crisp seeks to analyse the nature of Edwards's defence of this position, before assessing whether what Edwards says in defence of occasionalism in *Original Sin* is compatible with what he says elsewhere, in his *Miscellanies*. In so doing, Crisp takes issue with the way in which Sang Lee's influential reading of Edwards's metaphysics uses Edwards's doctrine of occasionalism. If God re-creates all things at each moment, then there is no room for anything to persist through time. Persistence is rather like the stills in a roll of film that make up a movie. They are distinct, discrete exposures, each capturing a moment in time, that can be run together and projected onto a cinematic screen to give the appearance of action across time.

In recent moral philosophy, there has been a renewed interest in the virtues, and in virtue theory as a metaethical position. Philip Quinn deals with this theme in Edwards's work, arguing that Edwards's dissertation on *True Virtue* represents an important and original contribution to virtue theory, from the perspective of Christian theism. Quinn claims, contrary to previous Edwardsian scholarship, that Edwards's philosophical argument in *True Virtue* can be separated out from his theological argument in his moral theory. This yields an interesting result: that Edwards's references to 'being in general' and 'being simply considered' are not oblique references to God (as is often assumed by Edwardsian scholars), but refer to all intelligent beings in a system of being. According to Quinn, Edwards does not mean to claim that true virtue consists exhaustively and exclusively in love to God, the being of beings, only that it chiefly consists in this (as well as other, lesser things with respect to other, lesser beings).

The Theology of Jonathan Edwards

Theologians have been predominant among recent commentators on Edwards's thinking. Perhaps the most influential among them has been Sang Lee. Stephen Holmes addresses Lee's work directly, arguing that Lee's reconceptualization of

Edwards's philosophical theology in terms of dispositions and habits is misguided, and yields a skewed conception of Edwards's overall programme. Holmes emphasizes the importance of the context in which Edwards developed his ideas. He argues that the evidence Lee adduces for his reformulation of Edwards's thinking is inconsistent with the traditional picture of Edwards. Moreover, far from presenting a more dynamic Edwardsian ontology, Lee's interpretation of Edwards is actually less dynamic than the traditional ontology that Edwards espouses.

Amy Plantinga Pauw turns her attention to the doctrine of divine simplicity. She argues that Edwards's conception of the Trinity makes the endorsement of a doctrine of divine simplicity extremely problematic, based upon the Edwardsian notion, captured in his early idealist metaphysics in *The Mind*, that 'one [being] alone cannot be excellent'. She is led to the conclusion that Edwards's aesthetic view of being (that harmony and beauty are shown in symmetry of relations between things) means that God must be a being-in-relation. And this is difficult to square with a traditional doctrine of simplicity.

Gerald McDermott has recently written on Edwards's views on other religions, from classical civilizations to Native Americans. He takes up this theme again in his essay comparing the work of Edwards with John Henry Newman in this respect.

Edwards endorsed the notion that God had originally given an oral deposit of revelation to Adam and his descendants that has trickled down into the teaching of non-Christian religious traditions, albeit in ever more corrupted forms. He also endorsed a dispositional doctrine of salvation – that a disposition of faith is what is necessary (though perhaps not sufficient) for salvation. McDermott contends that this means Edwards was not as hostile to some non-Christian religions as is sometimes thought. By contrast, Newman took a more robust approach to other religious traditions. Taking up Clement of Alexandria's view that there is a separate divine dispensation for 'pagans', he maintained that the relation between Christian and non-Christian religions is one of continuity, rather than discontinuity. The Church's mission is to build upon and purify the faith present in non-Christian religions, not to replace one notion of faith with another.

Michael McClymond also compares Edwards's thinking with another tradition, this time the Orthodox tradition, in the person of Gregory Palamas. Both Edwards and Palamas were deeply influenced by Neoplatonism, which led them to espouse a version of the doctrine of divinization. This is the view that Christians will enjoy the beatific vision of union with God in heaven, based, in particular, on 2 Peter 1: 4. However, as both Palamas and Edwards point out, this does not mean that Christians will share in the *essence* of God, only in his *nature*. Both writers developed their ideas in very different situations, Palamas building on the eastern notion of hesychistic, or 'quiet', prayer, and Edwards developing ideas drawn from the Cambridge Platonists. But there are interesting areas of convergence between the two, including the view that a 'divine light' conforms human beings to God's character; the immediacy of the connection between God and human beings in a state of grace; the notion of unceasing progress in the spiritual life beyond death; an emphasis on bodily affections in the spiritual life; and teaching on human participation in the nature of God. McClymond concludes that Edwards clearly does teach divinization, and suggests that this might offer a fruitful avenue of dialogue between Reformed and Orthodox Christians.

The year 2003 marks the tercentenary of Edwards's birth. It is hoped that these essays may commemorate this anniversary by demonstrating that Edwards continues to be a thinker with whom theologians and philosophers can fruitfully engage.

Paul Helm and Oliver D. Crisp

Notes

1. Miller, Perry (1949), *Jonathan Edwards*, New York: Sloane.
2. See, for example Holmes, Stephen R. (2000), *God of Grace and God of Glory, An Account of the Theology of Jonathan Edwards*, Edinburgh: T&T Clark; McDermott, Gerald R. (2000), *Jonathan Edwards Confronts the Gods, Christian Theology, Enlightenment Religion, and Non-Christian Faiths*, New York: Oxford University Press; McClymond, Michael J. (1998), *Encounters with God, An Approach to The Theology of Jonathan Edwards*, New York: Oxford University Press; and Plantinga Pauw, Amy (2002), *The Supreme Harmony of All, The Trinitarian Theology of Jonathan Edwards*, Grand Rapids: Eerdmans.
3. Examples include Chisholm, Roderick (1976), *Person and Object*, London: George Allen and Unwin, Appendix B; Quinn, Philip L. (1983), 'Divine Conservation, Continuous Creation, and Human Action', in Freddoso, Alfred J. (ed.), *The Existence and Nature of God*, Notre Dame: University of Notre Dame Press; and Wainwright, William J. (1990), '*Jonathan Edwards and the Sense of the Heart*', in *Faith and Philosophy* 7, 43–62.
4. (1961), *What is History?* Harmondsworth: Penguin.
5. See the following volumes of the Yale edition of Edwards's works: Edwards, Jonathan (1957), *Freedom of the Will, The Works of Jonathan Edwards Volume 1*, ed. Paul Ramsey, New Haven: Yale University Press, and (1989), *Ethical Writings, The Works of Jonathan Edwards Volume 8*, ed. Paul Ramsey, New Haven: Yale University Press; (1959), *Religious Affections, The Works of Jonathan Edwards Volume 2*, ed. John E. Smith, New Haven: Yale University Press; (1980), *Scientific and Philosophical Writings, The Works of Jonathan Edwards Volume 6*, ed. Wallace E. Anderson, New Haven: Yale University Press; and (1994), *The 'Miscellanies' Nos. a-500, The Works of Jonathan Edwards Volume 13*, ed. Thomas A. Schafer, New Haven: Yale University Press.
6. Lee, Sang (2000), *The Philosophical Theology of Jonathan Edwards, Expanded Edition*, Princeton: Princeton University Press.
7. See, for example, two recent monographs: Plantinga, Alvin (2000), *Warranted Christian Belief*, New York: Oxford University Press and Helm, Paul (1997), *Faith and Understanding*, Edinburgh: Edinburgh University Press, ch. 7.
8. See, for example Kvanvig, Jonathan L. (1993), *The Problem of Hell*, New York: Oxford University Press; Talbott, Thomas (1990) '*The Doctrine of Everlasting Punishment*', in *Faith and Philosophy* 7, 19–41; and Walls, Jerry L. (1992), *Hell: The Logic of*

Damnation, Notre Dame: University of Notre Dame Press.
9. See Wainwright, William (1988), 'Original Sin' in Morris, Thomas V. (ed.), *Philosophy and the Christian Faith*, Notre Dame: University of Notre Dame Press.

Chapter 1

Jonathan Edwards on Hell

Jonathan L. Kvanvig

Every religion offers both hope and fear. Each offers hope in virtue of the benefits promised to adherents, and fear in virtue of costs incurred by adversaries. In traditional Christianity, the costs incurred are expressed in terms of the doctrine of hell, according to which each person consigned to hell receives the same infinite punishment. This strong view of hell involves four distinct theses. First, it maintains that those in hell exist forever in that state (the Existence Thesis) and that at least some human persons will end up in hell (the Anti-Universalism Thesis). Once in hell, there is no possibility of escape (the No Escape Thesis), and the justification of and purpose for hell is to mete out punishment to those whose earthly lives and character deserve it (the Retribution Thesis).

There was a time when such a picture of hell engendered fear rather than a perceived need for defense, a time when traditional Christianity was more a cultural presupposition than it now is. The need for defense is felt much more strongly now than in the past, but the strong view of hell has always been in need of an adequate ground. For if reality is structured as traditional Christianity claims, some explanation is required for the strong view of hell in terms of God's nature and character. The alternative is to treat Christian doctrine as some collage of literary motifs drawn from an ancient collection of stories and writings, elevated to the status of accurate information through the power of myth. Traditional Christianity places higher demands on itself, insisting that it forms a coherent and accurate picture of the nature of God and his relationship to the created universe. When Christianity is taken in this theoretically serious way, questions of justification and explanation become pressing. In particular, those aspects that appear to threaten theoretical unity require explanation, and the strong view of hell is surely among such aspects, given the centrality of God's love in traditional Christianity and the lengths to which God will go in that gospel to redeem lost humanity.

Jonathan Edwards not only preached the doctrine of hell in astounding and disturbing ways, but also addressed these theoretical questions in as sound a way as can be found. I will argue for this claim by investigating how one might try to defend the strong view of hell, in order to show where Edwards's discussion fits into this larger picture, and then will investigate more carefully his own contribution to the question of the acceptability of the strong view of hell.

1

Requirements of a Defense of the Strong View of Hell

The question which must be answered by a defender of the strong view of hell is why anyone would think it is true. It is, of course, one quite natural interpretation of the teachings of Scripture on the subject, but it is far from clear that it is unique in this regard. Furthermore, if the strong view fails on theoretical grounds, an appeal to Scripture in defense of the view will be inadequate. So the prior question that must be asked concerns the theoretical adequacy of the view, and since the strong view is intrinsically a retributive account, we can begin by investigating that aspect of the view.

Any justification for retribution requires wrongdoing, ordinarily in terms of harm caused or harm intended, and neither source provides an obvious defense of a view of hell on which every person is equally guilty and all deserve an infinite punishment. Some people cause more harm than others, thereby rendering ineffective an appeal to the principle of 'an eye for an eye,' and some people intend, or at least appear to intend, more harm than others. There is some moral presumption in favor of the view that willing evil is as bad as doing it, but even if we grant this principle, we would need some equality of intended harm in order to justify the claim that everyone deserves an equal, infinite punishment. Furthermore, one would need to claim that every person was guilty of such an egregious act or intention that an infinite punishment is warranted. Perhaps such actions or intentions are possible, on some account akin to that given by defenders of capital punishment, but it is hard to see how everyone is guilty of such actions or intentions.

One might argue here that we ought to attend more carefully to the darkness of the human heart, and the fact that even the best and wisest of us carry enormous capacities for evil within us. I have no doubt that these claims are true, that the heart of human beings is deeply corrupt and full of all kinds of evil thoughts, but even granting very dark views about human nature will not sustain the strong view of hell. For it is implausible to deny that some inflict more harm than others and some intend more harm than others.

These factors lead straightforwardly to a search for another source of justified retribution other than that arising out of actual or intended harm, and the traditional answer has been to find such a source in the status of the one wronged. On this viewpoint, the degree of guilt incurred by a wrong action is a function not only of harm caused and harm intended, but also a function of the status of the one against whom the wrong is done. We can call this principle the 'status principle,' for short.

A facile dismissal of this defense would attempt to tie the plausibility of such an appeal to status to the moral experience within nonegalitarian societies. The claim would be that such an appeal could only be plausible to those involved in such societies, where, for example, the moral experience of killing a prince would be quite different from that of killing a serf. I think, however, that this dismissal is too quick. For the concept of status need not be interpreted in such a sociological fashion. Consider, for example, the appeal to status central to humanism. Even in an age emphasizing the moral dimension of the rights of animals, it is too facile to dismiss the humanistic elements of our moral experience as entirely unfounded. Even if it is *prima facie* wrong to kill any animal, it is implausible to think that the forced choice between the death of a human and the death of, say, a lizard is an unresolvable moral dilemma. Furthermore, notice that the moral choice here is difficult to explain in terms only of harm caused or harm intended, unless one builds into the idea of harm caused the idea that human life has an intrinsic value beyond that of a lizard. Such a viewpoint, I suggest, is nothing more than a recognition of the intuitive plausibility of some type of status principle.

If we attempt to defend the traditional doctrine of hell by appeal to the status principle, however, two central tasks face us. First, we must identify that on which status depends. Some wholly implausible ideas can be rejected immediately, such as defining status in terms of fame, or fortune, or longevity, or wisdom. If these ideas are implausible, however, what more plausible account can be given? Second, we need to find some function of harm caused, harm intended, and status to yield the result that an infinite punishment can be justified given some combination of these three factors.

This second task is exacerbated by the need for the value of the function to be infinite for all (unregenerate) human beings, for the strong view of hell requires that every person deserves an infinite punishment. Since there are clear differences among human beings in terms of harm caused and harm intended, there must be something about the feature of status that swamps these differences to yield a justified infinite punishment in every case. Moreover, there are clear differences among human beings in terms of the status of the objects of their wrongdoing. Some are thieves while others are murderers; some torture only lower animals while others torture human beings.

So we will need to identify some special action or class of actions that every person performs which triggers justified infinite punishment in order to defend the strong view of hell. As we have seen, it is difficult to find such an action when we look for it in terms of harm caused or harm intended, and it is difficult to find such an action when we look at the things of ordinary life which suffer harm or which we attempt to harm. The only other place to look for an adequate defense of the strong view is in actions which wrong God. Only by bringing God into the picture is there any hope of finding a wronged party with sufficient status to swamp the differences that exist in terms of harm caused and harm intended.

In addition, because all such wrongs deserve the same punishment on the strong view, the appeal to wrongs against God must be sufficient in itself to justify the infinite punishment of the strong view, regardless of any differences in terms of harm caused and harm intended. Not only must there be some way to sin against God which deserves infinite punishment, but it must also be the case that any sin against God requires such punishment. Otherwise God's presence in the moral story would be insufficient to justify an infinite punishment.

If sinning against God were not sufficient in itself to justify an infinite punishment, the strong view would have to be defended additionally in terms of the quality or quantity of wrongdoing that could justify an infinite punishment. Quality differences would have to trace to kinds or degrees of harm caused or harm intended, and we have already seen the failure of such appeals to justify an infinite punishment. So all that remains would be some appeal to quantity of wrongdoing against God. Such an account would be highly arbitrary, however. If one sin against God is insufficient to warrant infinite punishment, how could one deal with a larger number, say, fifteen, or five hundred? The only plausible, non-arbitrary answer would be that an infinite number of sins would make a difference, but it is hard to see how it is possible for finite beings to perform that many distinct sins, let alone something of which all humans are inevitably guilty. So, the best hope for a defense of the strong view of hell is to hold that God's status is so overwhelmingly high that it renders irrelevant any other moral differences. No matter how insignificant a sin is in terms of harm caused and harm intended, if it is a sin against God, it automatically becomes so serious that it deserves an infinite punishment. No weaker account of God's relationship to human sinfulness could give a theoretically satisfactory defense of the strong view of hell.

Once we have determined that any sin against God is sufficient to merit an infinite punishment, we must address the question of which of our wrongdoings count as sins against God and which do not. One might try to identify actions in which human beings make God the intentional object of their wrongdoing, aiming to harm him, or insult him in some way by their behavior. Yet it is not obvious that all people perform such actions, especially in an age of increasing atheism and agnosticism. For in such an age, it is a hard empirical claim to defend that atheists and agnostics affirm connatively what they refuse to endorse cognitively.

The difficulty of identifying some particular sin against God of which all are guilty suggests that a more egalitarian approach might provide more hope for success. On this egalitarian approach, all sins are equal, for all sins are against God, whether or not God is the intentional object of that sin. It is here that the work of Jonathan Edwards is most relevant, especially *The Nature of True Virtue*, for Edwards gives the most complete and detailed defense found in the literature of the claim that all sin is against God. It is this defense that I wish to examine and comment on here. I will argue, first, that though Edwards's explicit arguments need some emendation, the changes required are small and sufficient to yield an adequate defense of the claim that all sin is against God.

Edwards's Defense of All Sin Being Against God

Edwards classifies all behavior as either sinful or truly virtuous. True virtue, according to Edwards, consists primarily in 'love to being in general,'[1] and secondarily in a relish of, or delight in, the intrinsic excellence of benevolence.[2] Edwards connects this conception of virtue to God by identifying God with being in general: 'God is infinitely the greatest Being,' 'the foundation and fountain of all being and all beauty ... the sum and comprehension of all existence and excellence.'[3] God's pre-eminent reality, in this sense, prevents one from displaying true virtue and yet insisting 'on benevolence to the created system in such a manner as would naturally lead one to suppose' that it is 'by far the most important and essential thing.'[4] According to Edwards, 'a determination of mind to union and benevolence to a particular person, or private system, which is but a small part of the universal system of being ... is not of the nature of true virtue' unless it is 'subordinate to benevolence to being in general.'[5] So no person is truly virtuous who is not governed by a love of God and a delight in his beauty.

By contrast, then, sinful behavior is identified with attachment to private systems (such as individual persons or groups, special causes or concerns, including personal happiness, the well-being of all humans, and even the well-being of the entire created order) rather than benevolence to being in general. Edwards thus requires a proper motivation in order for one to avoid sin, and anything less than properly motivated behavior is sinful.

It is here that the relationship between God and being in general is central to Edwards's thinking. Once we have granted the identification between God and being in general, or at least the claim that the two are inextricably linked, Edwards concludes that one can only be truly virtuous by being motivated in a way that makes God central to that motivation. Because God must be central to virtuous behavior in this way, the central failure in sinful behavior is a failure to involve God in one's motivations, and hence to sin against God.

This argument requires as a premise the claim that any behavior aimed at something less than God himself constitutes an offense against God. One might wonder why this claim is true. After all, in the usual case we sin against a person by intentionally directing our actions toward that person. Mere failure to take the interests of a person into account when deciding on a course of action doesn't imply that when things go wrong, one's behavior constitutes an offense against that person. The decision to marry a certain person, for example, might harm some third party, but the marriage need not constitute an offense against that third party. So why are things different in the case of God?

There are two ways to try to answer this question, one ethical and the other metaphysical. Let us consider the ethical answer first. To do so, let us engage in the fictional project of reifying morality, allowing us to talk of offenses against morality. The question then is under what conditions one can commit an offense against morality. In particular, the question is whether it is ever possible to do something morally wrong and yet not commit an offense against morality.

Such a possibility could arise if there were a distinction between what is morally required of a person and what that person ought to do, all things considered (including the moral features of the situation). If there is such a distinction, then when deliberating about what to do, one first should determine what is religiously required, what is morally required, what is required in terms of self-interest, and so on. Each of these factors would then play some role in a function on all of these factors that yielded some overall obligatory course of action. The overall, obligatory course of action might, in any given case, be what is morally required, but it might also be what is religiously required, or required in terms of self-interest, or in terms of some other requirement (or maybe what is required is something different from what is required from each of these limited perspectives).

Suppose then that we are considering a situation in which what is obligatory, all things considered, is incompatible with what is morally required. In such a case, one ought to violate morality, because morality is just one factor to be taken into account when deciding what one ought to do. If one does as one should, one will have acted contrary to the demands of morality, but one will have committed no offense against morality. For on this theory of the relationship between morality and what one ought to do, there is a logical gap between honoring morality and doing the right thing, all things considered. Hence, one can fail to honor morality without offending against it. The explanation of this possibility is that one has an overriding reason to fail to honor morality, and it is the existence of this overriding reason that allows one to occupy the neutral position of failing to honor morality without committing an offense against it.

Suppose, however, (and much more plausibly) that there can't be any difference between what one ought to do, all things considered, and what morality requires of one (though, of course, there can be a difference between what one ought to do, all things considered, and what *conventional* morality, the moral viewpoint of one's culture, implies). In such a case, every wrong action constitutes an offense against morality. Morality always occupies the pre-eminent position in all matters of conduct on this view, so that even those who care not at all about morality and do not take its demands into account nonetheless offend against it when they act contrary to its demands. On this view of the relationship between what one ought to do, all things considered, and what morality requires of one, any deliberation that fails to honor the overriding nature of morality offends against it. Courses of action which show a weighing of reasons which does not grant pre-eminent position to moral reasons offend against morality for that very reason. For such courses of action betray a presupposition that the demands of morality might not be the same as what is required of us, all things considered, and that view is false and necessarily so.

Edwards's position against the possibility of a neutral position with regard to God can be defended by adopting this same view of morality as necessarily overriding. Some people do not care about morality and treat its demands as less than overriding, but they are wrong. And because they are wrong, any improperly motivated action constitutes an offense against morality, even if the action which they perform is one required by morality.

So if we adopt the plausible view that obligation, all things considered, is just morality, we can generate an ethical defense of Edwards's position if we can find a way to link together offenses against morality with offenses against God. The first

Edwardsian step here is to identify the appropriate object of moral concern with being in general, a step which will cause some to balk on the same grounds that they balk at utilitarian theories which require the common good to be the object of our moral concern. Such lofty aims are unrealistic or improper in some way, according to these objectors. More realistic and more appropriate is the view that the object of moral concern is local: our concern should be localized to a particular crying child in need of our help, for example.

I think we should be sympathetic to this complaint, for it is common and disturbing to find people who care in the abstract but not in the particular. They care about poverty but not about any particular poor people, and perhaps the problem is that moral concern at too abstract a level is simply not the ideal. Still, there is an important qualifier on moral concern displayed at the local level, for any concern to alleviate immediate and particular suffering, as in the case of a crying child, needs to be sensitive to the way in which other moral concerns can conflict with what is immediate and present. At times, the right thing to do is to leave the immediate and particular suffering as it is in service of some greater good or in order to respond to some more important concern. For example, a doctor might have to leave an elderly couple on the side of the road, unable to change their flat tire, in order to make it to an emergency surgery.

Such factors show that any concern for the local and immediate must be tempered by sensitivity to overriding information. Those in whom such sensitivity is present need not sacrifice moral concern for the immediate and present, but they also display a concern for the well-being of things that is quite general. Furthermore, without this very general concern, the concern for the immediate and present can lead to moral wrongdoing, so it is necessary for any attachment to the immediate and present to be governed or subordinated, as Edwards insists, to something more general. Moreover, this sensitivity must be completely general, since overriders concerning the immediate and present can arise from anywhere. Hence the need for sensitivity to overriders can be used to sustain Edwards's point that the appropriate object of moral concern must be being in general.

Edwards needs something more as well, however. He also needs some special relationship between being in general and God in order to maintain that improper motivation necessarily offends against God. Earlier, in describing Edwards's position, I claimed that Edwards 'identifies' being in general with God. Such a description suggests a relationship of identity, and if God were identical with being in general, then offenses against morality would automatically be offenses against God, given the centrality of being in general to proper moral motivation. Such an identification is not one Edwards would make, for not even an appeal to idealism, which Edwards does find attractive, can undergird the pantheistic implications of this kind of identification between God and being in general. Moreover, even if Edwards found the thesis palatable, there is no reason for anyone else to adopt it, and one cannot defend a difficult view of hell by appeal to controversial premises for which no adequate argument can be found.

Without such an identification between God and being in general, the ethical defense of the centrality of God to true virtue outlined above cannot succeed. All is not lost, however, for there is a metaphysical defense of the view which might work even if the ethical defense fails. That is, I believe Edwards has a metaphysical answer to the question of why God is central to proper moral motivation, even though the identification between God and being in general cannot be taken to be strict identity. That answer is in terms of Edwards's doctrine of continuous creation. Edwards says,

> God's upholding created substance, or causing its existence in each successive moment, is altogether equivalent to an *immediate production out of nothing*, at each moment, because its existence at this moment is not merely in part from God, but wholly from him; and not in any part, or degree, from its antecedent existence.[6]

This claim constitutes a straightforward denial of deistic tendencies to think that things have in themselves the power of self-sustenance. Edwards goes further, however, than merely to deny deism:

> If the existence of created substance, in each successive moment, be wholly the effect of God's immediate power, in that moment, without any dependence on prior existence, as much as the first creation out of nothing, then what exists at this moment, by this power, is a *new effect*; and simply and absolutely considered, not the same with any past existence, though it be like it, and follows it according to a certain established method. And there is no identity or oneness in the case, but what depends on the *arbitrary* constitution of the Creator; who by his wise sovereign establishment so unites these successive new effects, that he *treats them as one*, by communicating to them like properties, relations, and circumstances; and so, leads us to regard and treat them as one.[7]

Edwards here embraces the view that identity over time is an arbitrary construction by God; that there is no such thing as the persistence of a thing as an intrinsic property of that thing. Instead, persistence is a relation between things and some unifying activity on the part of God to constitute, arbitrarily, the existence of a thing which is the same over time.

How does this account of continuous creation help to defend the view that all sin is against God? Consider an analogy. Things can be related in such a way that harming a thing can constitute an offense against another thing related to it in an appropriate way. For example, property relations are often conceived of in this way, and certainly familial relationships are as well. If you intentionally deface a building belonging to me, you have committed an offense against me, and if you attack my child, you equally commit an offense against me.

These relationships that give rise to the possibility of such offenses can be more or less direct. For example, as a child grows and develops, wrongs done against the child are not quite as obviously offenses against the parent of the child. By the time the child has become an adult, it may be that wrongs done no longer constitute offenses against the parent. I do not know whether that is true, but it is at least true that they are less obviously wrongs against the parent.

The effect of Edwards's doctrine of continuous creation is to establish a direct and immediate relationship between God and the created order. Because of the intimate dependence, complete and total, of things on God, harm to the created order automatically constitutes an offense against the being on whom this order completely depends.

Unfortunately, Edwards's doctrine of continuous creation faces serious difficulties. Philip Quinn argues persuasively that Edwards's position implies that action is impossible. Quinn argues that for any action to occur, certain bodily movements must occur, and such movements essentially take time. An agent literally must persist through time in order for the action to be performed, and Edwards's view implies that such persistence is impossible: as he says in the above quoted passage, 'what exists at this moment, ... simply and absolutely considered, [is] not the same with any past existence.' Hence, if action requires persistence through time, then, on Edwards's view, action is impossible.[8]

Regardless of whether we endorse Quinn's criticism, there is no reason to think that persistence through time is impossible, and if it isn't, then Edwards has not yet given us an adequate defense of the claim that all sin is against God. I think his position is nonetheless suggestive, for there is a related, but slightly weaker thesis that can be used to achieve the same metaphysical result. For one need only appeal to the doctrine of divine conservation to support Edwards's account of how all sin is against God.

The standard way of denying the doctrine of divine conservation is by appeal to some analogy such as the watch–watchmaker analogy. God's relation to the universe, it is held, is like that of a watchmaker to a watch he builds, winds up, and puts aside to let it run on its own. This analogy is defective at its core, for what allows the watchmaker to stand back and let the watch run on its own is the structure of the universe that the watchmaker uses to his advantage in order to secure the continued operation of the watch. The watchmaker relies on the physical constituents of the universe together with the laws governing them to be able to create a watch which runs independently of the watchmaker. In the case of God, no such structure is in place for God to exploit in order to secure the continued operation of the universe, making the case of God's relationship to the universe radically different from that of the watchmaker's relationship to the watch.

This difference cuts to the heart of the matter, for divine conservation is false only if God creates things with a power of self-sustenance within them, a power involving a relationship between the present existence of a thing and its future existence. If this power were contingent, we would need an explanation why a thing continues to have that property even if God created the thing in question with that property initially. One might argue that the continued possession of the property is a continued effect of God's original creative act, but there is no medium that is independent of God and capable of accounting for such continuation. God can, of course, will that the property of self-sustenance continues to be a property of things, but it would obtain as a result of God's continual willing of it, not in virtue of God exploiting some medium, causal or otherwise, which ensures the continued presence of the property. So if there is a merely contingent power of self-sustenance in things, this contingency prevents any appeal to such a power in service of denying the doctrine of divine conservation.

That leaves as the only option that the power of self-sustenance is essential to the things that have it. Such a view is problematic for two reasons. First, since the power involves a relation to the continued existence of the thing, the power could be present only if the persistence of that thing were logically guaranteed. Yet nothing that contingently exists can have its persistence logically guaranteed.

One might claim that this objection depends on an account of the relation to its continued existence that is too strong. In particular, one might claim that the relation is one of *defeasibly* continuing to exist, that is, continuing to exist so long as some competing power doesn't prevent it from existing. On this construal, the power of self-sustenance would be analogous to laws of inertia in physics: things continue on as they are unless acted upon by some force.

Still, this picture of self-sustenance is problematic, for it is incompatible with the possibility that God created the very things he has created, but without such powers. Any view which treats the power of self-sustenance as essential to the things that have it must deny this possibility, for essential properties are those properties that a thing must have in order to exist. What this view implies, then, is something that appears to be false. God could have created each of us so that we continued to exist only by his activity of conservation, and this possibility shows that no power of self-sustenance is essential to us.

Therefore, the only plausible version of the self-sustenance doctrine is one that makes that property a contingent one, and we have already seen why no such contingent property can successfully avoid the doctrine of divine conservation. Such a property could obtain only given some medium for carrying the effects of an action that no longer exists. We are able to so act because the universe is structured causally and temporally so as to allow that which no longer exists to still have effects. Apart from such a structure, however, all that exists to explain the continued possession of the power of self-sustenance is God's resolve to continue carrying out his original decision. The power in question might exist, but its existence in no way removes the need for a doctrine of divine conservation. Instead, its continued presence is itself another call for that very doctrine.

Given this defense of the doctrine of divine conservation, we are in a position to see how God can be centrally involved in all instances of proper moral motivation for Edwards. This doctrine demonstrates the intimate relationship between God and everything that exists, throughout the entire history of the existence of things. No remoteness or distance between God and his creation can be maintained, and so wrongs done against God's creation constitute offenses against God, in a way mirrored darkly by wrongs done against one's offspring constituting sins against the parents.

Once it has been established that all sin is against God, the moral relevance of status becomes the crucial aspect of any defense of the strong view of hell. On any reasonable measure, however, God must be granted the very highest status. So Edwards's account and the refinements of it presented here provide a strong foundation for a defense of the strong view of hell.

Conclusion

I remain unconvinced, however, that the strong view of hell can be defended completely, even given this foundation. For even if all sin is against God, and sinning against God is the most serious wrong that could be committed, there is still the issue of mitigating factors in the theory of punishment to be considered. It is one thing to intentionally take a human life, and another thing to accidentally do so, and such mitigating factors place constraints on what sort of punishment is fair and just. If both wrongs are punished equally, the punishment is not fair, for the mitigating factor in the case of accidental death has not been taken into account. Something similar may exist in sins against God, for a person may commit wrongs with no thought or awareness of their relationship to God at all. The strong view of hell ignores such mitigating factors, and is problematic for that reason.

Still, though, there is much to be learned about the doctrine of hell from Edwards's defense of it. For the most puzzling feature of the strong view of hell is the severity of punishment for any wrong. Even if the defense is not successful for the entirety of the strong view of hell, Edwards's defense of how all sin is against God reveals how all of life is lived in the face of God and the justice in holding us responsible for this relationship.

Notes

1. Edwards, Jonathan (1970), *The Nature of True Virtue*, ed. William Frankena, Ann Arbor: University of Michigan Press, p. 4.
2. Ibid., pp. 3, 11.
3. Ibid., pp. 14–15.
4. Ibid., pp. 16–17.
5. Ibid., p. 18.
6. Edwards, Jonathan (1970), *Original Sin, The Works of Jonathan Edwards Volume 3*, ed. Clyde A. Holbrook, New Haven: Yale University Press, p. 402.
7. Ibid., pp. 402–3.
8. Quinn, Philip L. (1983), 'Divine Conservation, Continuous Creation, and Human Action,' in Freddoso, Alfred J. (ed.), *The Existence & Nature of God*, Notre Dame: University of Notre Dame Press, pp. 55–80.

Chapter 2

Jonathan Edwards and the Doctrine of Hell

William J. Wainwright

In spite of the notoriety of his Enfield sermon ('Sinners in the Hands of an Angry God'), Edwards's reflections on hell are not as widely known as they should be since they are scattered throughout his sermons, notebooks and theological treatises. This is unfortunate because no defense of the traditional doctrine of hell is better than his. Its failure would therefore reinforce the suspicion that that doctrine is untenable. The defense has three parts. Edwards attempts to show that (1) the eternal punishment of the wicked is a necessary consequence of God's desire to display his justice, majesty and holiness, that (2) it contributes to the good of the whole system, and (3) is just. I shall argue that Edwards's endeavor is partly successful and partly not.

I

'Wicked Men Useful in their Destruction Only' argues that people have a 'use,' namely, 'the glory of God [which] is the very thing for which [they were] made.' There are two ways in which they can serve this purpose. They can contribute to God's glory *in acting* or in 'being *acted upon*.' They 'cannot be useful *actively*,' however, 'any otherwise than in bringing forth fruit to God; serving God and living to his glory.' Those who fail to serve God actively must therefore serve him passively by being useful in their destruction – 'as a barren tree, which is in no way useful standing in the vineyard, may be good fuel.' Their destruction contributes to God's glory in two ways. First, God's end in creation is the exercise and manifestation of his perfections *ad extra*. The destruction of the wicked manifests or glorifies three of God's attributes – his 'vindictive [punitive] justice,' his 'awful majesty,' and his infinite holiness. Second, the destruction of the wicked increases God's glory by giving 'the saints a greater sense of their happiness and of God's grace to them.'[1]

The following argument supports Edwards's first claim:

1   'It is a proper and excellent thing for infinite glory to shine forth.'

2   'It is proper that the shining forth of God's glory should be complete; that is, that all parts of His glory should shine forth, that every beauty should be proportionably effulgent.'
3   God's glory includes his 'awful majesty, His authority and dreadful greatness, justice and holiness.'
4   Attributes like these are most clearly manifest in the punishment of sin. For example, if God did not 'permit and punish sin, there could be no manifestation of God's holiness in hatred of sin.' Therefore,
5   Sin and its punishment are necessary if all of God's attributes are to fully 'shine forth' (CDD 358–9).

In short, God inflicts eternal misery upon the damned because he wishes not only to 'show how excellent His love is' but 'also how terrible His wrath is.' The 'whole universe' will thus be called upon to behold and 'adore' not only his love but 'that awful majesty and mighty power that is to be seen' in the destruction of the wicked (SHG 460–61).

Edwards supports his second claim by this argument:

1   God's communication of himself *ad extra* consists in the knowledge and love of God, and the joy in him, which he bestows on the saints.
2   Unless God manifests each of his attributes, however, including his vindictive justice, majesty and holiness in the hatred of sin, the saints' knowledge of him won't be complete.
3   The love of the saints necessarily increases in proportion to their knowledge of God's greatness and excellency. But
4   As their knowledge and love of God increases, so too does their happiness, for the latter '*consists* in the knowledge of God, and a sense of His love' (my emphasis), that is, in their loving and being loved by him.
5   Wickedness and its punishment are thus necessary for the saints' knowledge and love of God, and for their joy in God (from 2, 3, and 4).
6   They are therefore necessary for God's communication of Himself *ad extra* (from 1 and 5) (CDD 359).

Note two things about these arguments. First, they are designed to show that the best world contains sin and the destruction of the wicked. If sound, they prove that the punishment of wickedness is a logically necessary consequence of God's exercising and manifesting his attributes *ad extra*, and of his fully communicating himself to creatures. Since the best world *is*, arguably, that in which God most perfectly expresses and communicates himself, wickedness and punishment are logically necessary conditions of the greatest good.

Note also that the arguments are interrelated. The happiness of the saints consists in their knowledge and love of God. Their love of God, though, logically depends upon their knowledge of God, and that depends upon his self-manifestation. God's self-communication consisting in the knowledge, love, and joy of the saints thus ultimately depends upon his self-disclosure. Yet that (as the first argument allegedly shows) entails sin and punishment.

Edwards's arguments aren't implausible. They are not sufficient to justify the traditional doctrine of hell, however. To do so he must not only show that wickedness and punishment are necessary ingredients of the best world. He must also show that wickedness and *everlasting* punishment are necessary. Does the full manifestation of God's justice, majesty and holiness, and hence the saints' knowledge of God, require *that*?

Edwards's strongest argument is his proof from God's holiness:

1 'God's nature' is 'infinitely opposite to sin.'
2 He has a disposition, therefore, both to (a) infinitely 'oppose it in his acts and works,' and to (b) publicly display his infinite opposition to it and displeasure with it (from 1).
3 The 'proper exercise and testimony of [opposition to and] displeasure against sin, in the supreme being and absolute governor of the world, is taking vengeance,' that is, public punishment, and the 'proper exercise and testimony' of *infinite* opposition and displeasure is *infinite* punishment. Given that,
4 God's dispositions are necessarily realized in the most fitting manner, it follows that
5 God inflicts an infinite punishment upon the wicked (from 2, 3, and 4) (Misc. 779).

Does 1 entail 2? It *does* seem to entail 2(a). As Edwards says, 'It is impossible, if God infinitely loves, and honours himself, as one infinitely worthy to be loved and esteemed, but that he should, from the same principle, proportionately abhor and oppose opposition to, and contempt of himself.' If the former is 'in its own nature decent and proper,' then so too is the latter (SS 488).

That 1 entails 2(b) may be less obvious, but Edwards thinks it unbecoming for 'the Sovereign of the world, a being of infinite glory, purity, and beauty, to suffer such a thing as sin ... without his ... giving some public manifestations and tokens of his infinite abhorrence of it' (SS 461). This, too, is plausible. Other things being equal, it is unfitting for the virtuous not to express their disapproval of wickedness and vice. By failing to openly disapprove of evil, they tolerate it or connive at it. Nor (other things again being equal) is it unreasonable to suppose that their expressions of disapproval should be in proportion to their abhorrence of the evils they disapprove of.

There is a further reason for thinking that 1 entails 2. 'If it be to God's glory that he is in his nature infinitely holy and opposite to sin; then it is to his glory to be infinitely displeased with sin. And if it be to God's glory to be infinitely displeased with sin; then it must be to God's glory to exercise and manifest that displeasure' (SS 462). In other words, if an attribute is excellent, then so too are its exercise and manifestation. So because God's opposition to sin is excellent, its exercise and manifestation are also excellent. It is thus reasonable to think that 1 entails 2.

The real problem is with 3. Edwards thinks that as 'the proper manifestations of God's power and wisdom' are 'mighty and wise works,' so punishment is the proper manifestation of his displeasure against sin (SS 462). But *why* is punishment the proper or most appropriate expression of God's opposition to sin? And why must it be *infinite*?

That the exercise and public manifestation of God's opposition to sin must at least *include* punishment is plausible given that God is the world's chief magistrate or 'moral Rector,' and that the punishment of wickedness and vice is fitting or appropriate whether or not it reforms the offender or deters others. Edwards makes both assumptions.

Yet why must the punishment be infinite? Presumably, because God's holiness and purity, and hence his opposition to sin, are infinite. Is this line of thought persuasive? It might be if Edwards could show that the expressions of God's *other* infinite attributes must be infinite.

But can he? The moon, after all, is finite although it is an expression of infinite power and wisdom. Even so, Edwards could perhaps argue that the *total* expression of an infinite attribute must be infinite in *some relevant respect* – that the world, for example, must be infinite because it is a product of infinite power and wisdom, or that the happiness of the saints must be infinite because it is the gift of infinite love.

But infinite in what sense? God's attributes are infinite in that they are unsurpassable. For example, God's beauty is infinite because nothing could be more beautiful and because no other beauty approximates it. (No other actual or conceivable beauty is half as beautiful, more than half as beautiful, almost as beautiful, and so on.) If the created expressions of God's attributes are infinite in an analogous sense, then they too are presumably unsurpassable in some relevant way. And there is reason to believe that Edwards thinks they are. The created world as a whole, for example, is the best possible, and hence a perfect (that is, unsurpassable) expression of God's infinite attributes. Viewed *sub specie aeternitatis*, the saint's happiness, too, is unsurpassable both because it is everlasting and because it asymptotically approaches God's perfection (EC 443, 459). By parity of reasoning, then, an infinite total expression of God's opposition to sin would be an unsurpassable expression of it – a punishment or penalty that is infinite in the sense that, in some respect, no punishment or penalty could be worse or even approximate it. The only punishment that clearly fits this description is permanent exclusion from God's presence. If we were created for beatitude, then a permanent exclusion from God's presence involves a permanent failure to realize our *telos*. In any case, in a theistic world, this evil is such that other evils (that is, all evils that don't include it) are incommensurable with it. No other evil that can befall us, or set of them, is as bad as this evil or even approximates it. So Edwards could argue that a perfect expression of God's infinite opposition to sin must involve the permanent exclusion of some (the sinful) from his presence. But this only takes Edwards close to his desired conclusion, not the whole way. For not only everlasting punishment but annihilation, too, involves permanent exclusion from God's presence.

Edwards thinks there are only three states – that in which there 'is nothing but good' (heaven), that in which good and evil are mixed (this world), and that in which there is nothing but evil (hell). It would be unfitting for the wicked to be placed in the first state. It would be equally unfitting for them to 'continue always' in the mixed state, for 'it is not fit that the barren tree should be allowed always to stand in the vineyard.' Edwards concludes that the wicked must therefore be placed in the state of unmixed evil (WUD 540–42). But this does not follow since an important alternative has been omitted, namely, the state in which there is *neither* good *nor* evil, that is, non-being.

Would annihilation be an *adequate* manifestation of God's infinite opposition to sin? Since it includes a permanent exclusion from the infinite good of God's presence, it is difficult to see why not.[2]

Yet suppose we grant that annihilation as well as the traditional hell adequately manifests God's infinite opposition to sin. Isn't there still a problem with either form of punishment? That is, wouldn't either form of permanent exclusion from God's presence obscure our grasp of an at least equally important divine attribute, namely, God's benevolence, or love to being in general? For example, wouldn't the saints' sense of God's goodness be tainted by their pity for the damned and horror at their fate? If it is, then God won't have succeeded in fully manifesting the love and goodness in which (according to Edwards) his glory principally consists.

This objection must be taken seriously but isn't conclusive. For a sense of God's love that is not tempered by a due sense of his infinite 'hatred of sin' may distort our view of his glory and beauty, and thus of his goodness. As Edwards says, 'A discovery of the love of God without an answerable discovery of the awful and terrible majesty and holiness of God, has a tendency to dispose the soul in some respects unsuitably towards God: there will not be a due reverence with love and delight ... 'Tis the will of God that when we rejoice, it should be with trembling and so [he] won't discover his love without [also] showing his terrible majesty' (Misc. 468).

I conclude, then, that it is at least not *clear* that anything less than permanent exclusion from God's presence will fully manifest his infinite opposition to sin. Yet even if this is true, is permanent exclusion from God's presence *just*? We will consider this question in the next section.

II

The principal objection to the traditional doctrine of hell is its apparent injustice. In inflicting everlasting misery upon the wicked, God imposes a penalty that seems to bear little or no proportion to the gravity of their offenses. Furthermore, in rejecting some while redeeming others who are equally undeserving, God appears to treat equal cases unequally.

A

Edwards's response to the first objection is clear. 'All sin, as it is against God, is infinitely heinous and has infinite demerit' (SS 459). It therefore deserves infinite punishment. How plausible is this?

In its 'primary' sense, 'true virtue consists in love to being in general' (TV 541); it aims at the general good. Those who love the general good, however, also love the disposition that promotes it. Thus the truly benevolent love benevolence as well as being.

But a truly benevolent person not only values benevolence because it promotes the general good; she also relishes it for its own sake. (Edwards calls this a 'truly virtuous complacence.') Hence, while true virtue 'most essentially consists in benevolence to being in general' (TV 540), there is a broader sense in which it includes both benevolence and a virtuous complacence, that is, both love toward being in general and a delight in that love's intrinsic beauty or 'excellence.'

God, though, 'is infinitely the greatest Being' and 'infinitely the most beautiful and excellent,' the 'foundation and fountain of all being and all beauty ... the sum and comprehension of all existence and excellence.' True virtue thus primarily consists in 'a supreme love to God, both of benevolence and complacence' (TV 550–51). Therefore, 'a determination of the mind to union and benevolence to a *particular person*, or *private system*, which is but a small part of the system of being ... is not of the nature of true virtue' unless it is dependent on or subordinate to benevolence to being in general (TV 554). For similar reasons, complacence in benevolence to particular persons or private systems is truly virtuous only when it is dependent upon or subordinate to complacence in God's benevolence. No one is truly virtuous, then, whose life isn't primarily governed by love of God and delight in his beauty. The noblest actions of those ruled by other principles are at best splendid vices.

But suppose we grant that if human behavior isn't motivated by the love of God, it isn't truly virtuous and is therefore sinful. Is it also *infinitely heinous*? Edwards believes that it is:

1 Sinful behavior is behavior motivated by an attachment to private systems rather than being in general. But
2 God is, 'in effect,' being in general (EC 461). Hence,
3 All sin is sin against God (from 1 and 2). But
4 God is infinitely worthy of regard. Since
5 An offense's gravity is principally determined by the worth of the being against whom it is committed,
6 There is 'infinite demerit in all sin against God' (OS 130) (from 4 and 5). Therefore,
7 All sin is infinitely heinous (from 3 and 6).

Premises 1, 2 and 4 seem plausible. In any case, I have no quarrel with them. Premise 5, however, is controversial and has been attacked by both Marilyn Adams[3] and Jonathan Kvanvig.[4] Since I have responded to Adams elsewhere,[5] I will focus here on Kvanvig's critique of my defense of the so-called 'status principle.'

In 'Original Sin,' I suggested that the principle is plausible if 'restricted to differences in ontological kinds and not applied to differences between more or less valuable members of the same kind.' So that, for example, whereas (other things being equal) offenses against morally good men and women may be neither more nor less grave than similar offenses against evil ones, offenses against archangels are worse than offenses against humans, offenses against humans are worse than offenses against dogs, and offenses against dogs are worse than wanton harm to flowers or crystals. A principle of this kind, I said, is 'all we need since God is a unique kind of being, and the value of the relevant kind (divinity) infinitely surpasses the value of other kinds.' Kvanvig considers three versions of my principle, arguing that each is inadequate. (1) A 'restricted' principle dividing reality into divine and non-divine beings is plausible only if it can be shown to follow from a 'more general status principle which makes reference to the division into kinds that results from carving nature (and supernature) at its joints' (Kvanvig 44f.). (2) A division into God, angels, humans, dogs, flowers, and so on, *does* divide things at the joints but is useless for our purposes because it is morally irrelevant. Wantonly destroying a dog, for example, isn't wrong because we have destroyed a *dog* but because we have destroyed something *sentient*. Being a member of an ontological kind isn't *itself* morally relevant although being of that kind may entail a property which is. We must therefore abandon 'ontological kind account[s] of status.' (3) The only version of the status principle that *might* work divides nature (and supernature) into morally relevant categories – persons and non-persons, for example, or sentient and non-sentient beings, or living and non-living things. Yet this won't do either. For God shares these properties with us and thus belongs to the same morally relevant kinds that we do. Other things being equal, offenses against rational beings or persons may be worse than offenses against beings that are merely sentient. But because God and we are both persons, the third version of the status principle does not imply that offenses against God are more grievous than those against our human neighbors. Kvanvig concludes that my status principle is indefensible or useless. Either way, it can't be used to defend Edwards's argument (Kvanvig, 40–49).

I do not find this convincing. In the first place, the division between divine and non-divine being *does* carve nature at its joints. Indeed, God and creatures are the two most fundamental ontological kinds, and the difference between them the most important ontological difference. (More on this below.) Secondly, although my examples may have been misleading, my intention was not to argue that *all* distinctions between ontological kinds are morally relevant but only that differences between certain *generic* ontological kinds – divine beings, angels, rational animals, animals, plants, or physical objects – are. Destroying a dog is worse than destroying a flower, not because dogs are *dogs*, but because dogs are *animals* and plants are not.[6] I agree, however, that the most perspicacious status principle will explicitly appeal to morally relevant properties like life, sentience and rationality or personhood.[7]

What, though, about Kvanvig's contention that a status principle framed in these terms is useless? That since the relevant categories include both God *and* us, it no longer follows that 'sinning against God is worse than sinning against your brother' (Kvanvig, 48). This seems wrong for two reasons. (And this is my third point.) First, Kvanvig seems to assume that the difference between God's sentience, or rationality, or moral agency and ours is a difference in degree and not in kind. He also assumes that differences in degree have little or no moral relevance. Both assumptions are dubious. Our sentience, for example, is a function of our animal nature and God's is not. Can his sentience, then, be the same kind as ours? Again, there may be only differences of degree between the sentience of oysters and the sentience of apes, but the difference in degree justifies differential treatment. Second, God is a member of at least one category that does not include us, namely divinity. It seems obvious to me at least that maximal perfection (and the self-existent holiness, omnipotence and omniscience on which it is parasitic) is a non-reducible morally relevant difference between God and us.

I conclude, then, that Kvanvig's objections to the status principle aren't compelling. Since the other premises of Edwards's argument are valid, we should accept its conclusion if its inferences are valid. But are they?

The inference from 3 and 6 to 7 is clearly valid. The inference from 1 and 2 to 3 is also plausible. For consider a parallel case. Susan is under the strongest obligations to her community and should regulate her behavior by a due regard for its interests. However, she is instead governed by an obsessive preoccupation with her children and, as a result, neglects the common good. In these circumstances, Susan has committed an offense against her community even if she didn't deliberately and self-consciously disregard its interests. Premises 4 and 5, however, do not entail 6. For it is logically possible that God's worth is infinite, that 'the gravity of an offense is a monotonically increasing function of the worth of the being offended' (so that 5 is true), but that the gravity of offenses against God remains finite.[8]

Is Edwards simply off the mark, then? Not clearly. For God's infinite worth together with the status principle at least *suggests* (although it does not prove) that offenses against him have infinite disvalue in the sense that no offense against a 'particular being' or 'private system' of beings could be worse or even approximate it in disvalue. (That is, no other offense is half as bad, more than half as bad, almost as bad, and so on.) In any case, 6 isn't *clearly* false.

But in the end this may not matter. For even if 6 is true, the most that follows is that sinful human behavior is infinitely heinous when considered objectively. It does not follow that sin deserves infinite punishment.[9]

The heinousness of an offense must be distinguished from the heinousness of the offender. That is, we must distinguish between the objective disvalue of acts which fall short of the law and the disvalue of the agents who perform them. Considered solely in relation to the law which proscribes it, a deliberate theft has the same disvalue irrespective of the person who commits it. Nonetheless, a wealthy, sane and educated man who commits a theft to show his contempt for the law is judged more harshly than a poor woman whose theft is at least partly the result of moral ignorance or confusion, and the pressure of circumstances.

A legislator charged with the task of drawing up criminal statutes in which fixed penalties are attached to certain types of offenses should primarily consider the objective disvalue of those offenses. A judge must also consider the disvalue of the persons committing them. Even when a crime is serious, it is sometimes unjust to apply the full rigor of the law because of the circumstances of the agent. In cases like these, the sentence should be reduced or suspended. It seems possible, therefore, for God, as legislator, to justly prescribe 'utter destruction' as the punishment affixed to offenses committed against his divine majesty and yet be unable, as judge, to justly inflict this punishment upon most of the sinners brought before him. In defending God against the charge of injustice, Edwards must not only show that he is a holy and just legislator, he must also show that he is a holy and just judge.

Even if sin is infinitely heinous in its own nature, an offender isn't infinitely heinous if he is unaware of the nature of his act or that act is (partly) involuntary. Now, common experience shows that our loves are restricted, partial, or private, and thus fall infinitely short of love to being in general. It does *not* show that our offenses against God are normally deliberate.[10] Nor does it show that they are fully voluntary. True virtue consists in love toward being in general, and vice in privileging private systems. Virtue and vice are thus dispositions of the heart, or affections. But our affective nature eludes our control. Corrupt dispositions and passions are therefore partly involuntary. Since wickedness implies a degree of self-consciousness and control which is lacking in most cases of human sin, it seems inappropriate to describe the persons who commit it as infinitely heinous.

Edwards would deny both claims. Like Calvin and St Paul, he believes that we have sufficient light to condemn us. He also thinks that our offenses are wilful: 'Sin ... wishes ill, and aims at ill, to God and man; but to God especially. It strikes at God; it would if it could, procure his misery and death' (Misc. 779).

There is truth, I think, in both contentions. It is at least arguable that everyone has at least *some* vision of the highest good, and thus (if God *is* the Good) of God. It is also true that all sin is, at least implicitly, directed against God. For privileging private systems implicitly commits one to 'striking at' being in general. Love of something entails 'hatred of,' or 'opposition to,' what apparently opposes it. So a love of private systems entails hatred of, or opposition to, what appears to oppose them. Since the good of being in general can conflict with the apparent good of private systems, loves centered on the latter involve an implicit hatred of, or opposition to, being in general or God, that is, an implicit tendency to oppose it.

The fact remains, however, that most offenses against God are neither fully self-

conscious nor wilful. Even if I intentionally sin against the highest good I perceive
and the good is in fact God, I don't intentionally sin against God *qua* God if I fail
to recognize that the two are identical. And even if an inordinate love of private
systems involves an implicit hatred of, or opposition to, God, the hatred or
opposition is (normally) *only* implicit.

It is not clear, then, that Edwards has shown that most sinners *deserve* an infinite
punishment even if, objectively considered, their offenses are infinitely heinous.
But in the end that may not matter. For one can be justified in withholding a good
even when the person from whom it is withheld can't appropriately be said to
deserve to be deprived of it. One is justified, for example, in refusing to bestow an
administrative post on a candidate who is unqualified for it. Nevertheless, if she
isn't fully responsible for her lack of qualifications, it seems wrong to say that she
deserves to fail. Similarly, if those with sinful dispositions aren't *fit* for heaven, then
God may be justified in withholding the good of eternal life even if it isn't true that
they *deserve* to be (permanently) excluded from his presence.

B

The doctrine Edwards defends maintains that God subjects some to punishment
while sparing others who are equally undeserving. But it seems unfair for God to
withhold his grace from John while bestowing it upon Mary, who is no better than
he. I will discuss Edwards's two most important responses to this objection: that if
John's protest (or a protest made on John's behalf) were legitimate, there would be
no such thing as grace (JG 394–95), and that '*unjustifiable* partiality is not
imputable to a sovereign distribution of his favors, though ever so unequally, unless
it be done unwisely, and so as to infringe the common good' (CDD 380, my
emphasis).

If John's protest is legitimate, then God, having bestowed his favor on Mary, is
obliged to bestow it on John. But what is *owed* (a debt) cannot be a gift or favor. As
Edwards argues in 'Divine Sovereignty,' grace is by definition a gift or present, not
something owed (Works 6, 486–7). To suppose that God is obliged to bestow his
grace on anyone is a contradiction in terms. Furthermore, if God is *obliged* to favor
us, then it is inappropriate to thank him for his favor since persons are not
appropriately thanked for fulfilling their obligations.

I believe that Edwards is correct in maintaining that grace is, by definition, a gift
or present, and that it makes no sense to say that someone deserves grace, or that
God owes him grace. But this isn't conclusive.

Consider the following three schemata:

1   A deserves to receive *x* from C (because of A's merit or some other
    qualification).
2   Irrespective of whether C has bestowed *x* on others, C has an obligation to
    bestow *x* on A.

3   If there are no relevant differences between A and B, then C has an obligation
to bestow *x* on A if C bestows *x* on B.

Form 3 propositions can be true even though related propositions of forms 1 and
2 are false. For consider the relation between parents and children. A father returns
from a trip. Neither of his two daughters *deserves* to receive a present from their
father, and he is under no obligation to bring them one, that is, he doesn't *owe* either
child a present. Nevertheless, *if* he chooses to give a present to one daughter, he is
obliged to give one to the other. Furthermore, since neither child deserved a present,
and since the father did not owe either of them a present, both should thank him.[11]

If this is correct, then the fact that grace is undeserved, and that God is under no
obligation to bestow his grace upon anyone, is not sufficient to refute those who
believe that *if* God bestows his grace upon Mary, who is no more deserving than
John, then God is obliged to also bestow it upon John.

Whether a form 3 proposition is true depends upon the nature of the relations
between A, B and C. Propositions of this form are not *always* true. As Edwards
observes, that someone goes out of his way to help a neighbor does not entitle his
other neighbors to demand similar treatment. Now, God stands to us in many
relationships. He is our bridegroom, redeemer, judge and king. But he is also our
father, and that creates a presumption in favor of the claim that if God chooses to
bestow grace upon one of his children, he is obliged to bestow it upon all others who
are no more undeserving.

A consideration of *other* relationships in which God stands to us may defeat this
presumption, however. The bridegroom analogy is particularly significant, for from
the fact that a bridegroom bestows love upon his bride, it doesn't follow that he
should bestow his love on another woman who is equally worthy of it. Romantic
love is inherently 'arbitrary' or 'capricious.' It *bestows* value on its object but is not
itself a *response* to objective value. The fact is that we employ diverse models to
express and explain the relation between God and human beings, and these pull us
in different directions.

I conclude, then, that whether or not God treats someone unfairly by not bestowing
grace upon him when he bestows it upon another who is equally undeserving depends
upon the relative importance of the models which suggest that God does have
obligations of this type. The importance of the father model in the Judeo-Christian
tradition suggests that he does, but other important models have different implications.

Whether Edwards himself can privilege the bridegroom analogy is doubtful.
Friendship, marriage and other forms of elective love are conceptually distinct from
benevolence since the former involve gratuitous choice and the latter does not. But
God's love, according to Edwards, is true benevolence – a love of being in general
which esteems everything in proportion to its real worth. Edwards distinguishes
God's elective love of the saints from his love of being in general but (in effect)
subsumes the former under the latter. God's elective love consists in his
predestination of some (and not others) to salvation. God's elective choices,

however, are determined by his will for the best and that, in turn, by his perfect love of being in general. Ultimately, God's choices are *not* gratuitous but only appear so because of our inability to fathom his reasons for them. In Edwards's view, God's love of created being is more like a wise father's benevolent love for his children than Tristan's love of Iseult or Damon's love of Pythias.

Edwards's second response may solve the problem created by the importance of the father model, however. If a father arbitrarily favors one child, he acts unwisely and infringes the common good (which, in this case, is the good of the family), for it is highly likely that his actions will produce pride, envy and resentment, and thus destroy the web of mutual affection which should bind a family's members together. Edwards should therefore argue that the goods secured by the unequal distribution of God's favors, namely, the manifestation of his 'vindictive justice' and 'awful majesty,' and of the freedom and sovereignty of his grace, together with the humility and gratitude which this evokes in the saints, contributes to the good of the entire system. The two cases, Edwards might say, are relevantly dissimilar. By treating his children unequally a human father impairs the (relevant) common good. God's unequal distribution of favors enhances it.

I do not find anything wrong with this *type* of response to the charge of unjustifiable partiality. Whether Edwards's *version* of it is adequate depends upon the truth of the claim that the unequal distribution of God's gifts most effectively contributes to the good of being in general. That it does so at least partly depends upon the adequacy of the arguments discussed in section I.

III

What, finally, are we to make of Edwards's apology? It undoubtedly leaves us uneasy. Some of this uneasiness may be due to a failure to take sin seriously, a lack of appreciation of its ugliness and horror. Some of it may result from failing to see that God is the 'chief part' of being, and that our obligations to rational being are therefore, chiefly, obligations to *him*. It cannot be explained entirely by these factors. Within the framework of the assumptions of classical Christian theism, the doctrine of hell implies that God has 'hated' certain persons from eternity. (For if God is omniscient and his decrees immutable, then, if he utterly opposes and rejects the damned, there is no time at which he does not oppose and reject them.) This is a stumbling block and an offense.

Nevertheless, Edwards has, in my opinion, shown that given certain not implausible assumptions concerning the infinite disvalue of offending God, the fittingness of retributive punishment, the value of God's self-manifestation and so on, the permanent exclusion of some from God's presence is consistent with the existence of a God of infinite greatness and excellency. I do not think he has shown that non-scriptural reasons can be given for the claim that this exclusion must take the form of everlasting punishment rather than annihilation.

Neither does it follow that the existence of a God of infinite greatness and excellency is compatible with the rejection of the countless numbers of men and women who are not fully aware of the nature of their sin, or *cannot* love being in general. Nor do I see any way to justify God's rejection of the reprobate if, as Edwards believes, God not only has made the vessels of his hatred but has also made them hateful. These positions are part of the system which Edwards was defending. To the extent that his arguments fail to support them, his defense is a failure. The significance of this failure, however, will depend upon whether Edwards's positions on these issues are essential to a Christian doctrine of hell. In my opinion, they are not.

Notes

1. 'Wicked Men Useful in their Destruction Only' (henceforth WUD), in Edwards, Jonathan (1817, 1847), *The Works of President Edwards*, vol. 6 of 10 vols, eds Edward Williams and Edward Parsons, Edinburgh and New York: B. Franklin, henceforth *Works*. Other relevant works are: 'The End of the Wicked Contemplated by the Righteous; or The Torments of the Wicked in Hell, No Occasion of Grief to the Saints in Heaven,' *Works* 4, henceforth EW; 'Sinners in the Hands of an Angry God,' *Works* 6, henceforth SHG; 'The Justice of God in the Damnation of Sinners,' *Works* 6, henceforth JG; Edwards, Jonathan (1970), *Original Sin, The Works of Jonathan Edwards Volume 3*, ed. Clyde A. Holbrook, New Haven: Yale University Press, henceforth OS; 'Satisfaction for Sin,' *Works* 8, henceforth SS; 'Concerning the Divine Decrees,' *Works* 8, henceforth CDD; Edwards, Jonathan (1989), *Concerning the End for which God Created the World and The Nature of True Virtue* (henceforth EC and TV, respectively), in *Ethical Writings, The Works of Jonathan Edwards Volume 8*, ed. Paul Ramsey, New Haven: Yale University Press; and Edwards, Jonathan (1994), *The 'Miscellanies,'* 501–832, *The Works of Jonathan Edwards Volume 18*, ed. Ava Chamberlain, New Haven: Yale University Press, henceforth Misc. followed by the Miscellany's number.
2. At one point Edwards argues that annihilation isn't punishment because we aren't conscious of having suffered it ('The Eternity of Hell Torments,' in *Works* 7, p. 471). But this is a bad argument. If it were sound, then, if naturalism were true, capital punishment wouldn't be punishment.
3. Adams, Marilyn McCord (1975), 'Hell and the God of Justice,' *Religious Studies* 11, 433–47.
4. Kvanvig, Jonathan (1993), *The Problem of Hell*, New York: Oxford University Press; henceforth Kvanvig.
5. Wainwright, William J. (1988), 'Original Sin,' in Morris, Thomas V. (ed.), *Philosophy and the Christian Faith*, Notre Dame: University of Notre Dame Press.
6. But can't Kvanvig simply rephrase his objection? Wantonly destroying a dog isn't wrong because the dog is an *animal* but because it is *sentient*. This is a distinction without a difference, however, for sentience is included in the essence animality. Kvanvig points out that 'explanatory relations are not constant under substitution of logical equivalents.' If God exists necessarily, then 'God exists' and '2+2=4' are logically equivalent. But the first explains the falsity of physicalism and the second does not (Kvanvig, 46). Nor (we might add) does the fact that P entails Q and Q explains R entail that P explains R. 'I exist' entails the conjunction '5 is the immediate successor of 4 and 4 is the immediate

successor of 3.' But the latter explains why 5 is a successor of 3 and the former does not. Nevertheless, when a property is not only entailed by another but is part of its essence (alternatively, is a defining feature of it), then if the former explains something, so does the latter. John's being already married explains why his marriage to Sue is bigamous but so too does his being already a husband.

7. But notice that persons (rational beings), sentient beings, living beings, and so on, are *also* ontological kinds. So this version of the status principle (like the second) 'divides nature (and supernature) at the joints.' The question isn't *whether* a division into ontological kinds is morally relevant but only *which* divisions into ontological kinds are morally relevant.

8. I owe this objection to Philip L. Quinn. Suppose that x is the worth of the being offended and that *y* is the gravity of the offense. 'Let $y=(1-[1/x+1])=([x+1/x+1]-[1/x+1])=(x+1-1/x+1)=x/x+1$.
   When x=0, y=0; [when] x=1/2, y=1/3; [when] x=1, y=1/2; [when] x=2, y=2/3; [when] x=10, y=10/11; [when] x=100, y=100/101,' and so on. 'As $x \rightarrow \infty$, $y \rightarrow 1- 1/\infty =1-0=1$.' (Correspondence, 16 February 2001. Quoted with permission. The algebraic equation was provided by Timothy Bays.)

9. That is, (as I argued in section I) a permanent exclusion from God's presence, whether taking the form of everlasting misery or of annihilation.

10. Edwards was not unaware of this difficulty. Miscellany 44 addresses the objection that 'the malicious or evil principle, which is the essence of sin, is not infinite' since persons who commit offenses against God do not actually have 'a full and complete idea of the infinite excellence and greatness of God,' and that it is therefore unjust 'to punish sin with an infinite punishment.' Edwards's reply appears to be this: just as our offense is, objectively considered, infinitely heinous because it is an offense against an infinitely great and excellent being, so our punishment is objectively infinite since it is everlasting. But just as our offense is not '*committed* infinitely' (my emphasis), so its punishment is not *experienced* as infinite because it is not experienced all at once. This won't do. For suppose we concede that the fitting punishment for an offense that is infinitely heinous when considered objectively, but is not 'committed infinitely' because of the ignorance of the offender, is a punishment that is objectively infinite but not experienced as such. Even so, everlasting misery isn't *clearly* a punishment of this kind, for it is *experienced in its entirety* even if it isn't experienced all at once and there is therefore no single moment at which its horror is fully appreciated. In any case Edwards fails to address the main point, namely, that because of their ignorance, men and women don't deserve to experience an infinite punishment, whether all at once or bit by bit.

11. Of course, there is a *sense* in which the father is obliged to give a present to his child. Given that he intends to bestow a present on his oldest daughter, Becky, he is obliged to bestow one on his youngest daughter, Sarah. Nevertheless, Becky and Sarah should both thank him. It can be appropriate to thank people for fulfilling their obligations when those obligations are voluntarily assumed. For example, if a person who is under no obligation to me sees that I am in difficulties and promises to help, it is appropriate for me to thank him for fulfilling his promise even though, having made it, he is obliged to help me. In the case we are discussing, any obligation the father incurs is a consequence of his freely deciding to give at least one child a present. It is therefore appropriate for both to thank him. (However, if the *only* reason why the father gave a present to one child was because, having freely bestowed a gift on his other and more favored daughter, he recognized his obligation to do so, then it is not clear that the first child owes her father any gratitude. The existence of the obligation in question does not preclude gratitude [which is my point], but if it is the *only* reason for the gift, then gratitude does seem inappropriate.)

Chapter 3

Edwards on Free Will

Hugh J. McCann

Jonathan Edwards's *A Careful and Strict Enquiry into the Modern Prevailing Notions of That Freedom of Will Which is Supposed to be Essential to Moral Agency, Virtue and Vice, Reward and Punishment, Praise and Blame* is as prolix as its title, as careful and strict as the title promises, and as relentless as the New England winter. For 311 pages, in the standard edition,[1] he pounds away at his Arminian opponents, repeatedly locating them in substantially the same infinite regress, and rejecting their notion of freedom as both irrelevant to true liberty and inconsistent with a proper understanding of God's knowledge and sovereignty. In large part, the tone is just a symptom of Edwards's time, in which polemical disputation was commonplace in theology. But it also signals the importance of the issue at hand – an age-old dispute in which human dignity is pitted against that of God, and to which a satisfactory resolution seems impossible. If we claim, as Arminius did, that human agents enjoy a kind of freedom that is antideterministic, God's power over the world appears limited, and his omniscience at least threatened. If by contrast we take the Calvinist stance, arguing that our deeds and destinies are fixed by divine decree, then our place in the world seems little different from that of our house pets. Some of us may be blessed with good dispositions and others not; but either way, our actions appear finally determined by factors utterly beyond our control. There is little of moral dignity in that, and it is hard to see, if it is so, how our destinies have been justly decreed, or even that the concept of justice applies to the case. Edwards's view of the matter is that of a good Calvinist: God's dignity comes first, and those who would subordinate it to man's must be shown to have misconceived things. But while Edwards's perceptions are in some ways very acute, his argument is not convincing, simply because the ordinary concept of freedom – whether it captures what really goes on in human action or not – is in fact the Arminian one. I will argue for this claim in what follows. More important, however, I want to suggest that to uphold the Arminian concept of freedom is not necessarily to diminish God's sovereignty or knowledge. On a proper understanding of the relation between God's will and our own, neither God's sovereignty nor our own moral authenticity need be diminished.

I

Edwards's position will be better appreciated if we first remind ourselves of what is at stake. Both he and his opponents believe in a God of maximal omniscience and sovereignty, whose power extends to every corner of the universe and all that occurs in it. Simply taken, this would mean that God's power over each human destiny is absolute, as it is over all else. And there is good scriptural backing for such a view, especially in the New Testament, where some doctrine of election seems clearly to be at work. There believers are told that they are chosen in Christ 'before the creation of the world to be holy and blameless in his sight. In love he predestined us to be adopted ... in accordance with his pleasure and will' (Ephesians 1: 4–5). This choosing is said to be 'in accordance with the foreknowledge of God the Father' (1 Peter 1: 2), and it is 'not because of anything we have done, but because of his own purpose and grace' (2 Timothy 1: 9). Indeed, as far as our own actions are concerned, even Hebrew Scripture speaks of God as having 'wrought all our works in us' (Isaiah 26: 12), and Christians are famously warned by Paul to 'work out your salvation in fear and trembling, for it is God who works in you both to will and to do according to his good pleasure' (Philippians 2: 12–13). The message here is clearly that our actions are in the control of God, who 'has mercy on whom he will have mercy, and hardens whom he will harden' (Romans 9: 18). If we accept this, what we say about human freedom has to be commensurate with a God whose power and sovereignty rule our every deed.

But what can we say in such a case? The passages cited appear to dictate a deterministic account of the will, in which the fiat of the creator settles our decisions and actions, and thereby our destiny. The impact of this might be softened somewhat if we hold that God accomplishes his ends through secondary causes – by having us always follow our strongest motive, perhaps – but in any case he controls all that we do. No such account is acceptable from the perspective of the Arminian, who defends what philosophers call *libertarian* freedom. From that perspective, any treatment of human decision and action in terms of deterministic causation inevitably entails that our deeds are selected *for* us, not *by* us. The selection may operate through our own acts of deciding and willing, but that makes no difference if these are caused by acts of will on God's part, or by our strongest motive. Granted, earlier actions of ours may at times influence later desires. But even then, on the causal account, our earliest actions must be caused by factors we do not control at all – by primitive longings ordained by God, or by his will directly. And then how can we be responsible? No one can resist the will of God: of necessity, what he wills must come to pass. Nor are we able to dictate what he wills, or to control in the end whatever environmental and psychological causes he might choose as means to bring about our behavior. But then, in a very real sense, none of what we do is truly up to us; and if that is so, justice seems no more than an empty word. How, if we are thus manipulated, can it be fair to punish us? We are not different, if determinism holds, from anything else in nature. Why, then, should it be that at death, a vicious dog faces only oblivion, whereas a vicious man faces damnation?

Utilitarian considerations are impotent here. It may be that earthly punishments help alter our motives, and hence our actions during life, and that this would be true whether we are determined or not. But the same does not hold in the eternal context, at least according to orthodox theology. At death, the state of the reprobate becomes irretrievable: their character is fixed and their motives beyond alteration, so their punishment cannot be justified by any hope of reforming them. The fate of the damned might, of course, have a deterrent effect on others here on earth. No doubt some whose destinies are still evolving find themselves moved to reform by consideration of the wrath to come. But even if we can convince ourselves that this has moral significance in a setting where all action is caused, it hardly follows that those already under condemnation are being fairly treated. Their punishment can be just only if they are responsible for their destinies, which by Arminian lights they are not if determinism holds. Moral responsibility requires that my will serve not only as the vehicle but also as the source of my unfolding destiny. Accordingly, the Arminian opts for a libertarian account of decision and action. The will is free. That is, what we decide and do is truly up to us, in that our decisions and actions are not causally determined by any combination of factors or circumstances, including the will of God. We are the masters of our own destinies; we possess a moral authenticity that places us above other animals, and makes us fit objects of eternal reward or punishment – thereby preserving a morally legitimate notion of divine justice.

II

Edwards, of course, is having none of this. He too is concerned to defend divine justice, but the Arminian strategy he finds unacceptable. Even if the libertarian conception of freedom is philosophically defensible – which Edwards will insist it is not – it is theologically unacceptable. To endorse this kind of freedom is, first of all, to court Pelagianism.[2] It looks as if we should be able, if we are free in this sense, to live a virtuous life entirely by our own resources; above all, we ought to be able to resist or accept the grace of salvation as we choose. Neither is possible for Edwards. Fallen human beings are incapable, without the interposition of God's grace, of doing anything truly acceptable in his sight (432), and salvation is strictly a matter of divine decree (433–4). The elect are chosen by God from the foundation of the world, and nothing any of us can do will alter our fate. This is in keeping with the complete and all-pervading sovereignty of God, which Edwards also upholds. Sovereignty consists in part, he says, in '[God's] will not being subject to, or restrained by the will of any other, and others' wills being perfectly subject to his' (380). If this is right, then whatever freedom is, it cannot allow us to act in ways that escape God's power and governance, or that subject his will to ours in any way. Our freedom cannot put God in a position of having to await our actions, and then react to them in order to achieve his ends. Yet this is precisely what the Arminian conception of freedom threatens to do.

But that is not all. Edwards's most extensive complaint about the theological implications of Arminian freedom concerns its implications regarding divine omniscience and foreknowledge. God's prior knowledge of human action is for Edwards an unimpeachable fact, manifested in the foretelling of specific acts such as Pharaoh's refusal to release Israel, and Peter's denial, as well as in a host of prophecies whose fulfillment could not have occurred without God knowing our behavior in advance (240–45). Indeed, the entire foundation of God's kingdom on earth would be based in nothing but guesswork unless God foreknew our actions (245). Such foreknowledge is, however, impossible if the libertarian account of free will is correct. This, says Edwards,

> may be proved thus; 'tis impossible for a thing to be certainly known to any intellect without *evidence*. To suppose otherwise, implies a contradiction: because for a thing to be certainly known to any understanding is for it to be *evident* to that understanding: and for a thing to be evident to any understanding is for the understanding to *see evidence* of it ... But if there be any future event, whose existence is contingent, without all necessity, the future existence of that event is absolutely *without evidence*. (258–9, Edwards's emphasis)

Edwards goes on to explain that what is evident must be either self-evident, or evident through its connection with something else. Neither is possible in the case of the operations of our will, if they represent an arena of Arminian contingency. They cannot be evident in themselves, since that would amount to their being logically or conceptually necessary; clearly, it was not logically necessary that Pharaoh refuse freedom to the Israelites. And if Pharaoh's action was free in the libertarian sense, it was exempt from causation, so there was no connection with anything else that would make it evident, either. In particular, there was no connection of the type that must ground divine foreknowledge, which has to be infallible. One might fairly claim that even on a libertarian scenario God had some evidence: Pharaoh was more likely, given his character, to refuse Moses' demands, the more so since God had hardened his heart. But that is not enough for certain knowledge, because it is consistent with Pharaoh deciding to let the people go, the possibility of which would render God's knowledge less than infallible. When things are infallibly foreknown, says Edwards, there is 'as great a necessity of their future existence, as if the event were already written down ...' (262).

It is not easy to escape this problem. One tactic is to adopt a Boethian stance on divine eternity. Boethius held that God exists outside of time, in a kind of eternal present to which all that goes on in the temporal world is equally accessible.[3] In a single act of awareness, God comprehends all of history, the future as well as the present and past, as though all were now occurring. If this is true, then God need not await our actions in order to know them; he sees them along with everything else, from his timelessly eternal vantage point. Thus, we might argue, our freedom poses no threat to God's omniscience. We can act entirely on our own in what is for us the future; yet God will not be ignorant of our deeds, because for him there is no future, just his timeless awareness, in which all is known. But this tactic, of which Edwards is well aware (266),[4] is at best partially successful. The difficulty is that the Boethian approach does not allow God to know *as creator* what our actions will be. Rather, it has him learning of our actions in light of our performing them, so that even though he is outside of time, his knowledge of our deeds is logically or metaphysically *posterior* to their occurrence. But his act of creating us must be logically *prior* to their occurrence, for unless we exist we cannot act. So while the Boethian maneuver may save us from having to say there is a time when God is ignorant of our decisions and willings, it requires that there be a phase of God's own activity that proceeds in ignorance of ours.[5] It is, moreover, a crucial phase, for if God did not know as creator that, say, anyone would ever sin, his providential governance of the world could not safely presume that fact.

A second tactic for restoring omniscience to God is owing to the sixteenth-century Spanish Jesuit, Luis de Molina, who held that God was able to know in advance how each creature he might create would behave in whatever circumstances that creature might be found – notwithstanding the fact that the creature enjoys libertarian freedom.[6] This so-called 'middle knowledge' is presented to God in what are known as *subjunctives of freedom*, each of which is known by him prior to creating the world. For example, he knew that if he created you in the circumstance where you had the opportunity to be reading this chapter right now, you would freely decide to read it. Armed with this knowledge, he could then create you in that circumstance – as opposed, say, to someone whose entire life was descriptively identical to yours until this moment, but who would have decided differently. In that way, it is alleged, God can govern the course of history without guesswork, yet without causing our actions. For he has the same kind of knowledge regarding the free decisions and actions of all possible creatures in all possible circumstances, and so can choose whom he will create, and how they will be situated. Thus, it appears, God's omniscience is safe, even though our actions are free.

Of the many difficulties this view faces, two are especially pressing. One is that it only worsens the threat to divine sovereignty posed by creaturely freedom. For now it appears to be settled even in advance of creation that some worlds, though they are certainly possible logically speaking, are nevertheless beyond the reach of God's creative power – for example, a world in which you exist, and are given the opportunity mentioned above to read this chapter, yet choose not to read it. This world is beyond God's reach, for it is settled a priori that, if created in the right circumstances, you will behave as you are doing now.[7] Needless to say, it is hardly in keeping with traditional belief that God's will should be thus subordinated to those of creatures as yet uncreated – indeed, some of whom may never be created –

nor is this a limitation Edwards is prepared to accept (395–96). In fact, however (and this is the second difficulty), it is not at all obvious that middle knowledge is possible, as becomes apparent if we are mindful of the way Edwards frames the omniscience problem. It is, as he says, a problem of *evidence*. Knowledge is not a matter of lucky guesses, or of believing, however fervently, what happens to be true. It requires justification, and it is not at all clear that there can be evidence to justify middle knowledge. Certainly, counterfactuals of freedom are not logically necessary. If your choice to read this chapter was free in the libertarian sense, it could hardly have been logically necessitated. And prior to the creation of the world, there could not have been contingent evidence to assure God that you would read it, either. Indeed, it seems clear that, had such evidence been available to God in advance of creation, it would only have curtailed his options still further. He would have been given the *fait accompli* that, come what may, he was going to create you, and you were going to decide to read this chapter. Middle knowledge is not, then, a possibility. Prior to the exercise of his own creative will, God can have no knowledge of how free creatures will behave.

III

Clearly, then, Arminianism faces serious theological difficulties. Unless a way can be found to bring libertarian freedom within the scope of God's creative will – something Edwards and his opponents both treat as impossible – both God's sovereignty and his omniscience must be denied, and with them the entire doctrine of the elect. This is too much for the Calvinism of Edwards – too much, indeed, for a great deal of Christian theology – and he accordingly rejects libertarian freedom. But he offers plenty of philosophical justification for doing so as well. Indeed, Edwards seems never to tire of belaboring the philosophical problems he sees in his opponents' position. Some of these are actually founded in a simplistic view he himself holds about the etiology of human action. There is no room in Edwards's position for a distinction between passive and active willing. That is, he sees no difference between merely desiring to perform some action, a state libertarians would likely view as passive and involuntary, and actively deciding to perform the act, or forming the intention to perform it. Rather, there is nothing to willing except preponderant desire or inclination. On this point, Edwards even takes issue with Locke, to whom he is otherwise heavily indebted. Locke is at pains to demonstrate a difference between desire and will,[8] but for Edwards, 'A man never, in any instance, wills anything contrary to his desires, or desires anything contrary to his will' (139). As for deciding or choosing, this comes to no more than developing a preference or preponderant desire:

> I have rather chosen to express myself thus, that the will always *is* as the greatest apparent good, or as what appears most agreeable, is, than to say that the will is

determined by the greatest apparent good, or by what seems most agreeable; because an appearing most agreeable or pleasing to the mind, and the mind's preferring and choosing, seem hardly to be properly and perfectly distinct. (144)

In short, there is really no difference between choosing some end and coming to have a preponderant desire for it.

Armed with this non-distinction, Edwards is able to refute with ease some standard libertarian theses. Consider, for example, the claim that at the very least, we must enjoy libertarian freedom in cases where we have no preponderant desire, where the alternatives before us appear of equal value. The Arminian might think we can choose as we please in such a case, but on Edwards's understanding this 'liberty of indifference' is a self-contradiction:

To suppose the will to act at all in a state of perfect indifference, either to determine itself, or to do anything else, is to assert that the mind chooses without choosing. To say that when it is indifferent, it can do as it pleases, is to say that it can follow its pleasure, when it has no pleasure to follow. (198)

As for the idea that we might actually choose in opposition to our strongest or preponderant desire, that is equally impossible:

[s]urely the will can't act or choose contrary to a ... prevailing inclination of the will ... That which the will chooses and prefers, that, all things considered, it preponderates and inclines to. It is equally impossible for the will to choose contrary to its own ... present preponderating inclination, as 'tis to prefer contrary to its own present preference, or to choose contrary to its own present choice. (205)

For Edwards, then, there is not even a logical possibility of the mind or will rising up against the force of inclination, and charting an independent course. Our inclinations may change with our comprehension of our circumstances, and of the value of the alternatives we face. But inclination or desire is all there is to willing, and to develop a preponderant desire is not just to experience the causal antecedent of an ongoing, deterministic process of intention formation. It is to complete the process, to form the intention, to decide.

This is, of course, far too easy, and we shall eventually have to return to this issue. But Edwards can be much more persuasive – for example, in his effort to show that Arminians cannot give a rationally acceptable account of how free will operates. Their claim is that, rather than being ruled by the most powerful available motive, the will has a power of self-determination, through which it is able to control its choices. Edwards sees no plausible way to parse this claim, and here his argument is much stronger. One possibility is that, like our other actions, acts of will are determined by choice, and that this is what makes them free. This suggests, however, that each act of choice, to be free, must be caused by a previous act of choice, threatening an infinite regress. The only way to halt the regress is to postulate an act of choice that is not the result of a prior choice. On the account at issue, however, this act would not be self-determined, not being brought about by the agent's choice, and therefore would not be free. But if it is not free, then neither are any of the other choices in the series, and the game is lost. (172)

This kind of argument is familiar in treatments of the will,[9] and Edwards reverts to it frequently (for example, 188–9, 235, 270, 344). As he proceeds to demonstrate, moreover, it raises a very difficult problem. The opponent might try to escape by denying that there is any act by which we determine our choices, yet still insisting that the will is self-determining. But this will not do. If the will is able to be self-determining, there ought to be some means by which this power is exercised, something the will *does* to set itself in motion. Otherwise, we appear to have a contradiction: a power we claim is wielded by the agent, but not through anything the agent does (175). Yet, the minute we postulate such a doing we are in trouble. If we make it some act independent of the choice to be determined, we court the vicious regress described above. Nor, as Edwards points out, can the viciousness be defused by making the sequence simultaneous. The libertarian may try this move, holding that the regress of acts is a legitimate possibility if it takes place all at once. But any regress deprives us of a point at which action is finally *initiated*, and if we try to cut it off by postulating a 'first choice,' not arising from any other, that choice will still fail, by the present theory, to be self-determined, and so fail to be free (177). The alternative maneuver is to claim that the act by which a choice is determined is not anything independent of it, but rather the very choice itself. This too, however, appears to fail. For, says Edwards, to claim this is to hold that the same exertion of the will counts as both cause and effect. That is not possible: a cause must be prior to its effect, if not in temporal order, then at least logically or, as Edwards puts it, 'in the order of nature' (178).

The problem to which these arguments point is endemic to libertarian treatments of human agency, which often seek to locate in agency itself a substitute for what their authors understand to constitute natural causation. We tend to think of ordinary event causation as an operation of existence conferral, in which the events and/or circumstances that make up the cause do not just issue in the effect, but actually bring it into existence – *ex nihilo*, as it were. Now it may be argued that this conception is in fact quite mistaken.[10] But once it is accepted, libertarians feel compelled to account for the existence of human decisions and actions in a new way, by appealing to some source apart from the events that surround our doings. And once those have been eliminated, there remain just two candidates: the creator, and the agent himself. The first does not appear promising, because invoking God's action as creator seems simply to reintroduce determinism, with divine fiat now causing our deeds. Thus we are left with the agent, who must now be held to bring his actions into existence, if anything does. As Edwards shows, however, this leads either to an unacceptable regress, or to a view that has acts of will being brought into existence as a part of the act itself. That is also impossible, since before the action occurs there is nothing to produce it, and once it is on hand its production is no longer necessary.

We should not conclude that there is no such thing as agency or self-determination. But Edwards's arguments do seem to show that whatever these consist in, it is not anything that counts as conferring existence on our own deeds. This puts him in a very strong position, for now the only apparent option left to the Arminian is simply to abandon the principle of sufficient reason: to hold that there is no accounting whatever for the existence of human choice and volition – not in God, nor in man, nor in nature. This is simply too much for Edwards to accept. It is not clear, for one thing, that in this case willing would be anything but a misfortune to the agent, something that befalls him instead of being done freely (271). But even forgetting this, such a move is out of the question. Anything that begins to be, Edwards insists, must have a cause (181). Without this principle, we cannot infer the existence of God from his works (182), or that of the world from our experience (183). Nor can we expect the world to be stable in its behavior. Rather, we must be prepared for it to take any course it pleases, for all sorts of things to appear from nowhere, and not look for an accounting, since there need be no order in the coming of something from nothing (184). Better determinism than this. And there is a further point, which we may add on Edwards's behalf: if our concern is to secure divine omniscience and sovereignty, we could hardly do worse than to espouse events, volitional or otherwise, whose appearance on the world's stage has no accounting whatever.

IV

And so we turn to Edwards the determinist, and here the position is as we would expect, with one proviso. All operations of the will, he claims, are determined by the strongest motive. The proviso is that since, for Edwards, willing in the sense of choice or decision simply *is* preponderant desire, motive cannot be the same as desire. Instead, it is 'the whole of that which moves, excites or invites the mind to volition' (141). So motive is not desire, but rather the totality of whatever awakens desire in us when apprehended – desire being the same thing as choice or volition once it becomes 'prevailing.' Obviously, there is no room here for libertarian freedom. What is more, Edwards cheerfully admits that since they are always caused in this way, there is a sense in which our choices are necessary. He calls this *moral necessity*, which is a 'sure and certain connection' between moral causes – in this case motives – and their effects (157). All of our willing is governed by this kind of necessity; we are never morally able to act otherwise than we do (307). But this does not interfere with responsibility. Just the opposite: we think of someone whose actions arise out of a deep-seated propensity to virtue as all the more to be praised and esteemed, whereas someone who acts out of deeply rooted malice or violence of character is considered that much more deserving of condemnation

(360). So the freedom required for moral responsibility does not involve the absence of determinism.

What it does involve is straightforward Lockean compatibilism:

> The plain and obvious meaning of the words 'freedom' and 'liberty,' in common speech is power, opportunity, or advantage, that anyone has, to do as he pleases. Or in other words, his being free from hindrance or impediment in the way of doing ... as he wills. (163)

On this kind of account, freedom has nothing to do with the connection between motive and will – that is, between antecedents of decision or volition and these mental acts. Rather, freedom concerns the relation between willing and its consequences, with whether decision and volition are able to issue in the behavior chosen. Where we are able to do as we please, so that a choice to do *A* would result in our *A*-ing, we have free will. The opposite of this is not causation, which Edwards holds operates throughout, but rather *constraint* or *restraint*, whereby we are either forced to do what we do not will, or prevented from doing what we do or might will (164). This kind of necessity – Edwards sometimes calls it 'natural necessity,' to distinguish it from the moral variety – excuses. A prisoner in a locked cell can neither be praised nor blamed for not leaving. But moral necessity does not. However determined his will may have been in committing the crime that brought him to his cell, the prisoner deserves to be there.

The formula that freedom is the power to do as we please is a favorite with Edwards. He employs it constantly, and tends to equate it with others that seem quite different – for example, statements from Church Fathers that speak of freedom of choice, or an ability of the soul to incline to whatever course it will (192). These sound as if freedom applies properly to willing itself, rather than to whether it can effect its intentions without impediment, but that idea is anathema to Edwards. He is aware, of course, that his Arminian opponents hold that for free will to obtain, we must be able to choose as well as act otherwise. Plugged into the formula, however, this simply comes to the ability to choose as we please, or to have chosen otherwise if we had chosen, leading to the same regress on which the Arminian notion of self-determination was alleged to founder (234–5). He is insistent, moreover, that the common notion of liberty has nothing to do with notions such as these:

> If a man is not restrained from acting as his will determines, or constrained to act otherwise; then he has liberty, according to common notions of liberty, without taking into the idea that grand contradiction of all the determinations of a man's free will being the effects of the determinations of his free will. (359)

If Edwards is right in all this – if choice is nothing but strongest desire, and freedom of will nothing but freedom of action – then he will have saved the day. Decision and volition will not violate sufficient reason; God's sovereignty and omniscience will be secure, since as creator he sets in motion a strictly determined history, the course of which can be planned entirely in advance. Above all, the Christian doctrine of election will be secured: the grace of salvation can be extended to whomever God wishes, in whatever strength he deems necessary to secure that person's conversion and eternal reward.

V

But how much of it is true? Edwards's objections to the libertarian concept of agent causation are, I think, well taken. I know of no way to make it plausible that we can confer existence on our own acts of will. And as long as their existence is not brought under the direct power of God as creator, I know of no way to preserve a thoroughgoing conception of divine sovereignty and omniscience. But the rest doesn't look very good. Consider Edwards's claim that choice or decision is the same thing as predominant desire. His strategy here is well conceived, since from a determinist perspective there is no reason why desire should be translated into action by any process other than coming to predominate. If we make decision out to be any more than this, it begins to have an antideterministic ring. But decision is a lot more, as can be seen even from modest reflection. Desire is in the main a dispositional state, a liking for one or another thing or action that may or may not lead one to pursue it if the circumstances are right. I may have a desire and not be thinking about it at all; I might even be asleep. Not so with choice or decision: it is a conscious event – something I do, and for which I am responsible. To make a choice is, moreover, to form an *intention*, a state in which, unlike the situation with desire, I am committed to pursuing the course I intend. There are more differences: desires may be strong or weak; they may be difficult to get rid of, and even more difficult to cultivate. Choice or decision, by contrast, is neither strong nor weak; and both our decisions and the intentions in which they issue are things we feel able to institute or expunge 'at will.'

It is possible to try to soften some of these differences. For example, besides dispositional desire, there is occurrent desire: the type of experience we all have with considerable frequency, of wanting one or another end. And it might be claimed that choice is to be identified only with conscious desire, thus assuring that what Edwards understands as decision will always be conscious. Not just any desire will do, of course, lest every felt inkling be made into a decision. But it might be held that whenever a desire is both conscious and predominant, it counts as a choice. This too, however, is unsatisfactory. Suppose I have a predominant and conscious desire to visit Florence for next summer's vacation, and that in fact I do decide to make the trip. Between now and next summer, I may experience the same desire again and again. But I will not decide again and again; once is enough. By contrast, I might experience the desire now and make no decision at all, since I still have lots of time to make up my mind. Strongest experienced desire is, then, neither necessary nor sufficient for choice or decision. Nor does it play the functional role that choice and intention do in deliberation and action.[11] To choose a course of action is to progress to a new frame of mind. There is a certain stability about intention: once I have decided to visit Florence, I am not likely to reconsider the issue unless a compelling reason comes up; nor should I. A predominant desire, by contrast, may be considered and reconsidered until a decision is made – or not made. Also, once I come to intend to visit Florence, I may be expected to form, in a timely way, further intentions that support the project – to choose an itinerary, a means of travel, and so on. Not to do so would be less than rational. Desire, even strongest occurrent desire, carries no such burden.

Intention formation is subject to other strictures of rationality as well. Ordinarily, it is irrational to aim at an objective one believes one cannot attain – to own the *Mona Lisa*, say. But there is no irrationality in desiring to own it, however strongly. Equally, it is normally irrational to form conflicting intentions – for example, to choose to spend my entire vacation at remotely separate locations. But I might well have equally strong desires to spend my vacation in Florence and to spend it in Athens, and no significant desire to spend it anywhere else. True, such desires do not count as choices for Edwards, but that is no impediment, for the desires might easily be combined into one: a single desire to spend my vacation in both places. Unquestionably, that would be a little on the zany side; but, like wanting most of all to own the *Mona Lisa*, it is not an exercise in practical irrationality. To intend to spend my vacation in both places, on the other hand, is such an exercise. And there is a reason for this contrast: it is useless to require that mental states over which we have no direct voluntary control exhibit consistency, either among themselves or with our beliefs. One might as well expect the wind to blow always from the west. Now we have no direct control over our desires, or their strength; at best, we are able to control them indirectly, by ordering our circumstances, cultivating tastes we find worthy of acquisition, and the like. Accordingly, we are not to be judged irrational if our desires, even our strongest ones, conflict at times with one another, or with what is feasible. We are, however, considered irrational if our decisions and the resultant intentions exhibit such failures. And that points to a reality that Edwards, along with many others, does not want to admit: our decisions are not to be identified with our predominant desires. Neither is it the case, in common life, that we take them to be driven by our wants, however strong. Rather, we believe, for better or for worse, that in deciding we rise above the buffeting of desire; we believe that as agents, we enjoy not just liberty of action, but also liberty of will. A look at the phenomenal character of decision and volition leads to the same conclusion. Unlike felt desire, deciding and willing are not passive occurrences, not things that happen to us, or could surprise us. Rather, they have the character of action: to decide to visit Florence, or to will the exertion that causes my arm to rise, are things that I do. They are, moreover, intentional doings, in which I feel I am in control. And they have these characteristics intrinsically: it is a conceptual impossibility for me to decide inadvertently to vacation in Florence, or to try by accident to raise my arm. This by itself is enough to undo the claim of Edwards, and many other determinists, that an uncaused act of will would have to be an accident that befalls the agent. We need not even enter into issues about causation to settle this matter, because the nature of these phenomena rules out any such danger. To say that I accidentally decided to visit Florence, or that my attempt to raise my arm befell me, is to utter a self-contradiction. Finally, decision and willing are things I am responsible for. The voice of conscience forbids more than wrong action. To form and harbor evil designs is itself evil; to will the exertion necessary to strike another is itself wrongdoing, even if sudden paralysis prevents the exertion from ever occurring. Pretty clearly, then, exercises of will have, at least in our understanding, all the features of voluntary, responsible behavior.

If this is so, and if moral responsibility requires that the agent have been free to do otherwise,[12] then we must enjoy that freedom in our choosings as well as in overt action. What, then, shall we say about the formula according to which such freedom comes to nothing more than the ability to act differently if we please, or if we will? On Edwards's understanding, a conditional analysis is in the offing here. 'I can *A*' is always 'I can *A*, if I choose,' which in turn goes to 'If I choose to *A*, I will *A*.' So to say that I can lift this rock is to say that if I choose or will to lift it, I will lift it. So far, so good, perhaps. But if responsible freedom belongs to the operations of will as well as to overt action, it must also be the case that I *can* choose to *A*, and – to turn Edwards's own argument against him – there the analysis clearly doesn't work. We get, 'If I choose to choose to lift this rock, then I will choose to lift it,' which is completely implausible, and leads to a regress. We can improve things somewhat if we ignore Edwards's failure to distinguish choice from prevailing desire. We can claim that choice is not identical with, but rather determined by, strongest desire, so that 'I can choose to lift this rock' becomes, 'If my strongest desire is to lift this rock, then I will choose to do so.' But this really isn't plausible either. For one thing, there are many situations in which we think the exercise of freedom is actually impaired by strongest desire – for example, where the agent suffers from addiction or psychological compulsion, or is affected by post-hypnotic suggestion. Such cases deserve careful treatment,[13] but surely if determinism were true we should *not* consider the freedom of such agents to be impaired, since certainly their decisions would be different were they not afflicted by compelling motives. So it doesn't work in this case to submit the concept of freedom to conditional analysis. And why should it, after all? This analysis treats the will as though it were imprisoned in the natural order – as though its operations were no more spontaneous, and finally of no greater moral interest, than those of our house pets. Why should we expect this to be our concept of freedom, if the phenomenology of willing is entirely the opposite?

It is, in addition, well known today (perhaps it was not, in Edwards's time) that 'I can, if I choose' need not be taken as implicitly conditional. J. L. Austin famously suggested that the *if*-clause in this statement is like the one in, 'There are cookies in the sideboard, if you want them.'[14] The idea in the latter case is not to suggest that your wanting them would put cookies in the sideboard; it is simply to raise the question whether you want some cookies – which are in the sideboard, whether you want them or not. Similarly, 'I can *A*, if I choose,' and 'I can *A*, if I want' can be read as asserting categorically that I can *A*, and then emphasizing that whether I shall is up to me, by raising the issue of whether I shall find *A* worthy of choice. That would certainly square with the reactions of lay persons when they are presented with the kind of analysis Edwards favors. Told that 'I can *A*' means simply, 'I will *A*, if I choose,' lay people promptly insist, in my experience, that this is not enough, that I must also be able to choose. And if they are then told that the latter means only that an alternative choice would be caused to occur were a prevailing desire present, they will say that a determined choice is no choice at all. Indeed, students do not even comprehend compatibilist analyses of freedom. They insist on reading compatibilism as saying that our choices are restricted by our desires, but that 'free will' operates among those that remain. This is hardly evidence of a successful conceptual analysis. If the compatibilist treatment of freedom were correct, we should have no more trouble getting students and lay persons to accept it than we have getting them to agree that a bachelor is an unmarried male, or a father a male parent. The fact is that we have next to no success. Pretty clearly, then, Edwards's understanding of freedom, and compatibilism in general, are on the wrong track.

VI

Where are we left? Evidently, Edwards is right in thinking human freedom must be subordinated to God's will as ruler of the universe, since only in that way can his sovereignty and omniscience be preserved, and the existence of our deeds accounted for. But he is wrong in thinking the operations of will are subject to natural causation – or, at least, he is wrong if the understanding of those operations that prevails in common life is correct. That, of course, is largely an empirical matter, which remains unsettled. As to the real nature of decision and volition, therefore, Edwards may yet prove to be right. But he is not right about our concept of freedom: in our thinking about action, we are wedded to libertarianism, and I think it would be a dislocating surprise for us to learn that our willings were part of the normal causal order. Is there, then, any other solution? I think there is, and that it is in some ways quite congenial to Edwards's way of thinking. We can hold that human choice and volition, though exempt from natural causation, are nevertheless a product of God's sovereign will as creator. That is, we may hold that God creates us doing the things we do, that the operations of our wills are simply part of what God himself wills in providing for our existence. The point of congeniality is that this fits very nicely with Edwards's own view of creation. Edwards did not believe that God merely created the world in the beginning, and then left it to run on its own; rather, he held that God must sustain the universe at each instant of its existence, that if he did not it would cease to exist.[15] On such a view, no special exertion is necessary for God to create us willing as we do; our deeds would owe their existence to the one, eternal act by which he creates the entire world, in all of its history. And if that is how things are, God's sovereignty and knowledge are complete: he exerts full control and authority over the world, and he knows how our actions will go simply by knowing his own creative will in the matter.

But how can we be free on such a scenario? True, we would be exempt from the buffeting of natural causes, but there is still supernatural causation to contend with. If our own willings are caused by God's, isn't that still determinism? Are we not still passive in all we do? I think the answer is No.[16] We need to remember, first, that nothing we might do can account for the existence of our acts of will. They, like us, must have their being in God. But we must also consider how this comes to pass. The mistake is to think some analog of natural causation is involved: for example, that God commands, 'Let Pharaoh refuse Moses,' and that this command then causes, by typical event causation, Pharaoh's refusal. That cannot be, because whatever event causation consists in, it is a contingent relationship, which like all contingent things owes its existence to God's creative will. If that required another command on God's part, we would be headed for another regress, and God would end up completely impotent. The only way to escape the regress is to say that in the case of the causal nexus, God's will is *directly* efficacious: that here, the *first* manifestation of God's creative will is not a command, but the very thing created. But if that is true with the relation of causation, it may as well be true for everything.

There is a useful analogy for understanding the view that emerges at this point. The best way to view divine creation is to treat it as akin to human creation: to hold that instead of being consequences of God's will as creator, we and our actions are the *content* of his will, in much the way the characters and events of a novel are the content of the author's imagination. The difference is that our existence is real rather than fictional. Otherwise, however, things are much the same. A novel is not, in the first instance, a book of inscribed pages; it is the story itself, subsisting in the author's mind. Yet the author does not enter into the tale, nor does she ever interact with her characters. Rather, she transcends them: nothing happens apart from her making it so, yet the characters are never acted upon, and their authenticity as agents is in principle unlimited. It is, I suggest, the same with God and us. We, along with our actions, have our being *in* him. Like the author, however, he does not operate *on* us at all. We are not, in our deciding and willing, passive before God's will: he wills that we decide as we do, yet he exerts no force upon us, and does nothing to us. The relation between his will and ours is, ironically enough, much too close for that. And precisely because it is so close, it leaves our moral authenticity intact.

This last claim may be doubted, especially if we are used to supposing that in exercising free will, we confer existence on our own choices. It was shown above, however, that this is not possible, and once the supposition is set aside, we can see that the present view leaves all that legitimately belongs to libertarian freedom untouched. Our acts of will are not produced by other events, or by any force that operates upon us. The sense of spontaneity that accompanies deciding and willing is accordingly justified. This, together with the fact that our decisions and willings are intrinsically intentional, gives us every right to feel we are in control of what we do. When we engage in decision and volition we are as active as we can be, and we mean to be doing precisely what we are doing, precisely when and as we are doing it. True, we cannot, in our choosings, defeat God's will as creator. But that is not because were we to try it, we would find ourselves opposed by an irresistible force. Rather, our very trying would be an expression of God's will, in which case there would be nothing to oppose. Does that make us unfree? I cannot see that it does, any more than the characters in a novel are made unfree by the fact that they have an author. Like them, we have no will or destiny independent of the will of our creator. But that does not subject us to causal determinism; nor does it put us in a position where our choices fail to be truly our own, truly active, or truly intended by us. This may not be all the freedom anyone ever wanted, but it is all we can ever have, and all we can meaningfully ask for. To be assured in addition that we have no author would add nothing.

VII

If the view I have defended is correct, we do enjoy libertarian free will, as usually defined. Yet the existence of our actions is explained in the same way as that of the world is. They owe their being to the creative fiat of God, whose sovereignty and omniscience are accordingly complete, and who is able to guide the entire course of history with the loving providence believers usually take to rule our destiny. More to the point, from the perspective of the present discussion, Edwards gets his way regarding the doctrine of the elect: our destinies are entirely in God's hands, and we will accept or reject the grace of salvation only in his accordance with his will. But Edwards's Arminian opponents also get their way: God's will for us does not undo our freedom, and we bear full moral responsibility for its exercise. Still, God is responsible too, and that raises a problem. We might wonder how God could ever will that we make decisions which violate the moral law, and especially how he could will the existence of anyone who is lost – assuming, that is, that some are. That is a deep problem, but it is not a new one. Edwards, in particular, would have to face it in any case, as would any other author who believes that in creating the world, God knows what he is doing.

Notes

1. Edwards, Jonathan (1957), *Freedom of the Will, The Works of Jonathan Edwards Volume 1*, ed. Paul Ramsey, New Haven: Yale University Press. Page references are to this source unless otherwise noted.
2. Edwards does not address Pelagianism independently in *Freedom of the Will*, but he

includes Pelagians with Arminians as proponents of the view of freedom he is attacking (for example, pp. 164, 203).

3. Boethius, *The Consolation of Philosophy*, Bk V, para. 6.
4. It is not clear, however, that he fully understands it. His criticism (pp. 266–7), which differs from the one I give, appears to accept the view that God is unchanging, yet to presuppose that he is still in time.
5. This talk of 'phases' is meant to be as accommodating as possible to the Boethian perspective: it prevents our having to say that God changes in learning of our actions, and so must be temporal after all. It is open, however, to the objection that such talk introduces unacceptable complexity into God's awareness. If talk of phases is rejected on that basis, as I am inclined to agree it should be, then the Boethian position collapses entirely.
6. Molina, Luis de (1988), *On Divine Foreknowledge: Part IV of the Concordia*, trans. Alfred J. Freddoso, Ithaca: Cornell University Press. For a thorough and careful defense of the Molinist position, see Flint, Thomas P. (1998), *Divine Providence: The Molinist Account*, Ithaca: Cornell University Press.
7. In Flint's terms, this is a possible world, but not one that it is *feasible* for God to create. *Divine Providence*, p. 51.
8. Locke, John, *An Essay Concerning Human Understanding*, Bk II, ch. 21, no. 30.
9. The classic modern statement is by Ryle, Gilbert (1949), *The Concept of Mind*, London: Hutchinson, p. 67.
10. See Jonathan Kvanvig's and my (1988), 'Divine Conservation and the Persistence of the World,' in Morris, Thomas V. (ed.), *Divine and Human Action*, Ithaca: Cornell University Press, pp. 13–49.
11. For an excellent treatment of the functional contrast between desire and intention, see Bratman, Michael (1987), *Intention, Plan, and Practical Reason*, Cambridge: Harvard University Press, especially chs 2 and 3, to which the points that follow are significantly indebted.
12. It is sometimes denied that this 'principle of alternate possibilities' is a condition for responsible behavior. See especially Frankfurt, Harry G. (1969), 'Alternate Possibilities and Moral Responsibility,' *Journal of Philosophy* 66, 829–39. Space does not permit discussion of this issue, but there are good reasons for thinking that the examples set forth to support this denial succeed only if one presupposes determinism. See Widerker, David (1995), 'Libertarian Freedom and the Avoidability of Decisions,' *Faith and Philosophy* 12, 113–18.
13. In particular, we should not suppose that in such cases, deterministic causation suddenly takes control of our decisions. It may simply be the case that when inordinate motives are at work, the agent's ability to appreciate sound reasons for action is impaired, so the choice is no longer fully rational.
14. Austin, J. L. (1961), 'Ifs and Cans,' in *Philosophical Papers*, ed. J. O. Urmson and G. J. Warnock, New York: Oxford University Press, pp. 153–80.
15. Edwards, Jonathan (1970), *Original Sin, The Works of Jonathan Edwards Volume 3*, ed. Clyde A. Holbrook, New Haven: Yale University Press, Pt IV, ch. 13, esp. pp. 397–405. Edwards had, in fact, a very radical view of divine sustenance. He seems to have believed time consists of discrete, denumerable instants, so that God must create the world anew at each moment. On such an account identity over time becomes highly problematic. Edwards held that it consists in no more than God's deciding to view pairs of entities inhabiting successive worlds as the same.
16. A number of the points that follow are argued at greater length in McCann, Hugh (1995), 'Divine Sovereignty and the Freedom of the Will,' *Faith and Philosophy* 12, 582–98.

Chapter 4

A Forensic Dilemma: John Locke and Jonathan Edwards on Personal Identity

Paul Helm

It is frequently argued that the religious tendency of John Locke's writings on the relationship between reason and faith, and particularly the two chapters at the end of the *Essay*, 'On Faith and Reason and their Distinct Provinces' and 'Of Enthusiasm', was in the direction of Socinianism, deism and worse. And certainly the work of the French *philosophes*, Condillac, Diderot and others, depends overtly on Locke. But *post hoc non est propter hoc*. And one thinker, at least, saw in Locke's views support for theological conservatism, the conservatism of Puritanism. Though in the sixteenth century Puritanism had been a radical movement, by the end of the seventeenth century it was intellectually played out, at least in England.

But not so in New England. Jonathan Edwards (1703–58), the New England philosopher and theologian, pastor, missionary and revivalist, saw in Locke's ideas material for the rational grounding, or re-grounding, of his inherited Puritanism. Not so much Locke's two chapters on faith and reason and on enthusiasm, though Edwards concurred with Locke's view that reason and religion have distinct provinces, and that enthusiasm was to be avoided, even though he drew the lines at rather different places than did Locke.

Rather, Edwards made use of the more central of Locke's philosophical positions. What Locke had to say about simple ideas gave Edwards a model for what he thought happened at religious conversion; what happened was the giving of a new simple idea, a new source of information and an insight into the nature of things denied to those who had to rely merely on the simple ideas provided by the operation of the five senses. What Locke had to say about human action in his chapter 'Of Power' Edwards utilized in his magisterial discussion of human freedom in his *Freedom of the Will*. And Edwards helped himself to what Locke had to say about the nature of identity, and particularly personal identity, in his discussion of how it comes to be reasonable that we are all implicated in the fall of Adam. In all these discussions, Locke was not used simply as a convenient peg on which to hang the coat of Calvinism; for according to Edwards's first biographer, Samuel Hopkins, Edwards read Locke while an undergraduate at Yale with 'more pleasure than the most greedy miser, when gathering up handfuls of silver and gold from some newly discovered treasure'.[1]

In this chapter I want to show in some detail how Edwards appealed to Locke on the question of personal identity; to see the seriousness and genuineness with which he took what Locke said, but also to try to understand how it was that the impact of Locke on Edwards, though genuine enough, came to be crowded out by other items on Edwards's agenda. More pointedly and poignantly than this, I want to try to indicate how those other agenda items neutralized and sterilized the influence of Locke at the very point where one might have expected that he could have been useful to Edwards.

I make no claims for the truth or even the plausibility of any of the views of the parties, but I shall concentrate solely on the issues of the interconnectedness and dislocation of the various ideas.

Locke on Personal Identity

Interest in the soul can take many forms; interest in the metaphysical nature of the soul, in its religious or spiritual capacities, and as the locus of personal identity and responsibility. This latter was Locke's primary interest in his famous treatment of personal identity – the soul as a forensic notion. He was concerned with 'that consciousness which draws reward or punishment with it'.[2] Because of this forensic interest, his thought about the soul had to have a strong epistemological dimension. If the question is how I can be presently responsible, and justly be held responsible, for something that occurred in the past, then there must be a way or ways of tracing a line from my present to my past. For Locke that line was traced by memory. Memory is the criterion of personal identity in this forensic sense. In what sense the employment of memory in these ways so as to secure, as Locke thought, the forensic connection, presupposes the soul in some other, deeper sense, is a further interesting question. Elsewhere[3] I have argued that consciousness is what a person consists in for Locke, and that our present memory is the fallible guide of continued past consciousness. But this issue is not of direct interest to us now.

Locke's position on the place of memory, and on the forensic character of personal identity, is expressed in his own words as follows:

> To find wherein personal identity consists, we must consider what person stands for; which, I think, is a thinking intelligent being that has reason and reflection and can consider itself as itself, the same thinking thing in different times and places; which it does only by that consciousness which is inseparable from thinking and, as it seems to me, essential to it: it being impossible for anyone to perceive without perceiving that he does perceive … For since consciousness always accompanies thinking, and it is that that makes everyone to be what he calls self, and thereby distinguishes himself from all other thinking things: in this alone consists personal identity, i.e. the sameness of a rational being. And as far as this consciousness can be extended backwards to any past action or thought,

so far reaches the identity of that person: it is the same self now it was then, and it is by the same self with this present one that now reflects on it, that that action was done.[4]

So personal identity, the identity of a person as a thinking, conscious being, goes where memory goes, and only there. (Here we forbear to discuss Locke's rather extravagant opinions on the character of consciousness, and his conflation of consciousness with self-consciousness.)

And Locke's forensic interest in all this comes out plainly in words such as these:

In this personal identity is founded all the right and justice of reward and punishment: happiness and misery being that for which everyone is concerned for himself, not mattering what becomes of any substance not joined to or affected with that consciousness.[5]

But is not a man drunk and sober the same person, why else is he punished for the act he commits when drunk, though he be never afterwards conscious of it? Just as much the same person as a man that was and does other things in his sleep is the same person as is answerable for any mischief he shall do in it. Human laws punish both, with a justice suitable to their way of knowledge; because, in these cases, they cannot distinguish certainly what is real, what counterfeit; and so ignorance in drunkenness or sleep is not admitted as a plea ... But in the Great Day, wherein the secrets of all hearts shall be laid open, it may be reasonable to think no one shall be made to answer for what he knows nothing of, but shall receive his doom, his conscience accusing or excusing him.[6]

Thousands of philosophy students, on the basis of what has been extracted from these passages in Locke, have been invited to entertain what is called the memory criterion of personal identity. On this reading of Locke, memory is what personal identity is, what it consists in. On this assumption it is all too easy to construct counter-examples to it based upon the fact that memory fades, or is fallible, or is interrupted. Thus we may suppose, for example, that a person's memory might be wiped clean, and then begun again. When with the aid of the new memory a person learns to use 'I', then it must refer to a new self, since memory is the criterion of personal identity and so for that person to say, 'I existed before my memory was wiped clean' is necessarily false. This looks to be an unacceptable result.

As a result of counter-examples such as these, in modern philosophical discussions of personal identity Locke's account has come to be supplemented (or supplanted) by the 'bodily' criterion of personal identity. But I do not think that Locke thought he was constructing a memory criterion in this simplistic fashion; as we have already seen, he was well aware of the facts of human fallibility and of interruptedness. The only time when memory will work infallibly, and take proper account of all interruptions to its operations, will be on that occasion which Locke referred to as the 'Great Day'. In the meantime memory is a rough and ready forensic tool; no more. Memory is a 'criterion' of backwardly continuous consciousness in the sense that it provides the best present evidence for that continuity; but, again, no more than that.

The great thing in all this, as far as we are concerned, is that for Locke it would appear that the identity of the human soul through a period of time is compatible with considerable changes in consciousness, just those changes which memory is capable of picking up. A person is the same person as at some previous time if there is sameness of consciousness, even though that consciousness is an awareness of the possession of a simple soul, but mere overlapping continuity, like the behaviour of cells in a growing tree. Locke explicitly draws the parallel:

> [d]ifferent substances, by the same consciousness (where they do partake in it) being united into one person, as well as different bodies by the same life are united into one animal, whose *identity* is preserved in that change of substances by the unity of one continued life.[7]

In the sections prior to discussing personal identity, when he is concerned with the identity of living things such as trees, Locke seems at times to advocate an even stronger thesis. He appears to claim not merely that the continuous identity of a tree is compatible with great change in the physical composition and organization of the tree from seedling to sapling to mature tree, but that continuous identity *requires* there to be such changes.

> In the state of living creatures, their identity depends not on a mass of the same particles but on something else. For in them the variation of great parcels of matter alters not the identity: an oak growing from a plant to a great tree, and then lopped, is still the same oak; and colt grown up to a horse, though in both these cases there may be a manifest change of the parts, so that truly they are not either of them the same masses of matter, though they be truly one of them the same oak, and the other the same horse.[8]

However, the key thing as far as the telling of our particular story is concerned is that for Locke awareness of personal identity through time is not awareness of something which has strict or absolute conditions of identity; it is the awareness of features of mental organization, compatible with and indeed requiring change over time. For what matters for the identity of living things across time is unity of organization, whether physical organization in the case of trees and animals or mental organization in the case of persons. For Locke personal identity is a case of what Sydney Shoemaker has called autonomous self-perpetuation,[9] continuity established through the connection between awareness of the present and of the past, a case of immanent causation.

The evidence of this connected mental organization is memory, either the memory we experience from the inside or which we fallibly impute to others, as when (according to Locke) in our rough and ready way we blame the drunk for what he does when drunk, assuming that he remembers what he did. If he did not remember, and we are mistaken in our imputation of blame, then the Lord will sort things out at the Great Day.

Edwards, Locke and Personal Identity

In the closing years of his life Jonathan Edwards wrote in defence of what he called the 'great Christian doctrine of original sin', arguing that it is a scriptural doctrine, that it is confirmed by experience, and that it is reasonable. It is in connection with his defence of the reasonableness of that doctrine that he utilizes what Locke had written on identity, including personal identity. He begins by adopting a Lockean approach to what he calls sameness or oneness among created things, as for example, in the following:

> A tree, grown great, and a hundred years old, is one plant with the little sprout, that first came out of the ground from whence it grew, and has been continued in constant succession; though it be now so exceeding diverse, many thousand times bigger, and of a very different form, and perhaps not one atom the very same ... So the body of man at forty years of age, is one with the infant body which first came into the world, from when it grew; though now constituted of different substance, and the greater part of the substance probably changed scores (if not hundreds) of times ... And if we come even to the personal identity of created intelligent beings, though this be not allowed to consist wholly in what Mr Locke supposes, i.e. same consciousness; yet I think it cannot be denied, that this is one thing essential to it.[10]

Unfortunately Edwards does not tell us here, or as far as I can discover anywhere else, what other essential features there are to personal identity besides same consciousness. Nevertheless it is clear that the spirit of his approach is Lockean, even if every detail is not. And I think that before long we shall be able to infer the other essential feature. That is, what Edwards takes from Locke is the idea that personal identity through time is not the unity of a simple and imperishable soul, but the unity of mental organization. This is a point to which I shall return.

Though Edwards does not say so, it is plausible to suppose that the target which (with Locke's help) he has in his sights is the idea of the natural indestructibility of the soul considered as a simple, indivisible substance, or as the form of a human being. If the soul is naturally indestructible, then a soul existing at t1 will exist at all subsequent times unless God annihilates it. For Edwards this was precisely to view God's relation to the soul the wrong way round, as we shall see.

Let us suppose, for a moment, that personal identity through time were strict and not loose; that is, that A is a person if and only if A is a metaphysically simple individual, a soul, and A's identity from time to time consists solely in being that soul through that time. Any change that A undergoes as a soul is accidental to his being that soul, and hence to his being A. Then there is only one possible way for A's life to be temporally extended, namely, by his soul, the soul that he is, being extended. Such an extension of A's soul is necessary and sufficient for the extension of A. It is Locke's denial of such a thesis that seems to have so attracted Edwards.

Edwards's Other Agenda

But Edwards had other irons in the fire besides an account of personal identity on broadly Lockean lines, and we must briefly turn to these.

The Divine Immediacy

One of these, the chief one, we might call his anti-deistic impetus. He was concerned to stress, against the deists, for whom the divine power was mediated through the power given to created things, that God's power was immediately exercised upon his creation, on all aspects of it equally.

Here is Edwards in full cry against the deists:

> That God does, by his immediate power, *uphold* every created substance in being, will be manifest, if we consider, that their present existence is a *dependent* existence, and therefore is an *effect*, and must have some *cause*: and the cause must be one of these two: either the *antecedent existence* of the same substance, or else the *power of the Creator*. But it can't be the antecedent existence of the same substance. For instance, the existence of the body of the moon, at this present moment, can't be the effect of its existence at the last foregoing moment. For not only was what existed the last moment, no active cause, but wholly a passive thing; but this also is to be considered, that no cause can produce effects in a *time* and *place* in which itself is *not* ... From these things, I suppose, it will certainly follow, that the present existence, either of this, or any other created substance, cannot be an effect of its past existence. The existences (so to speak) of an effect, or thing dependent, in different parts of space or duration, though ever so *near* one to another, don't at all co-exist one with the other; and therefore are as truly different effects, as if those parts of space and duration were ever so far asunder: and the prior existence can no more be the proper cause of the new existence, in the next moment, or next part of space, than if it had been in an age before, or at a thousand miles distance, without any existence to fill up the intermediate time or space. Therefore the existence of created substances, in each successive moment, must be the effect of the *immediate* agency, will, and power of God.[11]

There are, of course, Berkeleian and Malebranchian themes and echoes of themes here, but to discuss these now in relation to Edwards would take us too far afield.

Thus Edwards believed that anything that is created *could* not persist for more than a moment of time. Edwards must hold, therefore, that the present moment is a short period of time, since everything that exists in time exists for only a moment. Therefore the present cannot simply be the conceptual boundary between two periods of time; it must have duration. This, the immediate moment-by-moment dependence of all created things on God, is the first item in Edwards's agenda.

This view of creaturely dependence commits Edwards to the following thesis: that an individual at time t1 is not and cannot be strictly identical with anything prior to t1 but is a sum of four-dimensional parts, temporal parts, related by what twentieth-century philosophers call genidentity. A person perdures not through the powers and forces of matter (as in the modern materialist view of, for example, David Lewis) but by virtue of the will of God. This provides an answer to our earlier query about what else besides consciousness Edwards thinks is necessary for personal identity; nothing more is necessary for a time slice to be a time slice of a person, but what else is necessary (and sufficient) for a person perduring through time is the divine creation of successive time slices. So the difference (again using modern nomenclature) between Locke and Edwards is that Locke is an endurantist, whereas Edwards is a perdurantist with regard to personal identity through time. I shall consider this in more detail later.

Original Sin

The second item on Edwards's agenda concerns the forensic character of original sin.

In common with all orthodox Christianity Edwards accepted the doctrine of original sin upon scriptural authority, notably St Paul's teaching in Romans 5. When Adam sinned there is a sense in which all the human race sinned 'in' him, and in which Adam's posterity, being 'in' him, shared his guilt, and as a consequence is born with 'original sin'. Sin is transmitted through the human race by propagation, not by imitation, and the guilt of Adam's sin is imputed to his posterity.

As a result of the deep conviction that he had about the immediate dependence of the creation upon the Creator, Edwards developed a unique account of the relation between Adam and his progeny as part of his overall defence of reasonableness of the Christian doctrine of original sin. In Chapter III of this part of his work on original sin he offers what can best be described as a metaphysical excursus in an attempt to answer 'that great objection against the imputation of Adam's sin to his posterity ... that such imputation is unjust and unreasonable, inasmuch as Adam and his posterity are not one and the same'.[12] It is here that Edwards's Lockeanism comes into view, and also his perdurantist modification of Locke.

Edwards's argument is a reply to the claim that the relation between Adam and his posterity required by the doctrine of original sin is contrary to the nature of things. How can I be held responsible for what Adam did since I am not identical with Adam? Edwards replies, in effect, that not only is there an alternative metaphysical explanation of the nature of things to that implied by the deists, but that this alternative is the only one open to a theist. According to this alternative explanation, I am no more or less identical to Adam than I am to an earlier phase of myself. For both Adam and I are dependent things, and such unity as I have with an earlier phase of myself, or with Adam, is a unity constituted solely by the will of God. Whatever is dependent is immediately dependent upon God; and whatever is immediately dependent cannot persist for more than a moment.

> A father, according to the course of nature, begets a child; an oak, according to the course of nature, produces an acorn, or a bud; so according to the course of nature, the former existence of the trunk of the tree is followed by its new or present existence. In the one case, and the other, the new effect is consequent on the former, only by the established laws, and settled course of nature; which is allowed to be nothing but the continued immediate efficiency of God, according to a constitution that he has been pleased to establish.[13]

A thing's 'new and present existence' is therefore an existence that is numerically distinct from its immediate past existence. Nothing can exist for more than a moment; the fact that nature, the temporally continuous order of things, is as orderly as it is, is solely due to the wisdom and power of God, not to the inherent natures of things that he has created.

Edwards begins his positive account of the metaphysics of Adam's relation to his posterity by first offering a theologically sanitized version of Locke's view of identity through time which he gives in his *Essay Concerning Human Understanding*. Writing of the continued identity of trees and plants, Locke argued,

> [t]hat being then one plant which has such an organization of parts in one coherent body, partaking of one common life, it continues to be the same plant as long as it partakes of the same life, though that life be communicated to new particles of matter vitally united to the living plant, in a like continued organization, conformable to that sort of plants.[14]

Edwards argued in a similar way: 'God, according to an established law of nature, has in a constant succession communicated to it many of the same qualities, and most important properties, as if it were one.'[15]

'As if it were one', that is, as if it were numerically one, though in fact (of course) it is not and cannot be numerically one. From God alone is the power for Peter at t1 to be the same individual as Peter at t2, not numerically the same but the same in virtue of having many of the same qualities and most important properties that Peter at t1 had.

Edwards once again begins with the Lockean account of personal identity through time, according to which same consciousness is *necessary* for personal identity. That is, persisting personal identity requires having the same enduring consciousness. But this cannot be the whole story for Edwards, otherwise the deists would be given all the elbow room that they need. But, as we shall shortly see, Edwards understands this sameness in a rather different way from Locke. For it is here that Edwards's idea of creaturely dependence, mentioned earlier, begins to play a crucial role in the argument.

Locke had argued for identity as a succession of overlapping parts, the overlapping parts ordered by temporally continuous mental organization. From this it is a short step – but perhaps for Edwards a fatal step – to argue for identity as a succession of non-overlapping parts, a view particularly attractive to him given his view of creaturely dependence. According to Edwards a series of momentary parts, qualitatively similar in important respects, is treated both by ourselves and by God *as if it were* numerically one thing.

So far it may seem that all that Edwards is doing is adding a further, an explicitly theological, stage, an account in terms of divine creation, to the familiar Lockean account of identity. However, this second stage of Edwards's account contains a radical twist. He imparts this twist by emphasizing in unambiguous fashion that the divine upholding of all the forces of nature, including the laws of nature, is *immediate*. That is, any individual who exists at a time is caused to exist at that time only by an exertion of the power of God to cause him to exist. This divine power is causally *necessary and sufficient*, without the instrumentality of any other force or agency, to uphold that individual at that time. In particular, no created thing that existed at any moment prior to the moment in question could cause the existence of anything at that moment or subsequently, or contribute to its continued existence. For how could what has gone before contribute causally to what is present, Edwards asks, since what has gone before no longer exists? How can that which no longer exists now have any causal influence upon the present?

This requires a little explaining. What Edwards is saying is that nothing that is created exists, indeed can exist, for more than a moment, a vanishingly short period of time. Why not? Why could not something created exist for several moments? Because, according to Edwards, in order for this to happen what exists at an earlier moment would have to causally contribute to what exists later by enabling what exists to persist. But how could what no longer exists contribute to anything? What no longer exists has no causal powers; indeed, has no anything. Such a causal contribution would, in any case, be a kind of *creatio ex nihilo*, and would in Edwards's eyes rival and undermine the powers of the creator, because one created thing would be causing another created thing to endure, to extend its existence in time.

In order to see how radical this view is, we may usefully compare it with how Descartes argues in his *Meditations*. In the third *Meditation*, in arguing against the possibility that he has always existed, Descartes puts forward a very similar idea to that expressed by Edwards.

For though I assume that perhaps I have always existed just as I am at present, neither can I escape the force of this reasoning, and imagine that the conclusion to be drawn from this is, that I need not seek for any author of my existence. For all the course of my life may be divided into an infinite number of parts, none of which is in any way dependent on the other; and thus from the fact that I was in existence a short time ago it does not follow that I must be in existence now, unless some cause at this instant, so to speak, produces me anew, that is to say, conserves me. It is as a matter of fact perfectly clear and evident to all those who consider with attention the nature of time, that, in order to be conserved in each moment in which it endures, a substance has need of the same power and action as would be necessary to produce and create it anew, supposing it did not yet exist, so that the light of nature shows us clearly that the distinction between creation and conservation is solely a distinction of the reason.[16]

Like Descartes, Edwards tends to think of divine conservation as a continuous creation, and what we call natural causes are simply the factors which precede but which do not bring about what follows them. And nature is nothing, 'separate from the agency of God'; that is, there are no agents which have their causal power independently of the causal power of God. As Edwards puts it,

God's *preserving* created things in being is perfectly equivalent to a *continued creation*, or to his creating those things out of nothing at *each moment* of their existence. If the continued existence of created things be wholly dependent on God's preservation, then those things would drop into nothing, upon the ceasing of the present moment, without a new exertion of the divine power to cause them to exist in the following moment.[17]

This goes significantly beyond Descartes, in that what Edwards is here claiming is that no created being can be preserved in existence beyond a moment, not even by God. This is the fate of anything that is a dependent being. Nothing created that exists can exist for more than a moment. Despite Edwards's very strong avowal of divine sovereignty it would seem that not even God can preserve in existence for more than a moment a being as a numerically identical being or as one that has numerically identical parts through that period of time. By itself Edwards's argument from causation is not sufficient to enable him to conclude to the doctrine of temporal parts, since there would appear to be no inconsistency in the idea that although no past phase of a numerically identical individual (say, at time t1) could contribute causally to any present (t2) or future phase (t3), nevertheless God could causally uphold one numerically individual thing through the period t1–t3. And there are times when Edwards appears to take this view, a view very similar to that of Descartes. Thus at one point Edwards concurs with the view that the present existence of created substances is the effect or consequence of past existence, according to the nature of things.[18]

However, Edwards's stress on divine immediacy, his anti-deistic impulse, takes him beyond Descartes, to embrace an even more radical position. He claims that God's immediate creative or conserving activity

> is altogether equivalent to an *immediate production out of nothing*, at each moment, because its existence at this moment is not merely in part from God, but wholly from him; and not in any part, or degree, from its antecedent existence. For, the supposing, that its antecedent existence *concurs* with God in *efficiency*, to produce some part of the effect, is attended with all the very same absurdities, which have been shown to attend the supposition of its producing it wholly.[19]

So there are in what Edwards says two different doctrines about divine creation, identity and time. According to the first of these, if A is a dependent individual existing in time (as, according to Edwards, all individuals except God are), then A will not continue to exist for a moment longer unless God wills its continued existence. This is also the view of Descartes, as we have seen. But according to the second, the stronger doctrine, if A is a dependent individual, then A will continue to exist for a moment longer *only if God re-creates A for that moment*, and continues to re-create the individual for all succeeding moments of its existence. The re-created A is thus a numerically distinct individual from the first created A, though qualitatively similar, or even qualitatively identical.

These two accounts, the one that Edwards shares with Descartes, and the stronger account, are different in the following respect. It is compatible with the weaker doctrine that at any moment after the first moment of A's existence A may consist partly, or wholly, of numerically identical parts that A had at the immediately previous time. This is not only Descartes's view; as we have seen, it is Locke's view as well. By contrast, the second, stronger doctrine requires that A's existence at a time cannot consist in the persistence of any of the same parts, numerically speaking, that A had at an immediately previous time; or, if A has no parts, of A itself. This is because, according to Edwards, the existence of a created substance 'be wholly the effect of God's immediate power, in that moment, without any dependence on prior existence, as much as the first creation out of nothing'.[20]

Edwards's Forensic Dilemma

Let us now take stock. We have seen that what both Locke and Edwards have in common is a denial that personal identity consists solely in the persistence of a metaphysically simple soul through time. What they have in common is an important aspect of what Peter van Inwagen[21] has called the 'typically empiricist' view of thinking beings. On this view what makes a given sequence of thoughts the thoughts of a single thinker is the fact that the thoughts are in a certain causal sequence, organized in a certain way: a naturally overlapping sequence for Locke, a non-overlapping divinely produced sequence for Edwards.

So what for Locke makes the sequence of thoughts the thoughts of one person is that these thoughts are always conscious thoughts, and that there are appropriate causal relations between the thoughts in the sequence, the thoughts and their relations being imperfectly picked out by the imperfect operation of memory. We have to continue to bear in mind that when Locke says 'And as far as this consciousness can be extended backwards to any past action or thought, so far reaches the identity of that person', he was not primarily thinking about our presently fitful powers of memory but our powers of memory when effectively jogged by God. Or, if you like, he was thinking of God's powers of recall. Hence, as we have seen, his references to the Great Day.[22]

And, as we have also seen, for Locke this makes a plausible story to tell for forensic purposes. For it is plausible to suppose that what we are presently responsible for as regards the past is that there is a plausible story to tell that causally connects the past with the present. For there to be a causal story the causes and effects must last for more than a moment. That is, our memories, either unaided or divinely jogged, function forensically because there are facts of the matter about the past of a person which the present memories of the person are rememberings of.

But because of the other main item on his philosophical and theological agenda, his doctrine of divine immediacy, no such immanent causal story is available to Jonathan Edwards. Not only am I not numerically identical with anything simple or complex in the past; nothing in the present is numerically identical with anything in the past. There are no facts of the matter about continuous identity through time to which either divine or human rememberings can and must conform, since there are no objective, metaphysical facts of that kind. In matters of this kind God 'makes truth' simply because there is no alternative, and he makes truth not whimsically or in a random fashion, but in accordance with his own wise purposes. For given Edwards's doctrine of divine immediacy, and his ontology of temporal parts, nothing in all creation can persist for more than a moment. So what 'I' refers to when used in the present tense is a momentary self; what it refers to when used in the past tense is a phase of a four-dimensional human identity consisting of numerically distinct temporal parts. If I say 'I showered before I wrote this paragraph', the first 'I' refers to a numerically distinct individual from the second 'I'; they are united only by a wise God's continued creation. So the continued existence of what the 'I' thus refers to depends wholly upon things beyond what the 'I' presently refers to, namely the divine moment-by-moment re-creation.

So Adam is connected with the rest of the human race not because he is one with them by virtue of some immanent relation, but by being made one with them. By divine constitution, each individual, say Peter at t1, is genidentical, 'made one' with some non-identical part, Peter at t–1, and so on back to Adam. 'Genidentity' in its modern sense is not strictly the relation that Edwards employs here, for there is no immanent causal genesis of one temporal part by an immediately earlier temporal part. Rather, the causal agent is God. There is therefore no difference in principle between the unity of Peter at t1 and Peter at t2 and the unity of Adam at t–1 and

Peter at t1. Each unity is formed by the wise will of God. So Peter is made one with Adam. And Paul, in similar fashion, is made one with Adam.

But the relation which each of Peter and Paul has to Adam, whatever its exact features, is not transitive. Adam has been made one with Peter at t1 and with Paul at t1, but it does not follow that Peter at t1 and Paul at t1 are thereby made one with each other. They are not strictly identical, nor is there a relation of genidentity. They are not identical as Adam and Peter and Adam and Paul are identical because God has chosen not to communicate 'like properties, relations and circumstances' to Paul at t–1 and Peter at t1.[23]

For neither Locke nor Edwards is the identity of the person through time strict. No person persists in numerically identical fashion as a simple soul in a way in which changes in the features of consciousness are irrelevant, but Locke at least has immanent causal connectedness between these features, and so present qualities are the causal outcome of past qualities. And this connectedness is possible because there is qualitative overlap. For Edwards 'Peter at t1' and 'Peter at t2' denote wholly distinct objects related only by the (divinely instituted and maintained) genidentity, an instituting that makes it reasonable to suppose that each of us is genidentical with Adam, just as we are genidentical with certain past selves, and may therefore reasonably have his guilt imputed to us. It is our guilt because we are thus identical to guilty Adam, made so by a divine fiat which is both wise and reasonable, and for which strict identity through time, or even overlap across times, are not alternative possibilities.

So while for Locke there is an immanent causal story linking past and present directly, for Edwards no such story can be told. Instead Edwards tells the story of a constitution established by God,

> whereby the natural posterity of Adam, proceeding from him, much as the buds and branches from the stock of a tree, should be treated as one with him, for the derivation, either of righteousness, and communion in rewards, or of the loss of righteousness, and consequent corruption and guilt.[24]

Whatever one thinks of the theology, one needs the benefit of a few deep breaths in order to swallow the metaphysics of this arrangement, but (so it seems to me) fewer breaths to follow Locke.

But perhaps Edwards could regroup his forces at this point, in the following way. Perhaps he could invoke what we may call the doctrine of linear collective responsibility. Who is responsible for some evil action that Jones perpetrates at some time t6? Actions take time to carry out, as Philip Quinn and Delmas Lewis remind us.[25] Even if Edwards were to avail himself of a discrete (as against a dense) view of time (as presumably he must do), this will hardly help him, for his enthusiasm for divine immediacy leads him to stress the shortness of each such moment. But he might have argued that responsibility for an action taking from t1 to t6 is the collective responsibility of the set of those temporal parts of Jones existing from t1 to t6 which initiate, continue and complete, that action. These persons[26] – Jones at t1, Jones at t2 and so on – are not *jointly* responsible for the action, but *collectively* responsible for it in that each is responsible for his own phase of the action, just as a runner is responsible for his stretch of the relay. But Edwards did not follow this route, and perhaps there is some overriding reason why he did not do so, though such an approach does not seem uncongenial to his own cast of mind.

At the beginning I suggested that while Locke's philosophy contributed to the rise of deism, in the hands of Edwards it went the other way: it contributed to the rebuttal of deism, or at least to its repudiation. But now, in view of what we have learned, perhaps there is need to refine this opinion somewhat. Whatever help Locke may have been to Edwards, what Edwards lost, or was in very grave danger of losing, because of his stress upon divine immediacy, was the forensic focus in Locke's account, the very thing that he needed in order to defend the reasonableness of the 'great Christian doctrine of original sin'.

Locke's forensic focus was founded on the nature of things. But since for Edwards there is no fact of the matter (as far as the connection of the present with the past is concerned) apart from the will of God, there can be no memories, in the strict sense; for a person can remember only what is true. And though, if I am an Edwardsian, I may remember having a shower, I cannot truly remember having it, for whoever had the shower, it wasn't me.

So Edwards has to spurn the best chance he has from Locke of using memory to ground, in some way or other, responsibility for what occurred in the past in what is now occurring. One element of his philosophical theology, the idea of divine immediacy and of successive re-creation of the creation, is, as far as I can see, fundamentally at odds with another, his great Christian doctrine of original sin.

Notes

1. Cited in Cherry, Conrad (1966), *The Theology of Jonathan Edwards, A Reappraisal*, Garden City, New York: Anchor, p. 15.
2. Locke, John (1970), *An Essay Concerning Human Understanding*, ed. John Yolton, London: Dent, vol. 1, p. 283.
3. See Helm, Paul (1979), 'Locke's Theory of Personal Identity', *Philosophy* **54**, 173-85.
4. Locke, *Essay*, p. 283.
5. Ibid., p. 287.
6. Ibid., pp. 288–9.
7. Ibid., p. 281. 'Substance' in passages such as this, I take to refer to what Locke elsewhere calls a substratum. It matters not, for personal identity, whether the consciousness is upheld by one substratum or by several successive substrata. What matters is continuity of (conscious) mental organization.
8. Ibid., p. 276.
9. Shoemaker, Sydney (1997), 'Self and Substance', in Tomberlin, James E. (ed.), *Philosophical Perspectives 11, Mind, Causation, and World*, Atascadero: Ridgeview, p. 288 ff.

10. Edwards, Jonathan (1990), *Original Sin*, in Hickman, Edward (ed.), *The Works of Jonathan Edwards Volume 1*, Edinburgh: Banner of Truth, pp. 222–3.
11. Edwards, Jonathan (1970), *Original Sin, The Works of Jonathan Edwards Volume 3*, ed. Clyde A. Holbrook, New Haven: Yale University Press, pp. 400–401.
12. Ibid., p. 389.
13. Ibid., p. 401.
14. Locke, *Essay*, p. 277.
15. Edwards, *Original Sin*, pp. 397–8.
16. Descartes, René (1970), *The Philosophical Works of Descartes, Volume 1*, trans. Elizabeth S. Haldane and G. R. T. Ross, Cambridge: Cambridge University Press, p. 168.
17. Edwards, *Original Sin*, pp. 401–2.
18. Ibid., p. 401.
19. Ibid., p. 402.
20. Ibid., p. 40.
21. Van Inwagen, Peter (1990), *Material Beings*, Ithaca: Cornell University Press, p. 206.
22. Locke, *Essay*, p. 289.
23. The formal properties of Edwards's scheme are very similar to those of the materialist David Lewis. See Lewis, David (1983), 'Counterparts of Persons and Their Bodies' and 'Survival and Identity', in *Philosophical Papers, Volume 1*, Cambridge: Cambridge University Press. Like Edwards, Lewis holds to the doctrine of temporal parts. Nothing endures for more than a moment. And also like Edwards, unity through time, including personal identity, is a matter of sufficient similarity between immediately adjoining temporal parts. Being a materialist, for Lewis those parts are material, and the similarity is secured not by the transcendent causal activity of God but by 'bonds of lawful causal dependence' of an immanent, physical kind. (Ibid., p. 55.)
24. Edwards, *Original Sin*, in Hickman, *Works, Volume 1*, p. 225.
25. Quinn, Philip (1983), 'Divine Conservation, Continuous Creation and Human Action', in Freddoso, Alfred J. (ed.), *The Existence and Nature of God*, Notre Dame: University of Notre Dame Press, and Lewis, Delmas (1986), 'Persons, Morality and Tenselessness', *Philosophy and Phenomenological Research*, **47**, 305–9.
26. Delmas Lewis suggests that these persons are not persons but person parts, and that person parts are not persons. But this does not seem plausible. Naturally, the momentary parts are not the whole person, but they are wholly personal in that they are capable of initiating actions (to be continued and completed by later parts) or continuing or completing actions (initiated by earlier parts).

Chapter 5

How 'Occasional' was Edwards's Occasionalism?

Oliver D. Crisp

In recent philosophy of religion, there has been some attention given to the doctrines of divine creation and conservation of the world. This essay is an attempt to analyse where Jonathan Edwards's doctrine of creation and conservation should be placed along the continuum of views on these matters. First, we shall examine three candidate theories of creation and conservation. These comprise a strong conservation thesis, a continuous creation thesis and an occasionalistic thesis. Then Edwards's view will be placed alongside these others. In the process, we shall also see that his view involves a particular take on several central issues on the question of how persons persist through time. Finally, we shall turn to consider a recent objection to the notion that Edwards endorsed occasionalism, from Sang Lee's monograph, *The Philosophical Theology of Jonathan Edwards*.[1]

Three Views on Creation and Conservation

To begin with, let us take each of the three theses on creation and conservation just mentioned, in turn. Each of these views has received a considerable amount of attention in recent literature.[2] In what follows, I shall assume, unless otherwise stated, that a time index refers to a particular time slice, as do related terms like 'moment' and 'instant'. The notion of a time slice I am using is that of a temporally durationless moment. x refers to any given concrete particular, and t refers to a time index, primed as required.

A thesis which renders a creation + conservation doctrine I take to be a conjunction of the following two premises:

(C1) For all x, if x is contingent, then God creates x

and

(C2) For all x, if x is contingent, then God conserves x (at each time index at which x persists after creation).

Premise (C1) precludes the possibility that there are backwardsly everlasting contingent things. I do not make any claim about whether they begin to exist *in time*, though Edwards would have understood all contingent things as things which are created by God *with* or *in* time.[3]

I take it that (C2) is a conservation thesis which assumes that if x is a dependent, concrete individual existing in time, then x will not continue to exist for a moment longer *unless God wills its continued existence*. Hence (C2) could be co-joined with a further premise to make this strong conservation element explicit:

(C2') For all x, if x is contingent, then x *cannot persist through time without the conservation of God at all those temporal indexes at which it exists after t1*

where t1 expresses the first instant at which x is created. This excludes deism, which for present purposes I take to be the doctrine that involves the conjunction of (C1) with the idea that though any given x might be contingent, that contingency, though ontological, is not *radically* ontological. By that I mean that for any given x, if that x is contingent, then x is dependent for its existence upon God (given (C1)), but it is not *immediately*, *constantly* or *continually* dependent upon God's conservation at all times thereafter, at which x exists. At those subsequent indexes, x remains contingent, and therefore ontologically dependent upon the fiat of God. (God may decide to destroy the world in which x exists, or x itself, at some later index.) But x is not radically dependent upon the fiat of God after its initial creation. God empowers x to persist through time at all subsequent indexes at which x persists, such that God does not have to conserve x in existence at all those time indexes.

The conjunction of (C1) and (C2) (or, indeed, (C2')) also precludes a further possibility, that God may create an x which has the property of self-sustenance essentially (this might be taken to be a strong deist thesis). That is, it precludes the possibility that in creating x, God could give x the property of being able to continue to exist without the immediate conservation of God, moment by moment. Jonathan Kvanvig has recently provided an argument against the notion that God might create x with the essential property of self-sustenance. He claims that

> The property of self-sustenance cannot be essential to God's creation. If the property of self-sustenance is essential to a thing, then that thing cannot exist without bearing some special relation to its continued existence. Yet nothing can bear any kind of relation to its continued existence without continuing to exist! So the very fact that God could destroy the universe shows that neither it nor anything else in it has the property of self-sustenance essentially.[4]

So self-sustenance must be a contingent property of x. Even if God could have created x with this property contingently, this does not alter the need for (at least) a conservation thesis. For if this property is contingent, then some explanation needs to be given as to why it was originally endowed with this property, but also, more importantly, its continuing to possess that property. God might create x with the contingent property of self-sustenance, but that is no guarantee that x will continue to enjoy this property at all times subsequent to its creation, since God could withdraw it, because it is contingent.

Nor is it possible to claim that the contingent self-sustenance of x is a continued effect of God's original creation. Kvanvig observes that without some medium in which the effects of an action can carry over to a later time, no sense can be given to the notion of a later effect of an earlier action. There is such a medium in the created order itself, namely, laws of nature. So, Kvanvig maintains, lighting a match can be causally responsible for the subsequent forest fire, because of a sequence of temporally overlapping events, which are bound to the next event by laws of nature. The match burns, causing a leaf to smoulder, and in turn to flame; the leaf falls to the ground, causing the grass to smoulder, and so on. But there is no such medium between God and creation. There are no laws of nature to which God is responsible, or which act as a medium for his actions in creation. The only way in which God's actions can be said to have later effects is if God acts to bring these actions into effect at that later time. And once the causal medium is in place in the governance of creation, God can only ensure that the initial creative act is carried through to later times by sustaining the medium itself at the same time. So God's sustenance of the world still occurs at every instance of its existence as per (C1) and ((C2) versus (C2')).

Descartes appears to have endorsed a position similar in strength to the conjunction (C1) and (C2):

> But though I assume that perhaps I have always existed just as I am at present, neither can I escape the force of this reasoning, and imagine that the conclusion to be drawn from this is, that I need not seek for any author of my existence. For all the course of my life may be divided into an infinite number of parts, none of which is in any way dependent on the other; and thus from the fact that I was in existence a short time ago it does not follow that I must be in existence now, unless some cause at this instant, so to speak, produces me anew, that is to say, conserves me.

However, as his argument proceeds, it has often been seen as endorsing a continuous creation doctrine:[5]

> It is as a matter of fact perfectly clear and evident to all those who consider with attention the nature of time, that, in order to be conserved in each moment in which it endures, a substance has need of the same power and action as would be necessary to produce and create it anew, supposing it did not yet exist, so that the light of nature shows us clearly that the distinction between creation and conservation is solely a distinction of the reason.[6]

In keeping with this reading of Descartes, the strong conservation thesis of (C1) and (C2) could be developed into a doctrine of continuous creation in the following fashion:

(C3) For all x, if x is contingent, then God continuously creates x at each time index that it obtains.

The difference between (C3) and (C2) (and (C2')) is that a strong conservation doctrine does not mean that at each index at which an object obtains after its initial creation, God recreates that object *ex nihilo*. On (C2) and (C2'), although God conserves x after x's creation, he does not re-create x at each moment after his creation. That is, a strong conservation thesis preserves this notion of temporal persistence whereas a continuous creation thesis denies conservation, since nothing persists through time. Put more formally, the distinction between (C3) and (C2) is that if x is a dependent concrete individual, then x will continue to exist for a moment longer *if and only if God recreates x for that moment, and continues to re-create x for all succeeding moments of its existence.* This requires some explanation, not least because, if God recreates an object at different time indexes, then the following question could be asked: in what sense is the object re-created at t2 the same object as the one created at t1? Perhaps we can speak of different parts of the one spacetime entity existing at different time indexes. In this way, x would refer to all the aggregate parts of the whole spacetime entity. In that case, referring to the different spatiotemporal parts of x would involve priming x at each index, such that at t1 God creates x1 and at t2, x2 and so on. (C3) could be rephrased to capture this important point thus:

(C3') For all x, if x is a contingent spacetime entity, then God continuously creates those spatiotemporal parts of x at each time index that parts of x obtains, such that God creates x1 at t1 and x2 at t2 and so on, for every slice at which parts of x obtain.

Edwards also endorses this kind of thesis at one point in his discussion of creation and conservation in his treatise on *Original Sin* IV: III (hereinafter *OS*).[7] But Edwards goes beyond a doctrine of continuous creation to advocate occasionalism. The difference between a doctrine of continuous creation *simpliciter* and a doctrine of occasionalism is that occasionalism involves an additional premise (or perhaps premises) regarding the nature of secondary, or mundane, causation. As Philip Quinn has shown,[8] the doctrine of continuous creation does not commit its defender to the additional claim (made by occasionalists) that there can be no secondary causes (because, say occasionalists, God is the sole cause of all things, and all mundane causation is merely the occasion of God's activity. No created thing has the causal power to affect another). In fact, according to Quinn, continuous creation can be held alongside a commitment to the reality of secondary causes. He demonstrates this from an analysis of how his own continuous creation doctrine is compatible with several notions of what secondary causation involves, notions that are live options in the contemporary philosophical debate. These comprise Humean regularity theory; counterfactual analysis; and a necessitarian understanding of secondary causation.

Since all that is needed here is an indication that continuous creation does not entail occasionalism, we pause to consider one version of Quinn's theory, compatible with a Humean analysis, since this has the advantage of the weight of philosophical tradition behind it. We adapt Quinn's argument to the present purpose. Using a familiar analogy (familiar that is, in the causation literature) of a match being struck leading to the match being lit, we may formulate a continuous creation doctrine using Quinn's analysis thus:

(i)   God willing that match 1 is struck at t1 brings about match 1 being struck at t1.

(ii)   God willing that match 2 is lit at t2 + a slight temporal increment brings about match 2 being lit at t2 + a slight temporal increment.

This leads to the conclusion:

(iii) For all t, if, for some match, God willing that match exists at tn obtains and God willing that match is similar to match 1 obtains and God willing that match is struck at tn obtains, then, for some burning match, God willing that burning match exists at tn + temporal increment obtains and God willing that burning match is similar to match 2 obtains and God willing that burning match is lit at tn + temporal increment obtains.

So, God wills the existence of the match at each index of its existence. Or, in keeping with (C3'), God wills the existence of each temporal part of the match at each instance at which a temporal part of that match obtains. This yields a continuous creation argument similar to (C3) and (C3'). But if this is coupled with the regularity view of causation stemming from Hume,[9] all secondary causation amounts to is the constant conjunction of a particular x, or stage of x, with a particular (stage of) y.

The problem with this reading of continuous creation is that it seems to mean that natural causes, understood in this Humean way, in conjunction with a doctrine of continuous creation, involve occasional rather than true (that is, efficient) causes. In other words, how can there be room for secondary causes if a continuous creation thesis obtains, and all mundane causation is merely regularity as per Hume?

In answer to this, Quinn claims that his view entails nothing about *whether* or *how* events like the match being lit at t1 + temporal increment are brought about. It simply stipulates that *if* or *when* they do, they do so according to a Humean analysis. And though this may well mean that such events have only Humean rather than 'true' causes, in the sense understood by – for example – Malebranche, Quinn feels this is sufficient to his purpose, and is a result theists of an empiricist bent can live with.[10]

It may well be that this question of *whether* and *how* such causal events are brought about for theists like Malebranche and Edwards is precisely the point at issue (as far as they are concerned in the development of their own causal views). However, strictly speaking, Quinn has shown that continuous creation could be compatible with secondary causation on at least one reading of the matter, and that is all we set out to show. What Quinn's analysis demonstrates is that an important distinction can be drawn between continuous creation, understood as per (C3) and (C3'), and the notion that divine volition *also* brings about (that is, is the necessary and sufficient cause of) events in nature. The conjunction of these two things is not a consequence of his view as he sets it up in this argument, but is not precluded by it either, although Quinn himself does not subscribe to such a Malebranchean, or Edwardsian view.

Continuous creation does not entail occasionalism if Quinn et al., are correct. And up until this point, none of the theses we have outlined entails an occasionalistic view of causation. But if an additional thesis concerning the nature of causation is required to yield occasionalism, what might that thesis be? Such an occasionalist causation thesis involves the following line of argument (the argument applies equally to (C3) or (C3')):

(C4)   x has no causal efficacy or agency.

(C4a)   God alone is sole causal agent at all time indexes and for all contingent concrete particulars.

(C4b)   x, being contingent, does not persist through time long enough to have any causal influence on any other contingent concrete individuals.

And,

(C4c)   x is merely the occasion of God's activity at each time index.

(That is, x has no capacity for mundane, or secondary causation. God alone causes all things. x is merely the occasion of God's causing things to be as they are.)

Thus on (C3), x1 at t1 is numerically distinct from x2 at t2, though qualitatively similar, or perhaps identical with the previous x. But when conjoined with (C4), the continuous creation thesis of (C3) becomes an occasionalist thesis, since in addition to this, it claims that x1 at t1 cannot be the (partial or complete) cause of x2 at t2, since x1 and x2 do not persist long enough to affect adjacent temporal parts of x, and in addition, are merely the occasions of God's action. (We have already had cause to note in the previous chapter that Edwards also believed that nothing persists long enough to affect another thing.)

This leads us to consider the most controversial aspect of the foregoing, that is, (C4b). In light of (C4b) the following question arises: *why cannot x have a causal influence on any other contingent concrete individual?*[11]

It seems to me that the answer to this question is best found where the occasionalism outlined is understood to be compatible with a dense view of time. To extrapolate:

(C5)   Each index at which any given x exists is a temporally durationless slice.

This could be applied to

(C6)   For any x existing at t1 in a diachronic causal nexus, that x cannot persist long enough to have any causal influence upon y (or any other contingent individual in that nexus).[12]

This is because

(C6a)   If time is a densely ordered continuum (that is, an ordered continuum with no gaps), then either,
    (C6ai)   an earlier event has an interval between it and a later event, or
    (C6aii)   there is no interval between the two events.
(C6b)   If (C6aii), then the two events occur at the same time and are in fact one event, so the question of one event causing another cannot arise, whereas
(C6c)   If (C6ai), then x at t1 occurs before x at t2 and the two events are not temporally contiguous, such that the earlier cannot cause the later event.

So

(C7)   x cannot have any causal influence on any other contingent concrete individual.

Now, provided the dense view of time is coherent (which on current cosmological and mathematical theories it is), then the occasionalistic thesis appears to stand, and can be clearly distinguished from a continuous creation thesis, and, indeed, from a strong conservation thesis.

But another, related, question arises at this point. How does the occasionalistic thesis relate to an understanding of persistence through time, given that it appears to deny any persistence *per se*? Another way of putting this might be, is occasionalism consistent with either perdurantism or endurantism (as they are construed in the current literature)? At this point we pause to explain what each of these terms means, in as cursory a fashion as space allows:

(D1)   Perdurantism is the doctrine that all concrete individuals are made up of temporal parts, as well as spatial parts, that together constitute a whole individual. Thus all individuals are four-dimensional spacetime objects which are aggregates of their temporal parts.

(D2) Endurantism is the doctrine that all individuals exist wholly and completely at each index of their existence. And all individuals are numerically the same at each time index at which they obtain.

(D1) is usually taken to be compatible with a dense view of time; (D2) with a discrete view (though this should not be taken as an argument for entailment in these respects).[13] So, (D2) references to time indexes need to be modified accordingly.

Now, according to the foregoing argument, is the occasionalist thesis compatible with either perdurantism or endurantism? Initially, it appears that if it is compatible with either, it is compatible with (D2) rather than (D1).[14] However, I want to argue that it is in fact compatible with (D1) more than, or perhaps in a way that is more congruent than, with (D2). Let us explore this:

(C8) For any x to be x at t1, as well as x at t2, means that x perdures as an aggregate of temporal slices which God recreates *ex nihilo* at each index.

This is the case since, on a perdurantist ontology, temporal parts/slices are as much a part of a concrete individual as spatial parts, unlike (at least some forms of) endurantism.

But a case could be made to endorse a 'hard' endurantist ontology where nothing persists for more than a moment ('a moment' taken either densely, or discretely), and where at that moment x is numerically identical with all previous times at which it has obtained. This form of endurantism could be compatible with a dense view of time, provided that at each temporal slice x is numerically the same as at the previous time slice. But it seems to me that endurantism better fits a discrete view of time.

Nevertheless, the point of (C8) is that occasionalist ontology could fit the context of dense time along perdurantist lines, not that it could also fit a form of endurantism, though it might. The problem for this current ontology is that the occasionalistic thesis goes beyond perdurantism, making it redundant (at least, it does in Edwards's rendition of it in *OS* IV: III). This is because, on occasionalism, nothing perdures save God. All perdurance is an illusion.

So, would occasionalism better fit a hard endurantism of the four-dimensional variety? Only if at each time slice x remains numerically the same, and at each slice x exists wholly and completely. Both these theses are contentious, to say the least. Taking them in reverse order:

(E1) If x exists wholly and completely at each index that God recreates x according to (C3)–(C7), then at each instant in the sequence in which God recreates x, he recreates x completely and wholly *ex nihilo*.

And

(E2) If x exists as numerically the same (in all its parts and properties) at each time slice that God recreates x, then x cannot appear to change across time in an occasionalistic–endurantist ontology (where such change involves a loss, or replacement of at least some parts and properties of x).

So, on (E2), the endurance conditional of (E1) is made explicit. And it seems to me that given (E2), (E1) is highly unlikely for reasons that Reid's Whipping Boy and the Ship of Theseus thought-experiments make plain.

Moreover, it seems to me that Jonathan Edwards endorses occasionalism on a perdurantist background. We may now turn to consider this view.

Edwardsian Occasionalism in *OS*

What then, of Edwards's views in all this? Edwards developed a version of occasionalism in his defence of a traditional notion of the imputation of original sin from Adam to his posterity, in *OS* IV: III. That Edwards is led to espouse a form of occasionalism in his defence of this doctrine can be demonstrated by several citations from the text of *OS*, and by applying the apparatus of the previous discussion on conservation, continuous creation and occasionalism to these texts. First, Edwards shows that persistence through time and personal identity are dependent upon divine constitution:

> Identity of consciousness depends wholly on a law of nature; and so, on the sovereign will and agency of God; and therefore, that personal identity, and so the derivation of the pollution and guilt of past sins in the same person, depends on an arbitrary divine constitution ... For if same consciousness be one thing necessary to personal identity, and this depends on God's sovereign constitution, it will still follow, that personal identity depends on God's sovereign constitution.[15]

He then shows that God's constitution of things is such that all things continue to exist by the immediate power of God, upholding all created substance in being. This might be understood as a strong conservation thesis, similar in tone to a Cartesian view, or (C1) and ((C2) versus (C2')). However, Edwards goes beyond this. He maintains that preservation is a continuous creation *ex nihilo* by God of all created things: 'God's *preserving* created things in being is perfectly equivalent to a *continued creation*, or to his creating those things out of nothing at *each moment* of their existence.'[16] Moreover, 'It will follow from what has been observed, that God's upholding created substance, or causing its existence in each successive moment, is altogether equivalent to an *immediate production out of nothing*, at each moment.'[17]

This is compatible with (C3) and (C3'). This is a constitution which depends entirely upon the will of God, and is therefore arbitrary (that is, dependent on the divine will, or *arbitrium*). Edwards even goes as far as to say that

> All dependent existence whatsoever is in a constant flux, ever passing and returning; renewed every moment, as the colour of bodies are every moment renewed by the light that shines upon them; and all is constantly proceeding from God, as light from the sun.

In addition,

> It appears, if we consider matters strictly, there is no such thing as any identity or oneness in created objects, existing at different times, but what depends on *God's sovereign constitution* ... for it appears, that a divine constitution is the thing which *makes truth*, in affairs of this nature.[18]

This goes beyond (C3'), towards endorsing a position similar to (C4)–(C7). For if all created bodies are in a constant state of flux, and are constantly being renewed by God, then Edwards is certainly subscribing to a strong continuous creation doctrine. But if in addition to this, God ordains the truth of the appearance of persistence through time for any concrete particular, then no thing actually does persist, or is able to act as an agent in any respect, unless God makes this the 'truth' of the matter. The divine constitution ordains it all. This goes a considerable way towards demonstrating that Edwards was an occasionalist. The clincher is that Edwards's view of causation in his treatise on *Freedom of the Will* (hereinafter *FOW*) denies that a cause is ontologically more than an occasion: 'Therefore I sometimes use the word "cause," in this inquiry [*FOW*], to signify ... any antecedent with which a consequent event is so connected, that it truly belongs to the reason why the proposition which affirms that event is true.' But the relation that exists between the antecedent and its consequent, 'is perhaps rather an occasion than a cause, most properly speaking'.[19] Elsewhere, in, for example, *Miscellany 267*, Edwards denies that any contingent thing can exist for long enough to act upon a contiguous object as a cause:

> The mere exertion of a new thought is a certain proof of a God. For certainly there is something that immediately produces and upholds that thought; here is a new thing, and there is a necessity of a cause. It is not antecedent thoughts, for they are vanished and gone; they are past, and what is past is not.[20]

Edwards does not get much clearer than this on the subject of the nature of causation. However, this seems to provide good evidence that he endorsed a version of occasionalism, at least in *OS* coupled with *FOW*. But there is one other *Miscellany 1263*, where he takes up this theme, and which appears to conflict with this understanding of Edwards's views on persistence through time.

The Problem with *Miscellany 1263*

In turning to *Miscellany 1263*, we come to one of the disputed passages on which Sang Lee bases his argument in his monograph on Edwards's philosophical theology.[21] Lee uses several key passages from the *Miscellanies* in the course of his argument for a dispositional Edwardsian ontology,[22] but his criticisms of those who believe Edwards endorses occasionalism depend for much of their argumentative force upon his reading of *Miscellany 1263*. In that *Miscellany*, Edwards appears to believe that God creates 'arbitrarily', and then conserves his creation in an occasionalistic manner, but *according to established physical laws*. This sounds both confused and confusing. If this is Edwards's view (and on the basis of the argument mounted thus far, that has to be quite a sizeable 'if'), then it needs investigation, since this new perspective would tend to throw much of what has been developed thus far into disarray.

The context of Edwards's words in *Miscellany 1263* seems to be the (then) recent developments on aspects of the doctrines of creation and conservation with which he wished to take issue. Edwards recognized that the discoveries of 'natural philosophy' had meant that there were many who were willing to allow 'a present, continuing, immediate operation of God on the creation'.[23] But these thinkers claimed that God operates in his immediate conservation of the world according to fixed laws, laws which he himself determined from the beginning of creation, and according to which he must act in conservation, '[s]o that, though they allow an immediate divine operation in those days, yet they suppose it is [now] limited by what we call laws of nature, and seem averse to allow an arbitrary operation to be continued or even to be needed in these days'.[24] Edwards comments on this:

> But I desire that it may be well considered whether there be any reason for this. For of the two kinds of divine operation, viz., that which is arbitrary and that which is limited by fixed laws, the former, viz., arbitrary, is the first and foundation of the other and that which all divine operation must be finally resolved into, and which all events and divine effects whatsoever primarily depend upon. Even the fixing of the method and rules of the other kind of operation is an instance of arbitrary operation. When I speak of arbitrary operation, I don't mean arbitrary in opposition to an operation directed by wisdom, but only in opposition to an operation confined to, and limited by, those fixed establishments and laws commonly called the laws of nature.[25]

Edwards then goes on to use this distinction between what he calls a 'natural operation' and an 'arbitrary operation' to show that arbitrary operations are more glorifying to God, since God is an arbitrary being (that is, one who acts according to his own will – *arbitrium* – and is not subject to the constraints of physical laws). So, the more nearly arbitrary a particular operation is, the more closely it resembles the activity of God because such an operation does not utilize physical laws. In this respect arbitrary operations are more glorifying to God than natural operations. He goes on to say that after creation (an arbitrary operation), God conserves the world in being in secondary operations, which make use of physical laws such as resistance and attraction (a natural operation) brought into being at creation:

> in these secondary operations ... some use was made of laws of nature before established, such, at least, as the laws of resistance and attraction or adhesion ... that are essential to the very being of matter, for the very solidity of the particles of matter consists in them.[26]

Such sentiments do not sit easily with the argument of the essay thus far. Indeed, interpreters of Edwards who have followed Sang Lee's treatment of Edwards's ontology have tended to take up such aspects of Edwardsian thinking for the development of an Edwardsian 'dispositional ontology'. According to this view of Edwards, being is, for Edwards, 'essentially a network of laws that prescribe certain actions and events to take place on specified occasions. These laws are active and purposive tendencies, or dispositions, that automatically come into "exertion" when the specified circumstances are met.'[27]

In regard to the use Edwards makes of laws of nature in his metaphysics, Lee says,

> A law of nature, as Edwards uses the term, is a dispositional force or a habit with a mode of reality apart from its exercises. Thus, when God causes resistance, God follows the law that God had fixed: that a particular sort of resisting occurs at a particular point in space at a particular time. To put it differently, a body is essentially and abidingly a disposition – to have a particular kind of resisting caused by God to occur at a particular space and time.[28]

Our interest is not in the structure or detail of Lee's argument, or of any of those who have followed in his footsteps in the last few years, but in whether what Edwards says in *Miscellany 1263* is commensurate with the development of an occasionalism. Nevertheless, the fact that there has been a recent school of 'Edwardsian' thought, which has taken what Edwards says in places like *Miscellany 1263* as an endorsement of some kind of 'modified' occasionalism,[29] is worth bearing in mind. If Edwards does develop a consistent occasionalism, one which *is* commensurate with a form of temporal parts doctrine, then a Lee-style reading of Edwards is in trouble, at least with respect to their understanding of the occasionalistic aspects of Edwards's ontology. (And, of course, the same could be said by Lee, *vice versa*.)

Let us begin to examine this problem in *Miscellany 1263* in more detail. The argument Edwards presents here could be construed in three forms. In each proposition, where a word is enclosed in speech marks, it indicates a peculiar understanding of that term:

(A1) God creates 'arbitrarily' (that is, according to his will and fiat), and conservation is God's acting at each successive moment mediately through physical laws he has established.

(A2) God creates 'arbitrarily' (that is, according to his will and fiat), and all conservation takes place according to the immediate occasions of God's activity coupled with 'physical laws' themselves instigated by divine fiat at the point of actualization, which persist through time alongside the creation, and are co-dependent with creation upon God.

(A3) God creates 'arbitrarily' (that is, according to his will and fiat), and conservation is an illusion: God recreates all things *ex nihilo* each moment, including the 'laws' themselves, which appear to be physical constants at each index merely because God 'arbitrarily' deigns that they operate in such a fashion.

These three propositions would need to be more rigorously articulated if they were to stand as they are, but they will not need to. It is sufficient that they capture the essence of the three possible understandings of this *Miscellany*.

They are organized in order of strength. (A1) is the weakest reading, which is an uncontroversial version of creation and conservation as two distinguishable phases in God's activity as per (C1) and ((C2) versus (C2')). (A2) is the reading of *Miscellany 1263* that best comports with Sang Lee's understanding of Edwards's ontology. However, it is not quite the same as Lee's view. Lee appears to want to preserve some kind of 'occasionalism' in his dispositional ontology (how that might be achieved is less clear).[30] With this in mind, (A2) could be made more explicitly Lee-like with an additional premise to that effect. At the very least it could form the basis of a Lee-type reading of Edwards's ontology, which is sufficient for present purposes.

(A3) is, or could be understood to be, consistent with the reading of Edwards as an occasionalist. It is also the strongest of the three versions of his argument from *Miscellany 1263*. Its claim for the physical laws Edwards makes such use of in his 'natural operations' is that these are themselves dependent upon the 'arbitrary operations'. This obtains in such a way that, although they can be distinguished for the purposes of argument, they are ontologically indistinguishable in terms of their immediate and constant dependence upon divine fiat for continued existence *ex nihilo*, as is the case in occasionalism. So, on (A3) the use of 'laws' in *Miscellany 1263* serves merely a heuristic and descriptive purpose. It has no ontological payload (there are no laws that persist through time independent of divine fiat). Natural operations depend immediately upon arbitrary operations for their continued existence, and arbitrary operations are themselves the products of God's continued creation of the cosmos out of nothing; the distinction between arbitrary and natural operations of divine power serve merely to describe different levels of operation within the immediate dependence upon God of all created things, concomitant with Edwards's occasionalism. In short, for ontological purposes, both natural and arbitrary operations of God in 'conservation' are aspects of his moment-by-moment re-creation of the world out of nothing. In reality, nothing is conserved, everything is re-created at each moment by divine fiat, and even natural operations are the occasions of God's actions.

The problem of adjudicating between these three versions of the argument of *Miscellany 1263* is that all three readings appear to have some textual support in what Edwards says (at least, as far as this particular *Miscellany* goes). At times he speaks as if physical laws in their natural operations are somehow entirely separate secondary causes that persist through time once they have been created, as physical constants, as per (A1).[31] At other times in the *Miscellany*, he writes as if he envisages some form of (A2). And at still other points, what he says sounds like the developed occasionalism of *OS*, reflected in (A3).[32] It appears that it is precisely this plasticity in Edwards's thought that has led Lee astray.

That said, I do not propose to adjudicate this matter at all. It is sufficient for our discussion that (A3) be both commensurate with the argument for Edwards's occasionalism mounted thus far, and that (A3) is a legitimate reading of this *Miscellany*, such that it can be understood in a way which does not conflict with the mature Edwards in *OS*. To make this reading of the *Miscellany* clear, consider the following argument, where W1 refers to a particular world (which happens to be the actual world) along (A3) lines:

(1)   God creates W1.
(2)   In actualizing (1), God inaugurates a set of physical laws, L, which governs W1. This could mean:
(3)   God conserves W1 according to L (strong conservation thesis), or
(3')   God 'occasionalistically' conserves W1 according to L (which persists through spacetime), or
(3")   God occasionalistically 'conserves' W1 commensurate with (the appearance of) L.

(3") would better accord with Edwards's strong argument in *OS* outlined previously. But from *Miscellany 1263* (3), (3') and (3") seem plausible renderings of Edwards's thinking (alongside those outlined in (A1) and (A2)). Let us assume that (3") is a legitimate rendering of the *Miscellany 1263* argument, since it better accords with Edwards's argument in *OS* previously outlined. I take it to be a fairly uncontroversial presupposition in textual scholarship (of whatever kind) that, *ceteris paribus*, where an author is unclear, their work should be compared with other instances where they speak of the same issues with greater clarity. If so, it would follow that,

(4)   The occasionalistic 'conservation' of (3") means that God recreates W1 *ex nihilo* at each successive time index (t1 ... tn), but in such a way as to conform (or, more precisely, appear to conform) to L at each index.

Clearly, if 'conservation' here refers to an occasionalistic constant re-creation *ex nihilo*, then strictly speaking, any set of laws pertaining to W1 is itself arbitrary and 'persists' only in such a way that God's creation appears to exhibit consistency at different time indexes (that is, so that W1 does not at one moment work according to a strong law of gravity and the next a weak law, or whatever).

So, if Dean throws a ball at t1 and at t2 it is caught by Trevor as it falls to the ground, according to the law of gravity at work in W1, this is because God re-creates Dean, Trevor and the ball in their respective relations and states of affairs at both time indexes. This means that the illusion of physically persisting laws is preserved throughout the throwing and catching of the ball. Or, to return to the Edwardsian nomenclature of *Miscellany 1263*, for the purposes of natural and arbitrary operations, natural operations appear to persist through time (to any person who (apparently) persists through a particular period and observes Trevor and Dean's ball game). But in point of ontological fact, any such natural operations are entirely dependent upon arbitrary operations at every time slice in that period. To recapitulate: on the (A3) and (3") combination, natural and arbitrary operations merely describe different levels of divine activity in the ontology of Edwardsian occasionalism. Both are immediately dependent upon God's constant re-creation *ex nihilo*, and are, ultimately, divine actions.

Consequently, on at least one plausible reading of *Miscellany 1263*, Edwards's understanding of the role and function of what appear to be 'physical laws' is compatible with occasionalism, such as he develops elsewhere in *OS* and *FOW*. That this can be derived from the text of *Miscellany 1263*, and that this is a plausible understanding of what Edwards says there (as well as elsewhere), are all that needs to be satisfied, *pace* Lee, in order to show that, *if* Edwards was an occasionalist, then he was a consistent occasionalist. And, in addition, I think this provides good grounds for claiming that Edwards was, indeed, a defender of occasionalism.

Notes

1. Lee, Sang Hyun (2000), *The Philosophical Theology of Jonathan Edwards, Expanded Edition*, New Jersey: Princeton University Press.
2. Representative examples of this debate include Clatterbaugh, Kenneth (1999), *The Causation Debate in Modern Philosophy, 1637–1739*, London: Routledge; Pessin, Andrew (2000), 'Does Continuous Creation Entail Occasionalism? Malebranche (and Descartes)', *Canadian Journal of Philosophy* 30, 413–40; and Quinn, Philip (1988), 'Divine Conservation, Secondary Causes, and Occasionalism' in Morris, Thomas V. (ed.), *Divine and Human Action*, Ithaca: Cornell University Press.
3. This skirts considerable issues about the nature of time and its relation to the created order, which would lead beyond the purview of this essay. The phrase, 'with or in time' refers only to the point at which a given thing is created. At creation, Edwards, like Augustine, would have understood that God creates the cosmos 'with', rather than 'in', time. In *The Mind* he says, 'There is, therefore, no difficulty in answering such questions as these: What cause was there why the universe was placed in such a part of space, and

why created at such a time? For if there be no space beyond the universe, it was impossible that the universe should be created in another place; and if there was no time before the creation, it was impossible that it should be created at another time.' Edwards, Jonathan (1980), *Scientific and Philosophical Writings, The Works of Jonathan Edwards Volume 6*, ed. Wallace E. Anderson, New Haven: Yale University Press, p. 343, Corollary to [13].

4. Kvanvig, Jonathan L. (1993), *The Problem of Hell*, New York: Oxford University Press, p. 38. The argument that follows draws upon his discussion of conservation in this passage.

5. See, for example, Frankfurt, Harry (1999), 'Continuous Creation, Ontological Inertia, and the Discontinuity of Time', in *Necessity, Volition, and Love*, Cambridge: Cambridge University Press, pp. 55 ff., where he discusses the question of whether Descartes was advocating continuous creation or a strong conservation thesis. However, this reading of Descartes is not the only one possible. For an alternative account, see *The Causation Debate in Modern Philosophy*, pp. 26 ff.

6. Descartes, Rene (1970), *The Philosophical Works of Descartes, Volume I*, trans. Elizabeth Haldane and G. R. T. Ross, Cambridge: Cambridge University Press, p. 168.

7. He also defends an unambiguous continuous creation thesis in *Miscellany 346*: 'It [is] most agreeable to the Scripture, to suppose creation to be performed new every moment. The Scripture speaks of it not only as past but as a present, remaining, continual act. Job 9: 9; Ps. 65: 6; 104: 4; Is. 40: 22, 44: 24; Amos 5: 8; and very commonly in the Scripture.' Edwards, Jonathan (1994), *The 'Miscellanies,' Nos. a-500, The Works of Jonathan Edwards Volume 13*, ed. Thomas A. Schafer, New Haven: Yale University Press, p. 418.

8. In his essay, 'Divine Conservation, Secondary Causes, and Occasionalism'. Pessin argues for the same claim (in a very different way) in Malebranche. See 'Does Continuous Creation Entail Occasionalism?' p. 432.

9. The regularity view of causation is the traditional understanding of Hume's view of causation. It has been challenged in the contemporary literature by writers like Strawson, Galen (1989), *The Secret Connexion: Causation, Realism and David Hume*, Oxford: Oxford University Press, and Wright, John (1983), *The Sceptical Realism of David Hume*, Manchester: Manchester University Press. They claim Hume was a realist, not a reductionist, with respect to causal facts. Nevertheless, even the revisionists admit that 'The fact remains: the view that Hume held a Regularity theory of causation is still the standard view.' Preface to *The Secret Connection*.

10. 'Divine Conservation, Secondary Causes, and Occasionalism', p. 60.

11. This does not preclude the possibility of instantaneous causation. However, Edwards clearly forecloses this possibility, as well as that of backwards causation in (1957), *Freedom of the Will, The Works of Jonathan Edwards Volume 1*, ed. Paul Ramsey, New Haven: Yale University Press, p. 185: 'But that which in any respect makes way for a thing's coming into being, or for any manner or circumstance of its first existence, must be prior to the existence.' It is clear from the context that he means *temporally* prior. Moreover, 'The distinguished nature of the effect, which is something belonging to the effect, can't have influence backward, to act before it is. The peculiar nature of that thing called volition, can do nothing, can have no influence, while it is not. And afterwards it is too late for its influence: for then the thing has made sure of existence already, without its help.' Hence, I shall not develop a defence against these two potential alternatives here.

12. The following argument can be found in Kvanvig, Jonathan L. and McCann, Hugh J. (1991), 'The Occasionalist Proselytizer', in Tomberlin, James E. (ed.), *Philosophical Perspectives 5, Philosophy of Religion*, California: Ridgeview, p. 598.

13. Dense time is the view, roughly speaking, that time is composed of durationless instants,

such that where there are any two instants, there is a third between them. Thus time is a densely ordered continuum. Discrete time is the view that there are no smallest instants of time; all measurements of time must involve duration, even if the duration concerned is incrementally extremely small.

14. It might be thought obvious that if occasionalism is consistent with either of endurantism or perdurantism, it is could *only* be consistent with perdurantism. However, Mark Heller makes just this point with respect to Chisholm's view of Edwards in his (1990), *The Ontology of Physical Objects*, Cambridge: Cambridge University Press, p. 22.

15. Edwards, Jonathan (1970), *Original Sin, The Works of Jonathan Edwards Volume 3*, ed. Clyde A. Holbrook, New Haven: Yale University Press, p. 399.

16. Ibid., p. 401, author's emphasis.

17. Ibid., p. 402, author's emphasis.

18. Ibid., p. 404. A similar reading of *OS* IV: III can be found in Helm, Paul (1997), *Faith and Understanding*, Edinburgh: Edinburgh University Press, ch. 7.

19. *Freedom of the Will*, p. 180–81.

20. *Miscellanies*, p. 373.

21. *The Philosophical Theology of Jonathan Edwards*.

22. In particular, he uses *Miscellany 241* to ground his dispositional reading of Edwards, and several exerpts from Edwards's early philosophy, in particular Edwards's 'Of Atoms' and 'The Mind', in *Scientific and Philosophical Writings*.

23. *Miscellany 1263* in Edwards (1955), *The Philosophy of Jonathan Edwards from His Private Notebooks*, ed. Harvey G. Townsend, Eugene: University of Oregon Press, p. 185. It is not clear whom Edwards had in mind, though these views were being discussed in continental post-Cartesian philosophy at the time. See Clatterbaugh, *The Causation Debate in Modern Philosophy*, for discussion of this.

24. Ibid.

25. Ibid.

26. Ibid.

27. Morimoto, Anri (1995), *Jonathan Edwards and the Catholic Vision of Salvation*, Pennsylvania: Pennsylvania State University Press, p. 6. His book is a development out of Lee's work.

28. Lee (1999), 'Edwards on God and Nature: Resources for Contemporary Theology', in *Edwards in Our Time*, eds Lee, Sang Hyun and Guelzo, Allen C., Grand Rapids: Eerdmans, pp. 15–44.

29. It is not clear what Lee intends in his use of, what I have called, 'modified' occasionalism. For instance, 'it is God who constantly preserves the established general laws and causes actual existences according to those laws. But it is not a continual *creatio ex nihilo* in a simple sense. The divinely established general laws are given a permanence, and are in a sense not created *ex nihilo* every moment. Edwards' view is an occasionalism only in the sense that God moves the world from virtuality to full actuality every moment through an immediate exercise of his power. Edwards' view in not an unqualified occasionalist position, however, since the world has an abiding realism in a virtual mode.' *The Philosophical Theology of Jonathan Edwards*, p. 63.

30. In fact, this sounds more like some form of concurrence, coupled with a continuous creation thesis, than occasionalism.

31. Townsend, *The Philosophy of Jonathan Edwards*, p. 188.

32. Ibid., p. 185.

Chapter 6

The Master Argument of *The Nature of True Virtue*

Philip L. Quinn

My chief aim in this chapter is to explicate the main philosophical argument of Jonathan Edwards's *The Nature of True Virtue*. In chapter 1 of that dissertation, entitled 'Showing Wherein the Essence of True Virtue Consists,' Edwards argues for a metaphysical account of the nature or essence of true virtue and spells out some of the consequences of this account. I shall try to exhibit the merits of Edwards's views on true virtue by subjecting the argument of that chapter to critical examination. My effort is motivated by the conviction that Edwards has a contribution to make to contemporary discussions of virtue ethics; his views are of more than merely antiquarian interest. To be sure, they will need to be revised in some respects in order to bring them into alignment with our own sensibilities and way of thinking. But I shall try to show that Edwards's position has considerable plausibility if it is revised in fairly minor ways in response to criticism.

The revival of interest in virtue ethics in recent philosophy has influenced work in the areas of religious ethics and moral theology. In those areas, a lot of attention has been paid to the virtue theory of Thomas Aquinas and to its Aristotelian background. Focusing narrowly on this tradition would, however, expose Christian ethics to the risk of neglecting ways in which distinctively Christian virtue theories might be fruitfully developed. If I am right in claiming that Edwards's position can be made plausible, then it offers the prospect of a useful counterweight to Aquinas's perspective. Like Aquinas, Edwards made important contributions both to philosophy and theology. But his account of true virtue is closer to Platonic than to Aristotelian traditions, and its Christian roots are in Calvinism rather than in Catholicism. So bringing Edwards into contemporary discussions of Christian virtue ethics would broaden and thereby enrich them. And negotiating the differences between such contrasting perspectives might also help to deepen Christian ethical reflection.

Since I am a philosopher by profession, my approach to Edwards's account of true virtue is philosophical rather than theological. Though I do appeal at one point to some things he says about God in order to defend my interpretation of the argument under examination against an objection, I treat that argument as freestanding and evaluate it on its own philosophical merits. This leaves me open to an

79

objection raised by the editor of the volume of Edwards's ethical writings that includes *The Nature of True Virtue*. In his 'Editor's Introduction' to that volume, Paul Ramsey claimed that 'it is a grave error, now or ever, to separate Edwards' philosophy from his theology, or his moral philosophy from his theological ethics.'[1] Ramsey's feelings about this point were strong enough to prompt him to repeat it. He insisted that 'it is a mistake to treat Edwards' moral philosophy apart from his moral theology, his theological ethics.'[2] Because Ramsey was an accomplished Edwards scholar, this objection to my procedure deserves to be taken seriously. So I shall respond to it before I turn to the task of coming to grips with Edwards's views.

I acknowledge that for some purposes it would be a mistake to separate Edwards's moral philosophy from his moral theology. Edwards was a highly systematic thinker; he tried to knit the philosophical and theological components of his thought into a coherent unity. If one's purpose is to arrive at a comprehensive and complete understanding of his ethical views, it would be a mistake to separate his moral philosophy from his moral theology. Comprehensive and complete understanding would inevitably involve insight into how philosophical and theological themes fit together into systematic unity or fail to do so. But it does not follow that for all purposes it is an error to separate the moral philosophy from the moral theology. Nor does it follow that one cannot gain any understanding of Edwards's ethical views by treating his moral philosophy apart from his moral theology. And it seems to me there is ample textual evidence that it is legitimate to separate moral philosophy from moral theology if one's purpose is to explicate the argument of chapter 1 of *The Nature of True Virtue*, which is what I aim to do. For Edwards conducts that argument almost entirely in purely philosophical terms. The only instance in which he explicitly appeals to theological sources – Holy Scriptures and the views of Christian divines – is when he introduces the concept of love into his discussion; and even in that instance he is careful to confirm the point he is making by an additional appeal to other sources – the opinions of most considerable writers. Yet Edwards presumably thought he could get readers to understand the argument well enough to follow it without first explaining its connections to his theological views. And presumably he also hoped that he could persuade readers of its cogency without appeals to theological doctrines for support. It thus seems to me that considerations of charity in interpretation actually speak in favor of explicating and assessing this particular argument entirely in philosophical terms. So I think Ramsey's objection does not undercut the fairly limited project I aim to carry out in this chapter.

The chapter is divided into four parts. In the first, I consider Edwards's argument for the claim that true virtue consists in benevolence to Being in general. In the second, I discuss his argument for the further claim that the primary object of virtuous benevolence is Being, simply considered. The third part is devoted to what Edwards takes to be important consequences of his account of true virtue. And the fourth defends my interpretation of Edwards's conceptions of Being in general and

Being, simply considered, against an objection derived from remarks by Ramsey about how we are required to understand those conceptions.

Benevolence to Being in General

There is one respect in which the methodology Edwards employs in chapter 1 of *The Nature of True Virtue* resembles the methodology Aristotle endorses in the *Nicomachean Ethics*. At the beginning of book VII, Aristotle makes the following observation about his philosophical method:

> Here as in all other cases, we must set down the appearances (*phainomena*) and, first, working through the puzzles (*diaporesantas*), in this way go on to show, if possible, the truth of all the beliefs we hold (*ta endoxa*) about these experiences; and, if this is not possible, the truth of the greatest number and the most authoritative.[3]

For Aristotle, the way things seem to us and the common conceptions and beliefs we have about them should serve as the starting points for ethical theorizing, and one if its main goals should be to preserve and vindicate as many of our common conceptions and beliefs as the problem-solving dimension of theoretical activity will permit.

In *The Nature of True Virtue*, Edwards proceeds in accord with this Aristotelian method. He begins in chapter 1 with a list of what he takes to be common opinions about the nature of true virtue; the first item on the list is striking. Edwards claims: 'Whatever controversies and variety of opinions there are about the nature of virtue, yet all (excepting some skeptics who deny any real difference between virtue and vice) mean by it something *beautiful*, or rather some kind of *beauty* or excellency.'[4] Subsequent items on the list narrow down the kinds of things that possess the beauty in which virtue consists. It is a common opinion that virtue is not all of beauty; the beauty of a flower or a rainbow is not called virtue. It is also a common opinion that virtue is not all of human beauty; the beauty of a human face or voice is not called virtue. Virtue seems to be some sort of beauty of the mind of beings that have perception and will. According to Edwards, however, 'perhaps not *everything* that may be called a beauty of the mind is properly called virtue' (p. 539). There seems to be something beautiful about the minds that produce great speculative ideas in subjects such as philosophy or mathematics, but this beauty is a different thing from what is most commonly regarded as virtue. Properly speaking, virtue is the beauty of the qualities and acts of mind that are moral in nature. As Edwards sees it, it is common opinion that they belong 'to the *disposition* and *will*, or (to use a general word, I suppose equally commonly well understood) to the "heart"' (p. 539). He concludes that 'I shall not depart from the common opinion when I say that virtue is the beauty of the qualities and exercises of the heart, or those actions which proceed from them' (p. 539). In other words, to inquire into the nature of true virtue is just to inquire into what makes any habit, disposition or exercise of the heart truly beautiful.

It is easy to doubt that it would be part of common opinion among contemporary philosophers that moral virtue is a kind of beauty. No doubt they would agree that it is an excellence of some sort, but many would initially resist the suggestion that it is properly conceived of in aesthetic terms. I think much of the resistance can be explained by unfamiliarity. It seems to me that theologians would tend to be more open to this suggestion because theological aesthetics has recently attracted a good deal of scholarly attention.[5] But, as John H. Brown points out, 'twentieth-century philosophies of beauty are comparatively rare.'[6] Though Brown thinks a small revival of philosophical interest in beauty took place toward the end of the century, Guy Sircello and Mary Mothersill are the only philosophers he identifies as significant contributors to the restoration of beauty as a theoretical subject.[7] Given the absence of beauty from the thought of most contemporary philosophers, it is hardly surprising that many of them would be taken aback by Edwards's claim that moral virtue is a kind of beauty.

However, I think it would be unwise to dismiss Edwards's claim that moral virtue is a kind of beauty too hastily. Maybe the claim can be made plausible by means of an explanation of what Edwards must have been getting at when he spoke of moral virtue as a kind of beauty. In the Platonic tradition to which he was indebted, as Brown points out, thinkers usually understood beauty in terms of 'Apollonian values of order, clarity, harmony and balance as opposed to Dionysian values of profusion, sensuality and vehemence.'[8] And in the eighteenth century, Francis Hutcheson's analysis of beauty emphasized the characteristics of unity and diversity suitably combined.[9] So when Edwards speaks of beauty, we should take him to be invoking characteristics of this sort. It is at least *prima facie* plausible to suppose that moral virtue does have and is commonly believed to have some such characteristics. And, as we shall soon see, it is characteristics of this sort to which Edwards actually speaks in the course of his argument. It might also be doubted that Edwards is correct in distinguishing between a beauty of the mind that is properly called virtue and another beauty of the mind that pertains to the production of great speculative ideas. Anyone who is sympathetic to the idea of an ethics of belief is likely to think that there are intellectual or epistemic virtues as well as moral virtues in a narrower sense. And some very good work in recent philosophy has exploited analogies between epistemology and ethics in order to cast light on intellectual virtues whose sphere of action is the acquisition and maintenance of beliefs.[10] Hence it might be thought that minds which produce great ideas in philosophy or mathematics are beautiful because they have and exercise intellectual virtues, in which case this beauty of the mind would be properly called virtue.

It seems to me Edwards is not committed to denying that there are intellectual virtues. But even if there is a beauty of the mind that is properly called intellectual virtue but is distinct from the beauty of primary interest to Edwards, I think Edwards would be right to insist that there is yet another beauty of the mind which differs from both of them and is not properly regarded as a kind of virtue. Perhaps this can be made clear if we reflect briefly on Sylvia Nasar's recent biography of the mathematician John Nash, which bears the title *A Beautiful Mind*. As Nasar's book and the film based on it show us, when John Nash is praised for having a beautiful mind, he is not being commended for anything so humdrum as conducting his doxastic life in accord with intellectual virtue, which in fact he was unable to do for long stretches of time on account of debilitating mental illness.[11] His mind was instead being praised for being the source of mathematical ideas of extraordinary originality and power; it was being commended for its visionary qualities or its genius. No doubt qualities such as genius are mental excellencies, and I am prepared to grant that minds which possess them do have a kind of beauty. But I also believe Edwards is on the mark in holding that this beauty differs from the kinds of mental beauty that might reasonably be regarded as ethical virtue.

Edwards also takes it to be a matter of common belief that there is a distinction between true virtue and merely apparent virtue. He identifies true virtue with general beauty and merely apparent virtue with particular beauty. According to Edwards, general beauty is that by which a thing appears beautiful with regard to all its tendencies and its connections with everything it stands related to. By contrast, particular beauty is that by which a thing appears beautiful with regard to some of its tendencies and its connections with some of the things it stands related to. A musical example is invoked to illustrate this aesthetic distinction: 'As a few notes in a tune, taken by themselves, and in their relation to one another, may be harmonious; which, when considered with respect to all the notes in the tune or the entire series of sounds they are connected with, may be very discordant and disagreeable' (p. 540). As the example shows, a thing may have particular beauty relative to a restricted context but lack general beauty relative to a broader context. For this reason, Edwards finds it natural to identify true virtue with general beauty rather than particular beauty. He concludes: 'That only, therefore, is what I mean by true virtue, which is that, belonging to the heart of an intelligent being, that is. beautiful by a *general* beauty, or beautiful in a comprehensive view as it is in itself, and as related to everything that it stands in connection with' (p. 540). In short, true virtue is that kind of beauty which makes the heart of its possessor beautiful in a comprehensive view that takes into account its connections with everything it is related to.

Given the common opinions he has set forth and the identification of true virtue with general beauty he has argued for, Edwards is in a position to give his answer to the question of what the nature of true virtue consists in. It goes as follows: 'True virtue most essentially consists in benevolence to Being in general. Or perhaps to speak more accurately, it is that consent, propensity and union of heart to Being in general, that is immediately exercised in a general good will' (p. 540). Two questions about this definition of true virtue immediately spring to mind. Why does Edwards suppose that the attitudes which are constitutive of true virtue are consent,

Jonathan Edwards

propensity and union of heart? And why does he further suppose that in true virtue the object of these attitudes is Being in general?

Edwards has straightforward answers to both questions. The attitudes constitutive of true virtue are consent, propensity and union of heart because they are attitudes of the sort needed to render their possessor beautiful. As Edwards notes, 'beauty does not consist in discord and dissent, but in consent and agreement' (p. 541). Edwards requires for his account of true virtue attitudes that have aesthetic qualities such as harmony, agreement and balance. Perhaps consent, propensity and union of heart are not necessary for his purposes, but they are sufficient. And the object of these attitudes in true virtue is Being in general because that object is required to make the beauty of true virtue general beauty. Edwards supposes that beings capable of true virtue, or intelligent beings, stand in connection to the whole system of things. Hence he is committed to the view that, for intelligent beings, general beauty is beauty relative to the context of this whole system, which is to say, relative to Being in general. Putting the point in terms of a rhetorical question, he asks: 'And if every intelligent being is some way related to Being in general, and is a part of the universal system of existence; and so stands in connection with the whole; what can its general and true beauty be, but its union and consent with the great whole?' (p. 541). Thus Edwards's account of true virtue requires attitudes such as consent, propensity and union of heart in order to make true virtue a kind of beauty, and it requires Being in general for their object in order to make true virtue a kind of general beauty.

I fear that some contemporary philosophers will think that it is not possible to interpret Edwards's definition of the nature of true virtue in a coherent fashion. However, I believe the temptation to think that this is the case can be counteracted if one reflects on the views of a contemporary philosopher who takes the idea of aesthetic morality seriously. In a recent book, Colin McGinn expounds and defends the thesis that 'virtue coincides with beauty of soul and vice with ugliness of soul.'[12] McGinn calls this thesis the aesthetic theory of virtue (ATV); he spells out ATV in terms of supervenience. He develops his theory of aesthetic morality in the following way:

> let the supervenience base consist of the various virtues or vices: kindness, justice, generosity, compassion, steadfastness, and so on; cruelty, injustice, meanness, callousness, capriciousness, and so on. And let the supervenient properties be the kinds of morally aesthetic properties we have been considering; for simplicity we might just think of them as inner beauty and ugliness and grades of these.[13]

According to ATV, then, the aesthetic properties supervene on the ethical properties. On this view, as McGinn is careful to point out, it is not the case that all attributions of aesthetic properties are morally evaluative; the claim is not that some music, for example, is virtuous because it is beautiful. Instead, as he insists, 'virtue equals beauty *plus* the soul, to put it crudely. The particular *kind* of beauty proper to the soul is what virtue consists in.'[14]

Adapting McGinn's idea for application to Edwards's thought, we may coherently attribute to Edwards the view that the property of having general beauty supervenes on the property of having consent, propensity and union of heart to Being in general. The nature of true virtue consists of consent, propensity and union of heart to Being in general in the sense that having true virtue just is having consent, propensity and union of heart to Being in general. True virtue consists of a kind of general beauty in the somewhat different sense that having this kind of general beauty supervenes on having true virtue. In developing this account of true virtue, Edwards works backward from general beauty to the consent, propensity and union of the heart to Being in general, on which it supervenes. Hence general beauty is epistemically prior to the consent, propensity and union of the heart on which it supervenes. But this consent, propensity and union of the heart is metaphysically prior to the general beauty in question because it constitutes the base on which that general beauty supervenes. We therefore find in Edwards an example of a phenomenon that is quite common in philosophical positions: it is that the order of knowing is the reverse of the order of being.

Benevolence to Being, Simply Considered

Edwards makes four remarks that are intended to clarify his account of true virtue. First, if we suppose a union of heart to some particular being or beings that does not imply a tendency to union with the whole system of existence and is not inconsistent with emnity towards Being in general, this disposition to benevolence to a private circle or system of beings does not have the nature of true virtue. Such a disposition may have particular beauty and apparent virtue, but it will lack general beauty and true virtue. Second, we may describe true virtue as general benevolent love or kind affection because both Christian theology and moral philosophy agree that it consists in love of some kind. Third, we must not suppose that every loving act that is truly virtuous has Being in general, or the great system of universal existence, as its direct object; for, though true virtue consists in benevolence to Being in general, from this disposition there may arise exercises of love to particular beings, as objects and occasions present themselves to us. According to Edwards, what his account of true virtue implies is rather that 'no affections towards particular persons, or beings, are of the nature of true virtue but such as arise from a generally benevolent temper, or from that habit or frame of mind, wherein consists a disposition to love Being in general' (p. 542). And, fourth, we are to understand benevolence to Being in general to be restricted to intelligent Being in general, since Edwards wishes to exclude from the circle of ethical concern 'inanimate things, or beings that have no perception or will, which are not properly capable objects of benevolence' (p. 542).

The first three of these claims strike me as plausible developments of Edwards's position. I suspect, however, that many contemporary philosophers would baulk at the fourth. Impressed by their deep dependence on ecosystems of which they are parts, some would insist on expanding the circle of objects of benevolence to include their immediate biological environments or perhaps even the biosphere as a whole.[15] Others would argue for including inanimate natural objects of great beauty such as the Grand Canyon or the Grand Tetons. But, as far as I can tell, dropping Edwards's restriction to the narrow circle of intelligent Being in general would not seriously damage his position. Even if the circle of objects of benevolent love need not be so wide as to encompass Being in general without any qualifications at all, it does not have to be so narrow as to include only intelligent Being in general.

At this point in his argument, Edwards introduces a distinction between love of complacence and love of benevolence. Complacent love is defined as 'delight in beauty; or complacence in the person or being loved for his beauty' (p. 543). Complacent love therefore presupposes beauty in its object. Benevolent love is defined as 'that affection or propensity of the heart to any being, which causes it to incline to its well-being, or disposes it to desire and take pleasure in its happiness' (p. 542). Edwards considers it agreeable to common opinion to suppose that beauty in its object is not always the ground of benevolent love. Though he says he is not going to insist on this point, he notes that God's benevolence is often assumed to be prior to the beauty of many of its objects, and, indeed, prior to their very existence. What he thinks must be granted is that 'benevolence doth not necessarily presuppose beauty in its object' (p. 543). And it seems obvious that he is right about this. We can be benevolently disposed to things that are not beautiful. In particular, we can desire and take pleasure in the happiness of other intelligent beings who lack true beauty because they lack true virtue.

Edwards makes use of this distinction in what is easily the most enigmatic stretch of argument in all of chapter 1 of *The Nature of True Virtue*. Given his principle that virtue is the beauty of intelligent beings and consists in love, he claims, '[i]t is a plain inconsistence to suppose that virtue primarily consists in any love to its object for its beauty; either in a love of complacence, which is delight in a being for his beauty, or in a love of benevolence, that has the beauty of its object for its foundation' (p. 543). But Edwards does not argue directly for a claim of logical inconsistency. Instead, he observes that to suppose virtue primarily consists in any love to its object for its beauty is, given his principle, to suppose 'that the beauty of intelligent beings primarily consists in love to beauty; or, that their virtue first of all consists in their love to virtue' (p. 543). As he points out, this is going in a circle. What is more, it is easy to see that this circularity gives rise to an infinite regress. Edwards generates it quite crisply in the following passage:

> If virtue consists primarily in love to virtue, then virtue, the thing loved, is the love of virtue: so that virtue must consist in the love of the love of virtue. And if it be inquired what that virtue is, which virtue consists in the love of the love of,

it must be answered, 'tis the love of virtue. So that there must be the love of the love of the love of virtue, and so on *in infinitum*. (p. 544)

In other words, start with the proposal that virtue consists in the love of virtue. For the second occurrence of the word 'virtue' in the proposal, substitute words that express what the proposal tells you virtue consists in, namely, the words 'the love of virtue.' The result is that virtue consists in the love of the love of virtue. Repeat this procedure to get the further result that virtue consists in the love of the love of the love of virtue. And so on *ad infinitum*. But are the circularity and regress so vicious? If so, why exactly are they defects?

It seems clear to me that they are defects if we suppose that specifying what something consists in amounts to providing a philosophical analysis of it. An analogy may help us to see that this is the case. During the last half of the twentieth century, there was in epistemology a cottage industry devoted to revising the traditional analysis of knowledge as justified true belief in order to block Gettier counter-examples.[16] Imagine that in the course of this discussion someone had proposed as an analysis of knowledge that knowledge is true belief plus whatever else it takes to be knowledge. This proposal is circular and can be made to generate an infinite regress, and these facts are connected with its inadequacy as an analysis. For an analysis is supposed to take a complex and problematic concept and, so to speak, break it down into simpler components or, more precisely, explicate it in terms of concepts that are more primitive, better understood or something of that sort. And a circular analysis can perform none of these functions. So the proposal I have imagined would correctly have been adjudged to be an inadequate analysis. Similarly, the proposal that virtue consists in love of virtue is inadequate if a statement of what something consists in is supposed to perform the same functions as an analysis.

However, if the main point of Edwards's discussion of going in a circle and going on *ad infinitum* is to show that virtue cannot successfully be analyzed as love of virtue, there is a simpler and more direct route to the conclusion he wishes to reach. Once he has taken over from common opinion the view that benevolent love does not necessarily have beauty for its object, he is already in a position to claim that there can be instances in which virtue and hence benevolent love for intelligent being does not have its beauty and hence its virtue for an object. In other words, there can be cases of virtuous love that are not cases of love of virtue. And if this is so, virtue and love of virtue are not even necessarily coextensive, in which case love of virtue cannot be an adequate analysis of virtue. So I am prepared to grant that Edwards makes a plausible claim when he concludes that 'if the essence of virtue or beauty of mind lies in love, or a disposition to love, it must primarily consist in something *different* both from complacence, which is a delight in beauty, and also from any benevolence that has the beauty of its object for its foundation' (p. 544). And it seems to me independently plausible, just on intuitive grounds, that there can be virtuous love that is not directed to, and so is not love for, any beauty its object may have.

Edwards then argues that virtue cannot consist primarily in gratitude, which he defines as 'one being's benevolence to another for his benevolence to him' (p. 544). He notes that gratitude cannot be the first benevolence to which none is prior because gratitude is a response to prior benevolence, and he seems to think this gives rise to circularity of the sort he has rejected in previous argumentation. And immediately after having disqualified gratitude, he states a major conclusion:

> Therefore there is room left for no other conclusion than that the primary object of virtuous love if Being, simply considered; or that virtue primarily consists, not in love to any particular beings because of their virtue or beauty, nor in gratitude, because they love us; but in a propensity and union of heart to Being simply considered; exciting 'absolute Benevolence' (if I may so call it) to Being in general. (p. 544)

It is obvious that some of the ideas in this statement need explanation. As I see it, Being, simply considered, is to be understood as Being considered just as Being (or perhaps just as intelligent Being) or considered apart from any attributes (except perhaps for intelligence) that could differentiate one being from another. To say that the primary object of virtuous love is Being, simply considered, is to say that the attitude of love, when virtuous, is directed, in the first instance or most fundamentally, to Being, simply considered. And Edwards's technical term 'absolute Benevolence' refers to the kind of benevolence to Being in general, or the whole system of existence, that is excited or generated by virtuous love for Being, simply considered.

It also seems almost obvious that the argument Edwards offers for this conclusion is a failure. What his argument shows, if it is successful, is only that the primary object of virtuous love cannot be anything that gives rise to the sort of circularity and infinite regress he finds objectionable. This rules out candidates for the role of primary object such as virtue and beauty, but it clearly does not rule out all the alternatives to Being, simply considered. Think, for example, of terrestrial Being. From the assumption that virtue consists primarily in love of terrestrial Being, we cannot derive the circular claim that virtue consists primarily in love of virtue or, as far as I can tell, any other claim that is objectively circular. Edwards to the contrary notwithstanding, there is room left for conclusions other than that the primary object of virtuous love is Being, simply considered.

However, it is not difficult to see how theoretical considerations drive Edwards to suppose that the primary object of virtuous love is Being, simply considered. He has previously argued that virtuous love has as its object Being in general. For the sake of theoretical simplicity, he needs a primary object for virtuous love that is, at the very least, no narrower in extension than Being in general. Being, simply considered, suffices for this purpose, and so it is reasonable to postulate that the primary object of virtuous love is Being, simply considered. So, though Edwards does not have a proof for this claim, I am willing to allow that it derives some plausibility from the way it fits neatly into the philosophical theory he is engaged in constructing.

This neatness of fit is highlighted by the first of two remarks that Edwards makes about Being, simply considered. He says: 'The *first* object of a virtuous benevolence is *Being*, simply considered: and if Being, *simply* considered, be its object, then Being *in general* is its object; and the thing it has an ultimate propensity to, is the highest good of Being in general' (p. 545). The plausible thought behind the conditional claim is this: if virtuous benevolence extends to and, as it were, spreads itself over all of (intelligent) Being, simply considered, then it is guaranteed to extend to and, as it were, spread itself over (intelligent) Being in general or the whole system of (intelligent) existing things. And Edwards supposes that virtuous benevolence's ultimate propensity to the highest good of Being in general has consequences for its treatment of particular beings. The virtuous heart will seek the good of particular beings in so far as doing so is conceived to be consistent with promoting the highest good of the whole system of existence, and it will oppose any particular being that it conceives to be an irredeemable enemy of the whole system of existence.

Edwards's second remark about Being, simply considered, gives rise to a difficulty. He says:

> And further, if Being, simply considered, be the first object of any truly virtuous benevolence, then that Being who has *most* of being or has the greatest share of existence, other things being equal, so far as such a being is exhibited to our faculties or set in our view, will have the *greatest* share of the propensity and benevolent affection of the heart. (pp. 545–6)

In other words, the being that has the greatest share or degree of existence, if there is such a being, will, other things being equal, also have the greatest share of the virtuous heart's benevolence. As Edwards explains this principle of proportionality is governed by a *ceteris paribus* clause because it does not take into account the effects of the secondary object of virtuous benevolence. Edwards discusses it later, and it will be the topic of the next section of this chapter. The problem with the principle is its reliance on the idea that existence comes in larger and smaller shares or admits of degrees. This is an idea to which Edwards is firmly wedded. He insists that pure benevolence in its first exercise inclines to each being whose welfare is consistent with the highest good of the whole system of existence 'in proportion to the degree of *existence*,' and he observes in a footnote that 'I say "in proportion to the degree of *existence*" because one being may have more *existence* than another, as he may be greater than another' (p. 546). Yet many contemporary philosophers profess to find the very idea of existing to a greater or lesser degree unintelligible. Appealing to the concept of existence that underlies the existential quantifier or modern formal logic, they insist that it is incoherent to think of existence as coming in degrees. And some of them may add that the concept of degrees of existence is part and parcel of a now outdated metaphysical picture that is associated with the notion of the Great Chain of Being.[17]

I think Edwards can be defended against this objection. I agree that we cannot make sense of the idea of degrees of existence using the existential quantifier as it is usually understood, but I deny that the idea of degrees of existence is for this reason incoherent or unintelligible. Modern quantification logic is primarily a tool forged to serve certain philosophical purposes, and it serves those purposes very well indeed. However, there is no reason to believe that it is suited to serving all legitimate philosophical purposes. From the fact that it cannot serve the purpose of helping to make sense of the idea of degrees of existence, it simply does not follow that his idea makes no sense. All that seems to follow is that other tools will be required if this purpose is to be well served. I also agree that the idea of degrees of existence is old-fashioned, but I deny that it is on that account a bad idea. After all, some old-fashioned ideas are good ideas. Hence it seems to me that Edwards's use of the idea of degrees of existence in his account of true virtue does not by itself give us adequate grounds to reject that account.

There is a significant way in which Edwards's appeal to Being, simply considered, adds strength to the theory he is constructing. By insisting that virtuous benevolence is directed most fundamentally at Being, simply considered, he insures that virtuous benevolence will not in various ways be partial or biased. Not only will it not be restricted to those to whom we owe debts of gratitude; it will also not be directed exclusively to those who have special features on account of which they might be thought to deserve or be worthy of it. Nor will it be restricted to those who possess distinctive qualities that make them erotically attractive or desirable as intimate friends. Indeed, Edwards's appeal to Being, simply considered, as the primary object of virtuous benevolence may put him in an especially good position to deal with some hard cases familiar from contemporary discussion in biomedical ethics. Consider, for example, the irreversibly comatose and severely defective neonates. According to some theories, worthiness of moral respect depends on possession of properties such as freedom and reason that they apparently lack and have no prospects of coming to possess. Such theories have a problem of explaining why they are proper objects of moral concern. This need be no problem for Edwards. Even if the irreversibly comatose and severely defective neonates have smaller shares of existence than normal human adults, they do have shares of existence just because they exist. And since they fall within the limits of Being, simply considered, they are proper objects of virtuous benevolence. To be sure, there might be a problem for Edwards if we were to abide by his restriction of the circle of ethical concern to intelligent beings, for it could be argued that the irreversibly comatose and severely defective neonates fall outside the limits of intelligent Being, simply considered. However, this consideration seems to me to provide another good reason to revise Edwards's theory in order to relax that restriction.

The Secondary Object of Virtuous Benevolence

As Edwards's talk about a first or primary object of virtuous benevolence suggests, he holds that virtuous benevolence also has a secondary object. It is benevolent being. He asserts that 'a secondary ground of pure benevolence is virtuous benevolence itself in its object' (p. 546). He sees a general psychological connection between the two objects or grounds. It is that 'when anyone under the influence of general benevolence sees another being possessed of the like general benevolence, this attaches his heart to him, and draws forth greater love to him, than merely his having existence' (p. 546). According to Edwards, anyone who is governed by benevolent love of Being in general will have complacent love and a heightened benevolent love for other benevolent lovers of Being in general, out of gratitude, as it were, to them for their benevolent love of Being in general. Any lover of Being in general will therefore regard benevolent love of Being in general in another as his beauty and 'an excellency that renders him worthy of esteem, complacence, and the greater good will' (p. 547). In the end, then, Edwards acknowledges two objects of, or grounds for, benevolence. The first and more fundamental is sheer being. This allows virtuous benevolence to extend to all existing things, or at any rate at least to all intelligent beings, and to love them just because they exist. The second is virtuous benevolence itself, which is found only in some existing things. Virtuous benevolence loves them both on account of their existence and because of their virtuous benevolence, and so it has a greater love for them than it has for beings that lack virtuous benevolence.

Edwards concludes chapter 1 of *The Nature of True Virtue* with six observations that spell out details of his views on the secondary ground of virtuous benevolence. For the sake of completeness, I comment on each of them.

First, Edwards thinks benevolence to Being in general gives rise to love on the ground of benevolence by some sort of necessity. As he puts it, 'he that has a simple and pure good will to general entity or existence must love that temper in others that agrees and conspires with itself' (p. 547). So virtuously benevolent beings necessarily stand in some sort of special relation of concord or elective affinity to one another.

Second, for Edwards, moral or spiritual beauty is primarily an attribute of this secondary object, benevolent being, 'and the various qualities and exercises of mind which proceed from it, and the external actions which proceed from these internal qualities and exercises' (p. 548). But, third, all these things are morally beautiful mainly because 'they imply *consent* and *union* with Being *in general*' (p. 548). And, fourth, though this moral beauty is only a secondary ground of virtuous benevolence, it is the primary ground of virtuous complacence. Thus benevolent being is at once the second object of virtuous benevolence and the first object of virtuous complacence, and it is also the primary possessor of moral beauty.

Fifth, what Edwards describes as the degree of the amiableness or valuableness of true virtue 'is not in the *simple* proportion of the degree of benevolent affection seen, but in a proportion *compounded* of the greatness of the benevolent being, or the degree of *being* and the degree of *benevolence*' (p. 548). Virtuous benevolence is sensitively calibrated to the value of its object. When that object is the secondary object, benevolent being, the value of the object depends on its greatness, which in turn depends on both its degree of existence and its degree of benevolence. Hence, the value of a benevolent being is not a function of its degree of benevolence alone; it is a function of, and indeed is directly proportional to, both its degree of benevolence and its degree of existence. Thus, for instance, if two beings have the same degree of benevolence but differ in degrees of existence, the being with the larger degree or share of existence is more valuable than the being with the smaller share. But, by the same token, if two beings have the same degree of existence but differ in degrees of benevolence, the being with the greater degree of benevolence is more valuable than the being with the lesser degree. Clearly the principle that the being with the greater share of existence will have the greater share of the virtuous heart's benevolence holds in the first of these special cases. However, the being with the greater share of existence will not have the greater share of the virtuous heart's benevolence when a small difference in degree of existence is outweighed by a large difference in degree of benevolence. If a minor demon has slightly more existence but is much less benevolent than a saintly human, the human will be more valuable than the demon and will have a greater share of the virtuous heart's benevolence than the demon. In such a case the principle will not hold. Therefore, Edwards's earlier claim that the principle only holds when other things are equal is vindicated by this way of reckoning. It is defended by the following analogy: 'A large quantity of gold, with the same degree of preciousness, i.e. with the same excellent quality of matter, is more valuable than a small quantity of the same metal' (p. 549). In other words, the value of gold is a function of both quality and quantity, not just of quality.

Sixth, and finally, having previously contended that anyone who has a benevolent temper is bound to love benevolence in others, Edwards now argues that no one who lacks a benevolent temper can love benevolence in others. On his view, someone who loves benevolence in others values the disposition or inclination to promote the good of Being in general, while someone who lacks a benevolent temper does not value the good of Being in general. However, it is not possible to value the inclination to promote the good of Being in general and, at the same time, not to value the good of Being in general. For, according to Edwards, 'to love an inclination to the good of Being in general would imply a loving and prizing the good of Being in general' (p. 549). And so it turns out, as a matter of some sort of necessity, that all and only those who have the beauty of virtuous benevolence in themselves will love, or, to use Edwards's locution, will truly *relish*, the beauty of virtuous benevolence in others.

We are now in a position to summarize the account of virtue Edwards develops in chapter 1 of *The Nature of True Virtue*. Like other virtue theorists, Edwards takes virtue to be a disposition, propensity or habit. But unlike others, Edwards offers a monistic account of it: virtue is fundamentally just one disposition. To a first approximation, that disposition is benevolence or love, and, more precisely, it is to be understood as consent, propensity and union of heart. Because these qualities have such features as harmony and unity, they make their possessors beautiful, and so moral beauty supervenes on virtuous benevolence. Also to a first approximation, the object of virtuous benevolence is Being in general, and, for Edwards, Being in general is the whole or universal system of existence (or at least the whole system of intelligent existence). Upon closer analysis, however, it turns out that virtuous benevolence actually has two objects. Its primary object is Being, simply considered, which is Being considered apart from any attributes (except perhaps for intelligence) that can differentiate among beings. So the first ground in things for virtuous benevolence toward them is simply their existence. And anyone who has virtuous benevolence for (intelligent) Being, simply considered, will also have it for (intelligent) Being in general. The secondary object of virtuous benevolence is benevolent being. Hence the second ground of things for virtuous benevolence toward them is their own benevolence if they are benevolent. When virtuous benevolence is directed toward a particular being that is not itself benevolent, the positive value it discerns in such a being is directly proportional to its degree of existence. Virtuous benevolence loves such a being just because it exists and to the degree that it exists. When virtuous benevolence is directed toward a particular being that is itself benevolent, the positive value it discerns in such a being is directly proportional to both its degree of existence and its degree of benevolence, suitably combined. Virtuous benevolence loves such a being both because it exists and because it is benevolent in a way that is responsive to both its degree of existence and its degree of benevolence. And all and only those who possess the beauty of virtuous benevolence themselves will truly love or relish that moral beauty in others.

Final Objection Defeated

An important part of my strategy of interpretation has been to read chapter 1 of *The Nature of True Virtue* as a free-standing philosophical argument that can be understood, criticized and defended independently of its connection with Edwards's theology. In order to implement this strategy, I have taken Edwards's term of art 'Being in general' to refer to the whole system of existing things, leaving open the question of whether or not that system includes a deity. And I have taken his other main technical term 'Being simply considered' to mean Being considered apart from any differentiating attributes (except perhaps for intelligence), again leaving open the question of whether or not considering Being in this way involves considering a deity. I realize, of course, that in the last analysis these are not open questions for Edwards. He believes that God is a member of the whole system of existence, and he believes that considering Being apart from differentiating attributes involves considering God's existence. The issue is whether or not the argument of chapter 1 presupposes or in some other way rests on such beliefs.

A remark by Paul Ramsey suggests that it does. In a footnote on the first page of chapter 2 of *The Nature of True Virtue*, he claims that 'the internal argument of this chapter *requires* us to treat "Being itself, simply considered" and "Being in general" (and variants) as direct, respectful, or devout references to God, not as a metaphysical property or generality' (p. 550, editor's footnote). If we take Ramsey to be claiming correctly that God is the referent of the terms 'Being in general' and 'Being simply considered,' then Edwards is referring to God whenever he uses either of these terms straightforwardly in chapter 1. In this case, the argument of that chapter seems to have a theological presupposition. Or, to put the matter in a slightly different way, if Being in general just is God and Being, simply considered, just is God, then whenever Edwards refers to Being in general or to Being, simply considered, in chapter 1 he refers to God. In this case too, the argument of that chapter seems to have a theological presupposition. In either case, my strategy seems to fail. So it is incumbent on me to respond to this objection. The situation is complicated by the fact that the terms 'Being in general' and 'Being, simply considered' are not obviously referring expressions in the precise sense familiar to philosophers from debate in contemporary philosophy of language; it is not obvious that either of them functions, for example, as a proper name or a definite description. But dismissing the objection for this reason alone strikes me as a bit unfair, and so I shall spend some time examining some of the textual material that prompted Ramsey's remark.

Edwards begins chapter 2, which is entitled 'Showing How The Love Wherein True Virtue Consists Respects the Divine Being and Created Beings,' with the claim that 'from what has been said, 'tis evident that true virtue must chiefly consist in love to God; the Being of beings, infinitely the greatest and best of beings' (p. 550). Harking back to the previous discussion of Being, simply considered, Edwards reminds us of the principle that the being with the greatest share or degree of existence, if there is such a being, will, other things being equal, also have the greatest share of the virtuous heart's benevolence. He then explicitly introduces the assumption that God exists and has the greatest share of existence. Edwards writes: 'But God has infinitely the greatest share of existence, or is infinitely the greatest being. So that all other being, even that of all created things whatsoever, throughout the whole universe, is as nothing in comparison of the Divine Being' (p. 550). And though he does not bother to state it, the obvious conclusion is that God will, other things being equal, have the greatest share of the virtuous heart's benevolence or, what amounts to the same thing, that, other things being equal, true virtue chiefly consists in love of God.

Edwards does not claim that the created universe *is* nothing. When he says that it *is as* nothing, what he means is that it is puny in comparison to God. So if the term 'Being, simply considered' is a referring expression, it refers, for Edwards, to both God and the created universe, not to God alone. Otherwise put, the term 'Being, simply considered' has in its extension both God and the created universe. However, God is among the beings referred to or within the extension of this term only on the assumption that God exists. Edwards first introduces this assumption at the beginning of chapter 2; it is not presupposed by the argument of chapter 1. For all that the assumptions of chapter 1 allow us to conclude, the being with the greatest share of existence is an especially intelligent and noble extraterrestrial. If that were the case, it follows, by Edwards's principle, that this extraterrestrial would, other things being equal, would have the greatest share of the virtuous heart's benevolence, and true virtue would, other things being equal, consist chiefly in love for it. In other words, Edwards's principle and the argument in chapter 1 that is supposed to support it do not presuppose the existence of God.

It is not difficult to see that the term 'Being in general' presents us with a similar situation. If it is a referring expression, it refers to just those things that belong to the whole system of existence, and so it refers to God among other things only on the assumption that God exists. In other words, God is in the extension of the term 'Being in general' along with other things only on the assumption that God exists. But Edwards first introduces this assumption into the discussion at the beginning of chapter 2. In chapter 1, before he has done so, we cannot legitimately conclude that the term 'Being in general' refers to God as well as other things or has God along with other things in extension. The argument of chapter 1 does not presuppose any such theological facts about the reference or extension of this term; nor does it presuppose the existence of God.

In short, even if, as Edwards believes, the technical terms 'Being in general' and 'Being simply considered' refer to God among other things or have God among other things in their extensions, it is not a presupposition or assumption of the argument of chapter 1 that they do. Nor is this a consequence of that argument. And it is not even a presupposition, assumption or consequence of the argument of chapter 1 that God exists. Therefore the objection fails.

In this chapter, I have offered a sympathetic explication of the main philosophical argument of *The Nature of True Virtue*. I have also tried to defend Edwards's account of virtue against some objections, and I have proposed clarifications or revisions in order to enhance its credibility. My hope is that I will persuade philosophers interested in virtue ethics that Edwards's theory is a serious competitor for their allegiance. But I do not make the stronger claim that his theory wins in the competition against its rivals. In order to vindicate the stronger claim, more would need to be done. In concluding, let me mention just two issues that would require further discussion.

One is the question of how well Edwards's account of virtue fares in comparison with its competitors on topics outside the scope of my discussion. Because my focus has been on materials in chapters 1 and 2 of *The Nature of True Virtue*, I have not considered at length what Edwards has to say about merely apparent virtue. He has a great deal to say about it in chapter 6, which is about instincts of nature that in some respects resemble true virtue, and in chapter 7, which concerns reasons why things that lack the essence of virtue have been mistaken for true virtue. And, of course, other traditions of virtue theory also contain doctrines of the semblances or counterfeits of virtue.[18] In an evaluation of its overall merits, Edwards's theory would have to be subjected to an assessment on this issue that involves comparison with its principal rivals.

The other issue is how well Edwards's theory fares when the theology is brought on board and is viewed as a contribution to a distinctively Christian ethics. In this regard, Edwards's monistic virtue theory appears to be particularly promising. Contemporary agapeistic ethics centers Christian ethics on the gospel imperative to love God with all one's heart, soul and mind and to love one's neighbor as oneself (Matthew 22: 37–40).[19] It look as though it should not be at all difficult to align agapeistic ethics, which insists that love (*agape*) ought to extend in principle to everyone, even one's worst enemies, with Edwards's account of true virtue, which argues that benevolence ought to extend in principle to every being in the whole system of (intelligent) existence. Hence we have grounds for expecting that further exploration will show that agapeistic love coheres well with Edwards's virtuous benevolence. If this expectation is fulfilled, Christians will find there to be a consilience of the support Edwards's account of true virtue derives from his philosophical arguments and the warrant it derives from canonical scripture.

As I see it, the upshot is that I have shown that Edwards's virtue theory has a good deal of *prima facie* philosophical plausibility. I recognize, however, that this falls short of establishing that it is, all things considered, the best account of true virtue available to us.

Notes

1. Ramsey, Paul, 'Editor's Introduction,' in Edwards, Jonathan (1989), *Ethical Writings, The Works of Jonathan Edwards Volume 8*, ed. Paul Ramsey, New Haven: Yale University Press, p. 11.
2. Ibid., p. 33.
3. Aristotle, *Nicomachean Ethics*, 1145b. For helpful discussion, see Nussbaum, Martha C. (1986), *The Fragility of Goodness: Luck and Ethics in Greek Tragedy and Philosophy*, Cambridge: Cambridge University Press, ch. 8, pp. 240–63.
4. Edwards, Jonathan (1989) *The Nature of True Virtue* in *Ethical Writings*, p. 539. Hereafter page references to this work will be made parenthetically in the body of my text.
5. See, for example, Viladesau, Richard (1999), *Theological Aesthetics: God in Imagination, Beauty, and Art*, New York: Oxford University Press.
6. Brown, John H. (1998), 'Beauty' in Craig, Edward (ed.), *Routledge Encyclopedia of Philosophy*, vol. 1, London: Routledge, p. 683.
7. See Sircello, Guy (1975), *A New Theory of Beauty*, Princeton: Princeton University Press, and Mothersill, Mary (1984), *Beauty Restored*, Oxford: Oxford University Press.
8. Brown, 'Beauty', p. 681.
9. Hutcheson, Francis (1993), *An Inquiry Concerning Beauty, Order, Harmony, Design*, ed. Peter Kivy, The Hague: Martinus Nijhoff.

10. See, for example, Zagzebski, Linda (1996), *Virtues of the Mind*, Cambridge: Cambridge University Press.

11. Nasar, Sylvia (1998), *A Beautiful Mind: The Life of Mathematical Genius and Nobel Laureate John Nash*, New York: Simon and Schuster.

12. See McGinn, Colin (1997), ch. 5 'Beauty of Soul', in *Ethics, Evil, and Fiction*, Oxford: Oxford University Press. The quote is from p. 93.

13. Ibid., p. 97. The sorts of aesthetic properties McGinn has been considering are such things as being pure or being sweet and being foul or being tarnished.

14. Ibid. For McGinn, the soul is merely that to which virtue is correctly attributed; it need not be something of theological significance.

15. See Singer, Peter (1981), *The Expanding Circle*, New York: Farrar, Straus and Giroux.

16. See Gettier, Edmund (1963), 'Is justified true belief knowledge?', *Analysis* **23**, 121–3, and Shope, Robert K. (1981), *The Analysis of Knowing: A Decade of Research*, Princeton: Princeton University Press.

17. See Lovejoy, Arthur O. (1936), *The Great Chain of Being: A Study of the History of an Idea*, Cambridge: Harvard University Press.

18. For illuminating comparisons of what Confucian and Thomistic traditions have to say about semblances of virtue, see Yearley, Lee H. (1990), *Mencius and Aquinas: Theories of Virtue and Conceptions of Courage*, Albany: State University of New York Press.

19. See Outka, Gene (1972), *Agape: An Ethical Analysis*, New Haven: Yale University Press. A clear and concise survey of this strain in Christian ethical thought is found in Outka, Gene (1997), 'Agapeistic Ethics,' in Philip L. Quinn and Charles Taliaferro (eds), *A Companion to Philosophy of Religion*, Oxford: Blackwell.

Chapter 7

Does Jonathan Edwards Use a Dispositional Ontology? A Response to Sang Hyun Lee

Stephen R. Holmes

I suppose that some readers of my *God of Grace and God of Glory*[1] will have been surprised not to have seen more references to Sang Hyun Lee's *The Philosophical Theology of Jonathan Edwards*.[2] The basic thesis of the latter, that at the heart of Edwards's theology is a novel ontological scheme based on disposition, has, after all, become a standard interpretation of Edwards, built upon by a number of other works,[3] and, it would seem, generally accepted by most readers. My problem in knowing how to deal with Lee's work stemmed from two factors in my estimate of his book. First, I think it is an extremely powerful work, well written and seemingly convincing. Second, I think it is simply wrong in its main thesis. The latter meant that I could not make use of the work; the former that I could not dismiss it without considerable discussion, which would have broken the flow of my own argument. An uncomfortable silence was my, perhaps unhappy, compromise.[4] This chapter is an attempt to offer the sustained engagement that Lee's excellent work surely deserves, and in the process to explain why I cannot accept his conclusions. As such, I hope it will be of interest even to those who have not seen my earlier work.

Lee's central argument in his book is that Edwards developed a novel ontology: 'What Edwards accomplished in the course of his search for a philosophical understanding of the Christian faith was a thoroughgoing metaphysical reconstruction, a reconception of the nature of reality itself.'[5] Under the influence of his reading of Newton and Locke, Edwards rejected the old scholastic account of ontology which divided the being of things into substance and form, and put in its place 'a strikingly modern conception of reality as a dynamic network of dispositional forces and habits'.[6] This 'dispositional ontology', as Lee calls it, is claimed to provide the key to the unity of Edwards's thought – all else flows from here.

A disposition, or 'habit', is 'an active and ontologically abiding power that possesses a mode of realness even when it is not in exercise'.[7] Habits, or laws (as far as I can see, Lee makes no significant distinction between 'habit', 'law' and 'disposition'; if there is one, it is perhaps that habits are active dispositions, and

99

laws passive dispositions), are all that exist; God creates a nexus of dispositions,[8] and God himself is most properly conceived as 'the absolutely sovereign *disposition* of true beauty that is in an eternally complete exercise'.[9]

This last point is perhaps the most striking of Lee's claims. Reconceiving God as dispositional, according to Lee, involves giving an account of God's existence that is able to speak of the 'becoming' of God (p. 6, where this concept is explicitly linked to process thought). Creation is then seen as 'an increase or enlargement of God's own being' (p. 184), or a 'further actualization of God's own being' (p. 201), and the doctrine of the Trinity is reconceived in dispositional terms, with the Son and the Spirit being 'the eternal and absolutely complete repetitions of the Father's self-existent actuality' (p. 189).

Lee defends all this with a perceptive historical review of the notion of habit in Western thought (pp. 17–34), and with a wide selection of references from across the range of Edwards's writings. His scholarship and argument are alike impressive. For all these reasons, the influence of his book is unsurprising. However, there seem to me to be some good reasons for doubting Lee's conclusions, and alternative readings of the evidence he offers that are at least as convincing as his own. I want first to outline some historical and theological reasons why Lee's reconstruction of Edwards's thought is, to my mind at least, simply implausible, and then to sketch an alternative reading which, I will suggest, makes just as much sense of the key points of evidence, but is historically and theologically much less difficult to believe.

On the Theology of Jonathan Edwards

My fundamental problem with Lee's position is that I find his account of God, or rather his account of Edwards's doctrine of God, very difficult to believe in. This is not for any straightforward philosophical or theological reason – as far as I can see, Lee's picture is a coherent one, and it does not make any claims which can be dismissed as ridiculous in the present theological climate. It is, rather, for reasons of history: I cannot imagine Edwards, with the theological commitments he held to, coming up with anything like the doctrines that Lee tells us were at the heart of his system, and I believe that most if not all of the evidence Lee offers for his reconstruction can be explained as, or more, adequately by a less implausible account of what Edwards thought. Lee pays great attention to the Edwards's text, but little to his context, and if the reconstruction he offers is adequate to the former, it is my contention that it is wholly inadequate to the latter.

The consideration of Edwards's immediate precursors in Lee is restricted to a few pages on the idea of habit, under the title 'Ideas of Habit in Edwards' Background'.[10] Even in these pages, however, whilst some sustained attention is given to the immediate philosophical background (mostly Locke and Hume, but with passing references to Newton and the Cambridge Platonists), his account of the theologians from whom Edwards learnt his ideas is limited to a couple of paragraphs indicating that, when they mentioned 'habit', they preserved an Aristotelian–Thomistic account of it.[11] As far as it goes, there is nothing wrong with this: the Reformed Orthodox tradition from which Edwards learnt his theology was not especially interested in the idea of habit, and Lee's citations are sufficient to demonstrate that point. The tradition was rather more interested, however, in the doctrine of God, and when at the end of his book Lee makes a series of assertions about how Edwards reformulated that doctrine, some awareness of the context is surely necessary to give an accurate picture.[12]

This point is sharpened by the particular stance Edwards takes to this theological tradition. No attentive reader can be unaware of a basic theological conservatism within Edwards's thought: he inherited a relatively stable Reformed tradition of theology, which he knew well, generally upheld, and where he made minor amendments was both clear and defensive about the fact.[13] This tradition contained its points of controversy, of course, which Edwards naturally addressed, but in doing so he accepted that the questions were indeed the ones bequeathed to him, and generally (from his MA thesis on[14]) defended the more traditional position. Lee is aware of this conservatism, of course: in the opening pages of his book he speaks repeatedly of Edwards's 'restatement of the Augustinian–Calvinist theological tradition',[15] or of his desire to 'reaffirm in the *strongest possible* terms his theological tradition'.[16]

Two points must be made with regard to this. First, this conservatism is a conscious choice on Edwards's part. Recent historiography has demonstrated what Edwards's own writings indicate, that the crises of orthodox faith common to the intellectual world at least in the eighteenth century, were not excluded from New England by its distance from Europe. Even while Edwards was at college, after all, there was a serious scandal about the orthodoxy of Samuel Johnson, one of the tutors, and Edwards's defeat in the Breck affair demonstrates that a pastor of the day could hold clearly heterodox views and not be excluded from his pulpit thereby.[17] Gerald McDermott has recently demonstrated the extent of both the influence of Deism in Edwards's day, and Edwards's knowledge of it.[18] If Edwards is theologically conservative, it is not because he was unaware that other positions were either intellectually or socially possible.

Second, this *theological* conservatism is in marked contrast to Edwards's strikingly original philosophical constructions. He was, it seems, among the first on the American continent to have read Newton and Locke, and arguably amongst the first in the world to have appreciated the implications of what they had to say, and to have framed a convincing response. Lee's suggestion that Edwards offered a radical account of metaphysics can hardly be questioned, although what that account looked like is still an open question, I think. (Perry Miller, who began the recent upsurge of interest in Edwards, suggested it was a basically Lockean empiricism;[19] the majority line is probably that it is an idealism, similar to Berkeley's, although independently arrived at;[20] Lee's own suggestion, that it is based on a novel concept of disposition, is plausible and distinctive.)

This combination of philosophical radicalism and theological conservatism, while perhaps remarkable, is not unknown in the Christian tradition. Indeed, similar positions can arguably be found very early indeed, and inform some of the great works of the tradition. On the one hand, Origen's account of his theological method in the preface to *On First Principles* displays something of the same form, particularly in the suggestion that the Rule of Faith offers conclusions that must be believed, but that the way in which they may be derived and defended is open to investigation and reformulation.[21] On the other, both Aquinas and Schleiermacher may be read as attempting precisely this task, of restating inherited doctrine in a new philosophical idiom – respectively, Aristotelianism and post-Kantian Romanticism.[22] The impulse is also easy to understand: certain truths are given by revelation, and so may not be adjusted, leading to a doctrinal conservatism, but the way in which they are supported and arranged is open to human construction, which task then becomes urgent if a novel philosophical scheme becomes convincing.

Given this basic description of Edwards's position, any account of his thought must fulfil certain conditions. If a position he is suggested to have held is radical, then one of three things must be demonstrated to make the claim credible: that the position in question did not conflict with inherited dogma, and so was available for reformulation; or that, while there was a conflict with a traditional position, Edwards was not aware of it, and so proceeded as if the former condition obtained; or that he was consciously adjusting the theological inheritance. It seems to me that in fact (relatively uncontentious) examples of the fulfilment of each of these conditions can be found within Edwards's thought.

The first condition might characterize Edwards's approach to questions of substance metaphysics, which he addressed in some brief early essays, notably 'Of Being' and 'Of Atoms'.[23] Atomism, known from the teachings of Epicurus and Lucretius, had found a new popularity in the seventeenth century; Edwards set himself to analyse what these 'atoms', generally defined only as the smallest components of matter, were. Perceptively, Edwards argued that within the system the size of atoms was less relevant than their solidity, since their defining characteristic was utter indivisibility. If atoms are indestructible, then the force that preserves them must be infinite, and so the essence of being atomic is the action of an infinite force. Hence, argues Edwards, 'the certain unknown substance, which philosophers used to think subsisted by itself, and stood underneath and kept up solidity and all other properties ... is nothing but the Deity acting in that particular manner in those parts of space where he thinks fit'.[24] The position is novel – radically so, philosophically considered – but there is nothing within it that can be considered to conflict with inherited dogma.

The second contention is more difficult, as Edwards was unquestionably an able and knowledgeable theologian, but I would suggest that Edwards's account of the fallen human flesh of Christ might be an example. Edwards's habit of speaking of the human nature of Christ as sharing the weaknesses and vitiations common to post-lapsarian humanity, rather than the perfection enjoyed by Adam and Eve in the

Garden, aligns him with a minority position in the Christian tradition. There are precursors, particularly within Puritanism (Richard Sibbes and John Owen, for example), so he is not being wholly novel, but the position is certainly not mainstream.[25]

The third condition may be seen in the example I have already quoted, concerning the role of the Holy Spirit is the work of reconciliation; it may also perhaps be seen in Edwards's attempt to use Lockean psychology to solve an old Puritan controversy over the particular mental faculty that enjoyed priority in God's act of regeneration. Some writers had insisted that conversion was primarily a matter of a new understanding, or knowledge, of gospel truths, and so began in the mind; others suggested that it was instead fundamentally a matter of a new inclination to obey the gospel call, and so located first in the will.[26] Edwards's development of the novel psychological scheme advanced by Locke enabled him to cut through this debate by questioning the underlying faculty psychology, with its strong separation of intellect and volition, and instead to find an account of affecting knowledge that could unite the understanding and the will in a single act of regeneration of the whole human person.[27]

Given Edwards's abilities as a thinker, it seems to me reasonable to suppose that examples of the second sort might be expected to be rare and, where they do exist, to relate to insignificant or marginal doctrinal points. The extent of examples of the third sort might be open to debate, depending on how strong the influence of Edwards's basic doctrinal conservatism is taken to be, but I suspect that they will again be rare and will relate to relatively minor doctrines when discovered.[28] In particular, I suggest that where Edwards defends a particular doctrine, or makes significant use of it, to suggest that he adjusted it for either of the latter two reasons is implausible.[29] Now, it seems to me that many of the things Lee claims Edwards said about the doctrine of God fall into this category.

This argument is constructed in terms of probabilities, not possibilities, of course. That is, even if I am right, all that is demonstrated is that Lee's account is less likely to be adequate than one which explains the texts equally well but does not demand an unlikely relationship to the theological tradition on Edwards's part. I suggest that such an account is available. The next section of this essay will outline Lee's account of Edwards's doctrine of God against the tradition, and offer an alternative reading of the material which seems to me to deal with the evidence equally well, while being far more plausible in context.

Why Lee's God is Difficult to Believe in

The first half of Lee's book demonstrates that the notion of habit, or disposition, was not greatly employed by the theological tradition up to Edwards's day, and that there was a pressing need, following Locke and Newton, and perceived by Edwards, to find a replacement for the old substance metaphysics which had been generally assumed in the centuries preceding Edwards's birth. It further suggests that Edwards brought the concept of disposition to centre stage, and used it to create a new metaphysics. If this were the end of the argument, my analysis of Edwards's theological conservatism would have little relevance to it; Christian dogma has traditionally been understood as making few claims concerning ontology,[30] and so the relative novelty of Edwards's supposed employment of dispositional ontology could be explained by my first category above. Lee's book does not stop here, however. The second half of the book claims that this dispositional ontology was applied by Edwards to the divine being as well, which led to 'a basic modification of the traditional conception of the deity' (p. 6). If this is the case, then it is surely difficult to square with Edwards's theological conservatism.

Lee is clearly aware of the force of this sort of argument; early in his survey of his thesis he claims that Edwards 'reaffirm[ed] in the strongest possible terms his theological tradition within a thoroughly modern philosophical framework' (p. 4). What I hope to show in this section is that the 'basic modification' that Lee claims Edwards made is just that: a fundamental change in doctrine that would involve, if actual, Edwards having left orthodoxy and the theological tradition far behind. Chapter seven of Lee's book describes the doctrine of God conceived in dispositional terms that he ascribes to Edwards. It begins thus: 'The bold reshaping that Edwards gave to traditional Western conceptions of reality and knowledge presupposed an equally bold reconception of the very nature of God' (p. 170). This is precisely the point I am intending to argue, but it is perhaps worthwhile sketching some of the ways in which Lee's account of Edwards's theology is at odds with the theological tradition to which Edwards was indeed committed.

Lee offers an analysis of the implications of claiming that God is dispositional (pp. 183–4), composed of three points. First, it means that God's existence is pure activity: 'God ... does not first exist and then know and love, but rather he exists in and through knowing and loving' (p. 183). Second, in that disposition is 'a law of relations', for God to be dispositional implies 'the inherent relationality of the divine being' (p. 184). Finally, for God to be dispositional demands that 'God is inherently a tendency towards an increase or enlargement of God's own being' (p. 184). Now, it seems to me that the classical theism that Edwards inherited had no real problems in affirming the first two of these points, as I shall show in the next section, while the third is the crux of the matter. However, some comments are necessary concerning the implications of the way in which Lee claims Edwards worked out the first two points, and particularly the peculiar, indeed heterodox, character of the trinitarian theology Lee ascribes to Edwards.

Lee's account of the inner-triune life describes the Father as 'at once the divine primordial actuality of true beauty *and* the divine disposition to exert himself' (p. 188). The exertion of the divine disposition results in the being of the Son and the Spirit. Lee traces this through Edwards's employment of the Augustinian ideas of the Son as the perfect idea of the Father and the Spirit as the perfect love shared by the Father and the Son. Edwards does little original with this tradition, in my estimation, but Lee's attempts to read his discussions in dispositional terms end up painting him as developing a startlingly new account, which discards, or at least redefines, the basic grammar of orthodox trinitarian theology that was developed by the patristic theologians and enshrined in the ecumenical creeds.

Certain ways of talking about relationships of origin within the divine life are basic to this grammar. Father, Son and Spirit are one in essence (*homoousios*), but are three distinct subsistences (*hypostases*). Being one in essence, the only differentiating features of the divine persons are the hypostatic properties that pertain to their several relationships.[31] Thus, the Father is distinguished from the Son and the Spirit solely by being unbegotten, the Son from the Father and the Spirit by being begotten, and the Spirit is distinguished by procession. Given all this, it is crucial that the relationships of origin of the Son and the Spirit are described as different: were they not to be, there would be no differentiation between the second and third hypostases and so no meaningful doctrine of the Trinity.[32]

Within the Latin West, a second point prevailed, finally enshrined in an adjustment to the Creed, the *filioque* clause. The procession of the Spirit, it was asserted, was an act not of the Father alone, but of the Father and the Son acting together as a single divine principle. The dispute about the *filioque*, and the Western tradition, was still a standard part of the Reformed Orthodox theological tradition that Edwards inherited.[33] (That many theologians today would be unhappy with the latter, and some with the former, of these constructions is besides the point, of course: they are standard within the theological tradition, and to deny them in Edwards's day would be to align oneself with the Deists or Socinians.)

Edwards employed, as Lee notes, the fashion, derived from Augustine and developed within a Christian Platonist tradition with which he was familiar,[34] of discussing all this using a psychological analogy. The Son is the Father's perfect knowledge, or Idea, of himself, which being perfect is ontologically actual;[35] the Spirit is the ontologically actual love that the Father has for the Son and the Son for the Father. To know and to love are different acts, and the Spirit originates in the shared single act of Father and Son, and so such pictures are true to the grammar described above.

In Lee's hands, however, this language is twisted in ways which the grammatical rules will not accept. Both the generation of the Son and the procession of the Spirit are described as 'exercise[s] of the Father's disposition' (p. 192). Although there is an attempt to link this to the psychological language, and so differentiate between these two exercises (so that the procession of the Spirit is 'a further exercise (this time affectional) ...' p. 192), this is vitiated by the insistence that talk of 'knowing' and 'loving' is merely analogical,[36] whereas dispositional language is an accurate reflection of who God essentially is. Given this, the trinitarian grammar that demands that the origin of the Spirit is different from the origin of the Son is seriously endangered by Lee's constructions.

Further, Lee's account of the relations of origin within the Trinity considered in dispositional terms cannot incorporate the *filioque*; the Father's disposition is repeated a second time in the spiration of the Spirit; the Son has no part to play in this process, and there is certainly no suggestion of the Father and the Son acting as a single divine principle. The most Lee can offer is an asymmetric account of the Father's love for the Son: 'God's love of his Idea of himself' or 'a *reflexive* affection for God's self-knowledge' (both p. 192; emphasis original). The inadequacy of this is clear two pages later when Lee, after quoting Edwards asserting that 'the Holy Spirit is the act of God between the Father and the Son', is forced to acknowledge that Edwards talks of the Spirit as 'the consenting relation between the Father and the Son' (p. 194). There are, I think, only two ways to make sense of this in Lee's terms: either the Father and the Son act together as a single disposition in the procession of the Spirit, or the Spirit possesses peculiar hypostatic properties that are not derived from the relations of origin, a contention that (as Edwards would have well understood) simply destroys classical trinitarian dogma. Unless Lee can offer an account of the divine disposition that answers these two points, his reconstruction of Edwards's theology demands that Edwards completely cast aside positions that were basic to the doctrine of the Trinity he inherited.[37]

With the dynamism of God's being, again, Edwards is merely repeating what a long tradition had said, in my estimation, but is made to deny fundamental points by Lee's reconstruction. The central point here is the distinction traditionally drawn between the internal dynamic of God's life, in the generation of the Son and the procession of the Spirit, and the external dynamic, in the creation and preservation of the world. This distinction is once again a part of the 'grammar' of theology, a basic position that may be supported or developed in many ways, but which provides a rule of how to speak Christianly about God and the world. The particular issues at stake here are the linked patristic arguments concerning on the one hand the doctrine of the Trinity, and on the other God's omnipotence and aseity as expressed in the doctrine of creation. By distinguishing sharply between the generation of the Son and the creation of the world, it is possible to assert that the Son is *homoousios* with the Father and eternal, while the world is neither, but instead created *ex nihilo*. Again, the same distinction protects the status of creation as a free act of God, while also asserting that the generation of the Son is a necessary act: God can be God without the world, but God would be less than he in fact is without the Son.

Lee's description of Edwards's account of God's dynamism is again couched in dispositional terms, with first the generation of the Son and the spiration of the Spirit being the exercise of the divine disposition, and then the creation and directing of the world being a 'further exertion of his *original dispositional essence*, which is already fully exerted within God's internal being' (p. 199).[38] Lee acknowledges that Edwards always hedges his linkages of God's activity *ad extra* to God's activity *ad intra* with protective phrases (for instance, on p. 196, where Edwards is quoted as insisting that these 'are not the same kind of exercise of [God's] perfection'). However, the only content Lee can give to this difference in kind is to repeat the language of *ad intra* and *ad extra* (p. 197), which hardly does justice to Edwards's language (which repeatedly and clearly correlates the *ad intra/ad extra* distinction with a second, and independent, distinction in kind).[39]

Now, this distinction in kind is the one that protects the difference between the generation of the Son and the creation of the world; Athanasius called the former an *ergon phuseos* and the latter an *ergon theleseos*, and recognized that the theological repudiation of Arianism turned in part on this point;[40] Aquinas cemented the place of the distinction in scholastic discourse, using more Edwardsian terms.[41] Classical theism recognized that to fail to make this distinction robustly in some way is to either endanger the deity of the Son, or to risk ascribing deity to the world. Yet Lee's reconstruction of Edwards's theology suggests that Edwards was unable or unwilling to give any significant content to this distinction.

The failures I have been outlining thus far, however, appear to me to be venial sins: in each case, I think that a lack of attention to the context of Edwards's work has resulted in an account that is implausible, but I can imagine ways in which Lee's basic thesis might be rescued: a dispositional account that was adequate to the basic trinitarian and christological convictions of the (Reformed) Church is conceivable, thus far, even if Lee does not manage to offer one. The third implication that Lee claims belongs to a dispositional doctrine of God is however a mortal error: if to be dispositional means to believe in God's self-enlargement, as described by Lee, then there is no possibility of a dispositional account coexisting with an orthodox Christian theism, and if Edwards really thought what Lee claims he thought, then he had left Reformed Orthodoxy behind just as thoroughly and just as surely as Socinius had 150 years before. Or so I shall argue.

'The consequence of Edwards' conception of God's creation of the world as the exertion of God's original dispositional essence itself is that the world is in some sense a further actualization of God's own being ... Further ... the world is internally related to God's *own* life' (pp. 201–2). Lee will even, albeit in a borrowed phrase, talk about God 'continually "creating himself"' (p. 196 n. 59)! These statements are, as Lee is honest enough to admit ('Edwards attempts ... to replace the older notion of God as the absolutely self-contained *actus purus* with the dynamic conception of God as at once eternally actual and inherently and inexhaustibly self-enlarging' (pp. 203–4)), simply incompatible with classical theism. To hold such things requires (at least) redefinition of (at least) God's simplicity, aseity, infinity, eternity, omnipotence, impassibility and immutability.[42] If Edwards really did this, then he would have to acknowledge that he was much further from the Puritan orthodoxy that he is so often pictured as the champion of than any Arminian or Papist. Let me, however, first demonstrate the drastic effects I am claiming for Lee's arguments.

Lee claims that what God essentially is, is a disposition. The Christian tradition, whilst it tended to be unhappy with questions about God's ontological status,[43] would use language of 'pure actuality' or (better) 'pure act' when necessary.[44] This language, although derived from Greek philosophical intuitions, was borrowed by Christian theologians because it is useful in protecting certain important implications of central doctrines such as creation *ex nihilo* and the Trinity. Central to these is the suggestion that there is no potentiality in God's life (hence the full slogan: *actus purus sine ulla potentia*); God's perfection is such that there is nothing that he could be that he is not, fully and perfectly, from all eternity to all eternity.[45]

If this is the case, then clearly God does not change (immutability), is sufficient to his own existence (aseity) and totally unaffected by anything done by any created being (impassibility),[46] is not subject to change over time (immutability, eternity), and is sufficient to all effects that he should intend (omnipotence). Finally, God on this account is not doing many things, but is one act: being Father, Son and Spirit, eternally, perfectly and unchangeably. This is the doctrine of divine simplicity.[47] On this account, of course, any talk of the 'self-enlargement' of God, or of the 'becoming' of God, is immediately excluded. The logic demands that God is already infinite, and so enlargement of any sort is not a possibility, and God is already absolutely perfectly all that he is, or could be, so any change, any act of 'becoming', would involve a lessening of his perfection, and so is unthinkable. Equally, for God to be in any way affected or changed by a creature, or for any aspect of his perfect life to depend upon a creature, would endanger the distinction between creature and Creator which is at the heart of classical theism. God's being would in some sense depend upon the world, and so the gratuity of the act of creation would be undermined. Further, the trinitarian dogma that God's desires are fully supplied in his own eternal life would be compromised.

It is, I think, beyond doubt that Edwards accepted this complex of doctrines and arguments. It was accepted without question within the tradition he inhabited, was standard fare in the textbooks he studied, and in the theologians he quoted from and recommended in later life, and echoes of it appear throughout his writings.[48] Thus, I suggest (for the reasons outlined in my account of Edwards's basic theological conservatism above), it is extremely unlikely that he adopted a novel doctrine of God which undermined basic features of this account. A 'dispositional' account of God, inasmuch as it demands that there is unfulfilled potential in God's life, and so the possibility of God's 'self-enlargement' or 'increase', would have been unthinkable to Edwards. Jonathan Edwards did not use a dispositional ontology.[49]

What of Lee's textual evidence that he did? There is not space in this essay to deal with it all, but some characteristic moves can be noted. First, while Edwards will use the language of God's self-communication, or even emanation, it is always (I think) qualified in some way:[50] creation is 'an exercise of the same perfections of His nature. But it was *not the same kind of exercise*' (quoted in Lee, p. 196). In another place, Edwards's statement that 'God's own happiness is "enlarged"' rapidly becomes 'God's own life' being 'enlarged' in Lee's text, a rather different thing (pp. 201–2). As I have indicated above, in other cases Lee interprets a phrase of Edwards's assuming the words are loaded in ways demanded by his reconstruction, when the same phrase can be interpreted perfectly sensibly in another way. I am not suggesting, of course, that Lee fails to be responsible to the texts; rather, I am trying to indicate that the textual evidence he amasses, while impressive, is not overwhelming, and leaves room open for argument.

On the Living God

I acknowledged above that the argument was couched in terms of probabilities, and so that a more plausible account of the textual evidence was also needed before Lee's account could be dismissed. I have offered my own account of Edwards's doctrine of God, and his gracious acts in creation and redemption, in my *God of Grace*; I submit that this is at least as adequate to the texts as Lee's, and far more adequate to the context, in that I can show how Edwards was faithful with the Reformed Orthodoxy which he wrote to uphold.[51] I want to examine just one point that seems to be driving Lee's reconstruction before I end this essay, however.

Lee's great concern in his book would seem to be with the 'dynamic' nature of Edwards's vision. The central achievement of his dispositional ontology is supposed to be a shift from the static medieval category of 'substance' to the thoroughly modern, dynamic and relational category of disposition. This point can be found throughout Lee's text, but for example notice: the title of the introductory chapter, 'The Idea of Habit and Edwards' Dynamic Vision of Reality' (p. 3); the comments about process theology on p. 6; the statement of the thesis of chapter 3, 'one does not even begin to understand Edwards' world view without noticing that he introduced an essentially new understanding of the very nature of reality, replacing substance metaphysics with a dynamic and relational conception' (p. 47); the quotation from Anderson on p. 54; chapter 4 ('Being as Relational and Dynamic' p. 76), *passim*; and the discussions of the doctrine of God towards the end of the book. It would thus seem to be a central concern of the text.

Linked to this rhetoric of dynamism in Lee's account is a repeated use of terms like 'becoming', which contain echoes of Jüngel, of course, but are more explicitly linked to process thought in Lee's text.[52] It seems that Lee accepts and assumes the standard process-based critique of traditional Christian doctrines of God which has been borrowed and amplified by some more generally orthodox modern theologians under the influence of the historiography of von Harnack and certain readings of Barth. On this account, Christian theology has been thoroughly infected by Greek metaphysics, and a whole raft of concepts that are alien to the God of the Gospel have become standard in discussions of the divine attributes. Chief amongst these are aseity, simplicity, impassibility, immutability and eternity. These doctrines, it is asserted, are more Neoplatonic than Christian, because they remove any sense of dynamism from God's life, and instead describe him as a static, unchanging, unfeeling monad.

This critique is echoed with approval in the introduction to Lee's book, where we read of 'the demand to see the divine being as more dynamic than classical theism' (p. 4); we are further told that 'Jonathan Edwards had already confronted this modern question of the being and becoming of God and had worked out a highly innovative solution that introduced dynamism into the very being of God without compromising God's prior actuality' (p. 6), and that he 'introduced an element of dynamic movement into the heart of the divine being' (p. 6). At least one of the reasons, then, why Lee finds a novel doctrine of God within Edwards's *corpus* is his belief that the traditional doctrine of God lacks a necessary dynamic element. Indeed, given the repetitions of the point in Lee's book, this would seem to be a significant concern. It is however mistaken, and the God of Lee's reconstruction is actually less dynamic than the God of traditional orthodoxy that Edwards believed in.

In classical Christian theology, God is *actus purus* – pure act, or (better) 'action';[53] his essence (ontology) is his *esse* – usually translated 'existence', but one does not need to be a Latinist to see how intolerably lame that is, surely; '*esse*' is a verb, a 'doing word' (to quote my primary school teacher!). In God being and act are one; God is pure action, pure activity; pure dynamism. Further, the classical slogans claim that he is *actus purus sine ulla potentia* – there is no potentiality in God whereby he could be more active or more dynamic.[54] Inasmuch as Lee's account has God continually seeking new ways to be more dynamic, further exercises of his disposition, it is clear that Lee's God is in fact less dynamic than the God of the tradition. So, I suggest that one of the main reasons Lee offers for Edwards's supposed departure from the tradition is simply mistaken – and Edwards would have known it was mistaken. For all the (many) merits of Lee's work it is simply mistaken in its main thesis. Jonathan Edwards did not need a dispositional ontology, and he did not use a dispositional ontology, or so I have sought to argue.

Notes

1. Holmes, Stephen R. (2000), *God of Grace and God of Glory: An Account of the Theology of Jonathan Edwards*, Edinburgh: T&T Clark.
2. Lee, Sang Hyun (1988), *The Philosophical Theology of Jonathan Edwards*, Princeton: Princeton University Press.
3. See especially Morimoto, Anri (1995), *Jonathan Edwards and the Catholic Vision of Salvation*, University Park: Penn. State University Press, but also McDermott, Gerald R. (2000), *Jonathan Edwards Confronts the Gods*, Oxford: Oxford University Press, and Plantinga Pauw, Amy (2002), *The Supreme Harmony of All*, Grand Rapids: Eerdmans.
4. I further suppose, and certainly hope, that at least some readers of the work, familiar with the contours of Lee's argument, will have perceived that throughout chapters 2, 3 and 4 of the book I offer a sustained and conscious attempt to read Edwards differently to Lee on the central issues that drive his argument.
5. Lee, p. 3.
6. Ibid., p. 4; see also pp. 10–14.
7. Ibid., p. 7; see also pp. 34–46.
8. Ibid., pp. 47–114.
9. Ibid., p. 173 (for quotation) (my emphasis); pp. 170–241 for the exposition of the point.
10. Ibid., pp. 22–34.

11. Owen, Ames, Flavel and Shepard are mentioned in the text of pp. 24–5; in addition a work of van Mastricht's is cited in n. 26 on those pages.
12. Between pp. 170 and 241, in which Lee treats the doctrine of God, the extent of the notice taken of this Reformed theological context is a single reference to Calvin in a footnote (n. 41 on p. 190) (there are also very occasional passing references to the wider Christian tradition: one to Aquinas, one to Augustine, and so on). This reference shows Lee indicating that a point which he clearly regards as contentious in his reconstruction of Edwards is in fact in line with the tradition; clearly, he is not unaware of the possible force of the sort of arguments I am advancing.
13. For example, see his defence of a minor modification to the role of the Holy Spirit in conversion in Edwards, Jonathan (1971) 'Treatise on Grace', in *Treatise on Grace*, ed. Paul Helm, Cambridge: James Clarke, pp. 25–75 and p. 68.
14. This was entitled *Quaestio: Peccator non iustificatur coram Deo nisi per iustitiam Christi fide apprehensam*, and defended Calvinist orthodoxy in the face of the incipient Arminianism revealed at Yale by the defection of two of its tutors to Anglicanism the year before.
15. Lee, p. 3.
16. Ibid., p. 4 (my emphasis).
17. The Springfield, MA church was in the process of calling the Revd Robert Breck to be its minister in 1734 when Edwards and others demonstrated his Arminianism; despite a painful battle, Breck was eventually called.
18. McDermott, *Jonathan Edwards Confronts the Gods*.
19. Perry Miller (1949), *Jonathan Edwards*, New York: William Sloane, *passim*, but especially pp. 52–68.
20. See, for example, Wallace Anderson's editorial introduction to Edwards, Jonathan (1980), *Scientific and Philosophical Writings, The Works of Jonathan Edwards Volume 6*, ed. Wallace E. Anderson, New Haven: Yale University Press.
21. Origen (1936), *On First Principles*, trans. G. W. Butterworth, London: SPCK. See especially §§2–10.
22. Notice particularly in this connection Schleiermacher's striking and deeply conservative assertion that there is nothing in *The Christian Faith* that is original except the arrangement. He claimed to be doing no more that restating Reformed Orthodoxy in a new language.
23. These can be found in Edwards, *Scientific and Philosophical Writings*. Anderson's introduction to this volume is an invaluable resource for consideration of Edwards's more philosophical writings. See also my own discussions of this point in *God of Grace*, pp. 80–90.
24. 'Of Atoms', p. 215.
25. For a discussion of some of the issues at stake, and a useful survey of the main figures in Christian history who have taught this position, see Kapic, Kelly M. (2001), 'The Son's Assumption of Human Nature: A Call for Clarity', *International Journal of Systematic Theology* 3 (2), 154–66. For a review of Edwards's comments on the point, and how they fit into his immediate context, see again my *God of Grace*, pp. 135–8.
26. On which point see Cherry, Conrad (1966), *The Theology of Jonathan Edwards: A Reappraisal*, Garden City: Doubleday, pp. 1–14.
27. See ibid., pp. 15–24.
28. Indeed, my own reconstruction of Edwards's thought (in Holmes, *God of Grace*) suggests that he preferred to embrace incoherence, rather than give up or adjust a part of the doctrinal inheritance (perdition). The validity of this account is for others to judge, of course.
29. With the caveat, of course, that Edwards might have changed his mind on certain issues – but this would need to be demonstrated.

30. The recent popularity of the suggestion that trinitarian dogma does in fact make ontological claims concerning the primacy of persons and relationships does not obliviate this point; it in fact supports it, in that those advancing such claims recognize that their point of view is either novel, or something that was known to the Fathers but forgotten since, or at best a minority report in the tradition.

31. So both Gregory of Nazianzus (*Orations* 28:16; 30:8–9) and Augustine (*De Trinitate* V.6).

32. *What* these relationships are, or how they are different, are matters generally considered to be incomprehensible; *that* they are different, however, is vital. The classic statement of the case is in Gregory of Nazianzus' *Theological Orations*, sermons central to the achievement of the trinitarian settlement enshrined in the Nicene Creed.

33. See, for example, Turretin, Francis (1992), *Institutes of Elenctic Theology* vol. 1, trans. G. M. Giger, ed. J. T. Dennison, Phillipsburg: P&R Publishing, 1992, pp. 309–10. Edwards clearly assumes the *filioque* in several places, for example: 'the Holy Ghost is that love of God and Christ that is breathed forth primarily towards each other, and flows out secondarily towards the creature' ('Treatise on Faith', p. 63); or 'The Holy Spirit is the act of God between the Father and the Son, infinitely loving and delighting in each other ...' (*Miscellanies* 94).

34. Particularly through the Cambridge Platonists: Ralph Cudworth, Henry More, and so on, whom he cites with approval from time to time. See Anderson's introduction to *Scientific and Philosophical Writings* for some discussion of their influence on Edwards.

35. There are various ways of defending this ontological conception. I suppose that Edwards's so-called idealism, within which he asserts that the fundamental reality of all things is God's knowledge of them, would be the most obvious solution for him, but variations on the theme of Anselm's ontological argument can also be applied.

36. 'Edwards, as I noted above, follows the analogy of the self as the self, the self as knowing, and the self as loving', p. 192.

37. I am conscious that some readers of this chapter will be philosophers, and so that some of this analysis may appear a little abstruse. I should note then that, theologically considered, these discussions are so basic that they are still standard in first-year undergraduate courses, in Britain at least; in Edwards's day, with the threat of Deism and Socinianism looming large, they were endlessly rehearsed. Edwards could no more have been unaware of them than a philosopher today could be unaware of the basic contours of Kant's thought.

38. There is not room in a chapter of this length to engage in discussions of the texts Lee cites in support of his positions, but this point provides a good illustration of the way most of them can be dealt with. Lee first cites Edwards as saying 'The disposition to communicate himself, or diffuse his own FULLNESS, which we must conceive of as being originally in God as a perfection of his nature, was what moved him to create the world,' and then follows it with a phrase from the same discussion concerning 'God's communicative disposition in general' (p. 199, referring to the 'Dissertation Concerning the End for which God Created the World'). All of this makes perfect sense, and is unexceptional, considered in terms of classical theism ('perfection of [God's] nature' is a standard Reformed term for 'divine attribute', of course). If one accepts Lee's primary contention that the word 'disposition' carries ontological weight in Edwards's writings, then his interpretation of these texts follows, but it is not demanded by anything within Edwards's discussion itself.

39. For the purposes of this essay, the best demonstration I can offer of this point is to refer the reader to those phrases of Edwards's that Lee quotes on pp. 196–201; I do not suppose that anyone familiar with Edwards's corpus, and particularly the 'Dissertation Concerning the End ...' and the *Miscellanies* entries that preceded it, can fail to realize that these examples could be repeated *ad nauseum*, if not *ad infinitum*, however.

40. So Barth, *C.D.* I/1 p. 434, who cites *Or. c. Ar.* 2:29, but the reference appears to be wrong. *Or. c. Ar.* 1:29 might be meant.
41. *Summa Theologica* Ia q. 41 art. 2, where the distinction is between 'necessary' and 'voluntary' acts of the will. This language would have been mediated to Edwards by Turretin, *Institutes* 3:14 & 29.
42. That such doctrines are presently under attack is not the point here, of course: those attacking them seem to accept that they went virtually unquestioned (except by the Socinians and others who left orthodox Christianity behind) until Schleiermacher's day.
43. Hence the doctrine of divine incomprehensibility, the teaching that we may know that God is, but not what God is.
44. Edwards demonstrates his acceptance of this traditional term when he uses it as a premise in a trinitarian argument in *Miscellanies* 94: 'the pure and perfect act of God is God, because God is a pure act'. This is precisely the position Lee claims Edwards dispensed with in coming up with his dispositional ontology: 'Edwards attempts ... to replace the older notion of God as the absolutely self-contained *actus purus* with the dynamic conception of God as at once eternally actual and inherently and inexhaustibly self-enlarging' (pp. 203–4).
45. Again, this point is explicit in *Miscellanies* 94: 'this is God, because that which acts perfectly is all act, and nothing but act'.
46. Divine impassibility is, despite the misunderstandings of many who have written to oppose what they assumed it to mean in recent decades, not fundamentally the teaching that God cannot 'suffer' in the usual modern sense of that term. It is rather the teaching that God cannot be affected in any way by creation. Thus, God cannot 'suffer' in the old sense of the term, 'to be subject to' (as in 'to do and to suffer', or 'to suffer fools'). On this, see Weinandy, Thomas G. (2000), *Does God Suffer?* Edinburgh: T&T Clark, *passim*, but see especially p. 38 (for a definition of impassibility), and pp. 168–70 (for a careful statement of the ways in which God, although impassible, might be said to 'suffer' in the modern sense).
47. On which see my own (2001), ' "Something Much too Plain to Say?"': Towards a defence of the doctrine of divine simplicity', *Neue Zeitschrift für Systematische Theologie und Religionsphilosophie* **43**, 137–54. I should say here that I am aware of, if not especially sympathetic to, the various serious philosophical questions as to whether this traditional theism is coherent in various particulars. Such modern debates are not to the point in this discussion, however: Edwards was schooled in this tradition and remained convinced by it, rightly or wrongly.
48. For a helpful set of references to all these attributes, see Gerstner, John H. (1992), *The Rational Biblical Theology of Jonathan Edwards vol. II*, Powhatan: Berea Publications, pp. 3–36. See also the phrase that Lee quotes on p. 202: where God is stated to be 'self-existent from all eternity, absolutely perfect in himself, in the possession of an infinite and independent good ... above all need and all capacity of being added to or advanced, made better or happier in any respect'. Quite.
49. It might be that the first half of Lee's thesis, that Edwards uses dispositions in his discussions of the created world, can be rescued, but I doubt it. First, I find the textual evidence unconvincing, although there is not room to go through it here; second, Edwards is quite clear (in the 'Dissertation on the Nature of True Virtue' and elsewhere) that 'being' is univocal, so if this is not an adequate account of God's ontology, it is not an adequate account of any ontology; third, it seems to me that Berkeley's critique of Locke's employment of the category of 'substance' applies equally well to the use Lee claims Edwards made of 'disposition': if one believes in God's active providence, there is no need for such concepts (this is precisely the thrust of 'On Atoms', for instance); I suppose that Edwards, whose critique of 'substance' language follows very similar

lines, would have seen that to replace it with a similar 'occult property' was simply pointless.

50. Attentive readers of Edwards will know his fondness for qualifying comments such as 'as it were', and just how much can be implied by such qualifications at times.

51. In *Original Sin, The Freedom of the Will*, and so on.

52. For the linkage see, for example, comments in the introduction on pp. 4–7, or the comments on p. 189. Lee is not claiming that Edwards is a process theologian born out of time, and is clear as to the differences in his 'dispositional' system and process thought, but the suggestion that classical theism lacks dynamism, and that both process theology and Edwards find ways to meet this lack, is pervasive.

53. I have already indicated Edwards's agreement with this point above. 'Pure act' is an adequate translation so long as 'act' is understood in the now slightly archaic sense of 'the doing of a thing', rather than the standard modern sense of 'the thing done'. Given the potential for confusion, however, 'action' is preferable, at least in my estimation.

54. Lee's attempts to claim that his dispositional reconstruction of Edwards's theology preserved the key features of this account demonstrate his misunderstanding of it; repeatedly, we are told that God, under this scheme, is already 'fully actualised' or possessed of 'absolute and eternal prior actuality'. This is simply not the point; God is absolute and eternal action, not just actuality.

Chapter 8

'One Alone Cannot be Excellent': Edwards on Divine Simplicity

Amy Plantinga Pauw

Jonathan Edwards was only twenty years old when he wrote in his 'Miscellanies' notebooks, 'one alone cannot be excellent, inasmuch as, in such case, there can be no consent. Therefore, if God is excellent, there must be a plurality in God; otherwise, there can be no consent in him.'[1] Excellency, though Edwards appears never to have defined it directly, seems to be a harmony or consent of diverse elements. This concept was so important to his thought, Norman Fiering has suggested, that 'Edwards perhaps intended to rank [it] with the classical transcendental attributes of being.'[2] Edwards's youthful declaration that excellency was at the core of divine reality stayed with him throughout his life, nourishing his reflections on the Trinity[3] and funding his mature writings on religious affections, true virtue and God's end in creation.

Edwards's convictions about God's excellency put him at odds with a broad theological consensus about the nature of divine perfection. As Wallace Anderson points out, 'it seems evident that his new concept of being, when applied to the divine perfections, stands in sharp contrast to the long tradition of philosophical theology into which he was born. God's goodness is not grounded in the absolute unity and simplicity of his being, but belongs to him only as he constitutes a plurality involving relations.'[4] Defying a distinguished theological tradition that linked maximal unity with maximal existence, Edwards insisted that 'In a being that is absolutely without any plurality there cannot be excellency, for there can be no such thing as consent or agreement.'[5] Since 'God is the prime and original being, the first and the last, and the pattern of all, and has the sum of all perfection,'[6] ontological perfection must be redefined in terms of God's internal plurality. Though the divine simplicity tradition left traces in his theology, there are abundant indications of his departure from its strictures that are both more deliberate and more integral to his thought as a whole than his casual use of it. Excellency largely supplanted simplicity as a marker of divine perfection in Edwards's thought.

The doctrine of divine simplicity specifies that 'Whatever such sorts of distinction or complexity there are, none is to be found in God.'[7] Christian articulation of the unity of God was indebted to the notion of divine simplicity from early on, particularly as mediated by the Neoplatonist philosopher Plotinus.

Simplicity doctrine reached the peak of its philosophical development in the medieval period, whose dominant ontological style Nicholas Wolterstorff has characterized as 'constituent ontology.' In this ontology created entities are articulated composites, in which different constituent parts play different roles.[8] *Part* ordinarily refers to a piece of matter, and clearly all material substances are composed of constituent parts. But for medieval theologians, immaterial substances too have *parts*, if they have a distinct essence and properties. Composite entities are dependent on their constituent parts and thus vulnerable to change and dissolution. They obviously fail to exemplify ontological perfection. God, by contrast, is perfectly simple. Just as God has no bodily parts, neither is God 'composed' of various immaterial properties or substances. In God there is no admixture of elements or constraints from beyond the divine being itself, and hence God is not vulnerable to change or dissolution. Anselm expressed God's freedom from the limits of creaturely existence in his inimitable style of philosophical prayer:

> there are no parts in You, Lord. Instead of being composite, You are something so one and so identical with Yourself that in no respect are You dissimilar to Yourself. Indeed, You are Unity itself, divisible in no respect. Therefore, life and wisdom and the other characteristics are not parts of You but are all one; and each of them is wholly what You are and wholly what all the others are.[9]

God is perfect Being, in whom maximal unity and maximal existence coincide.

Affirming that God is simple within a constituent ontology involves certain unusual metaphysical claims about the lack of distinctions in God. Wolterstorff notes three 'theistic identity claims' made by medieval theologians on the basis of divine simplicity: 1. God is not distinct from God's essence; 2. God's existence is not distinct from God's essence; 3. God has no property distinct from God's essence.[10] Because God does not belong to the creaturely realm of composition, simplicity doctrine also 'serves to qualify the application of all creaturely discourse' to God, and thus has profound metalinguistic implications.[11] God transcends all the linguistic distinctions and modes of analysis that are used in comprehending finite objects. Our forms of speech are intrinsically inapt for talking about a God who is both simple and subsistent:

> the conceptual and linguistic resources at our disposal enable us to speak either of something subsistent and complex or of something simple and non-subsistent, but they give us no way to speak of something as both simple and subsistent. Hence when we speak of God, we are forced to misrepresent Him so far as the *modus significandi* [way of signifying] of our terms is concerned.[12]

We can speak of good persons and of the quality of goodness, but neither of these forms of speech is adequate when speaking of a simple God. We also predicate various distinct qualities of God such as goodness, wisdom and power. But this linguistic practice too falls short. These different qualities do not reflect distinctions within God's simple being; they rather express 'different cognitive fixes'[13] on God from within the limitations of human speech and comprehension.

Over the centuries divine simplicity doctrine has served to guard theological convictions about God's self-existence and transcendence. It obviates 'any reduction of God to the mythological level of a changing Zeus or Apollo, ultimately as helplessly embroiled in the ambiguities of world history as the devotees to whom they respond.'[14] Simplicity doctrine signals the deep asymmetry in Creator–creature relations. While every created thing depends on God, God depends on nothing for God's being and attributes: God is the unconditioned condition of everything else. The notion of divine simplicity demands an apophatic reticence about the nature of God's being. God is profoundly other, not just the largest, most perfect item on the inventory list of the universe. At the same time, theologians have commonly extrapolated from the concept of divine simplicity positive assertions of God's consistency and faithfulness. Theological function, more than philosophical coherence, explains the staying power of simplicity doctrine across diverse traditions of Christian faith.[15]

Adherence to the doctrine of divine simplicity has also created large problems in Christian theology for theories of divine predication and doctrines of incarnation and Trinity. Within a framework of wholly undifferentiated divine simplicity, a large chasm separates God's economic dispensation from the intrinsic divine reality. Even an upholder of traditional simplicity doctrine like Hans Urs van Balthasar found a need to modify it by 'a theology of trinitarian divine love,' so as to 'integrate talk of the divine simplicity, infinity and perfection with a responsiveness and liveliness in God which can go beyond the notion of an unchanging, altruistic love.'[16] As we shall see, Jonathan Edwards's metaphysical modifications of the simplicity tradition so as to accommodate 'trinitarian love' were even more drastic.

In contrast to the constituent ontology of the medievals, Wolterstorff describes the 'dominant contemporary ontological style' as 'relentlessly relational': 'We don't think of entities as being composites of constituents but as standing in multiple relationships with other entities.'[17] In its own way, Edwards's ontology was also 'relentlessly relational,' and this may account for the difficulty he had in integrating simplicity doctrine into his theology. In his rejection of substance metaphysics in favor of a 'new concept of being,' Edwards put forth 'a very different view of the formal and intelligible structure of reality'[18] than that of his major philosophical contemporaries. According to the valuable interpretation of his ontology pioneered by Sang Hyun Lee, Edwards posited disposition and habit rather than substance and form as the building blocks of reality. He thereby introduced 'a dynamic element into the very fabric of being,' including the being of God.[19] Dispositional reality is intrinsically oriented to repetition and enlargement. While remaining fully actual, God's reality is at the same time fully dispositional, so that 'God's own inner being can only be thought of as inherently relational or as going out of oneself to the other.'[20] Whereas the simplicity tradition created problems for a 'theology of trinitarian love,' Edwards's dispositional ontology establishes a profound fittingness between God's economic dispensation and God's inner being.

Though Edwards's new concept of being resisted the weight of the divine simplicity tradition, his theological inheritance exerted a strong counterbalance. Virtually all the Reformed scholastic and Puritan theologies with which Edwards was familiar upheld divine simplicity. Following the Catholic scholastic tradition, simplicity was often placed in a controlling position in Reformed scholastic systems of theology. For example, Peter van Mastricht, for whom Edwards expressed enthusiastic admiration,[21] and Francis Turretin both put simplicity at or near the head of the divine attributes treated in the doctrine of God. Thus it affected the understanding and articulation of all the other attributes of God, and of how these different attributes related to each other and to the divine essence. Van Mastricht chronicled how simplicity undergirds the traditional affirmations of God's aseity, immutability, infinity, eternality, perfection and wisdom.[22] For example he argued that if God is *a se*, that is, truly independent and self-sufficient, God's existence and nature cannot be 'dependent' on any constituent parts. Likewise God's immutability requires that God not be composed of parts subject to dissolution. Turretin found a correspondence between simplicity and the abstract terms attributed to God in Scripture, such as Life, Light and Truth.[23] God is not only said to *have* Life, as one would affirm of a composite, subsistent being; God is said in Scripture to *be* Life, which can only be said of a simple being, for whom there is no distinction between essence and properties.

The Johannine affirmations about God as Love and Life were also favorite *entrée* points for Puritan affirmations of divine simplicity. John Cotton, for example, found in the affirmation of 1 John 1: 2, 'Christ is life eternal,' a proof of Christ's simplicity; 'for,' as Cotton declared, 'these speeches are no Hyperbolies.'[24] Though in a less systematic way than the Reformed scholastics, Puritan theologians also tended to define the 'oneness' of God so as to accord with the doctrine of divine simplicity, and were sensitive to the far-reaching theological implications of the doctrine. This concern to uphold divine simplicity does not appear connected to particular theological controversies or divisions within Puritan circles. Cotton's broad assertion of divine simplicity is typical:

> God is not compounded, but free without mixture, he is without all causes besides himself, he is of himself, from himself, and by himself, and for himself: and as he is not compounded of causes, so he is not compounded of subject, and adjunct; man is one thing, and his learning and wisdome another thing: but God and his wisdome are not two distinct things; God and his love are the same.[25]

Cotton admitted that the notion of God's simplicity breaks the 'rule of Logick' concerning the proper predication of attributes, but he ascribed this to the divine mystery: 'There is no reason of this truth, because he is above reason.'

Facets of Edwards's theology reflect this legacy of divine simplicity. For example, in *Freedom of the Will* he contrasted God, who is 'of perfect and absolute simplicity,' with 'derived dependent beings, who are compounded, and liable to perpetual mutation and succession.'[26] In No. 308 of the 'Miscellanies' notebooks he affirmed in a standard way the identity of the trinitarian persons with the divine essence:

> we don't suppose that the Father, the Son, and the Holy Ghost are three distinct beings that have three distinct understandings. It is the divine essence understands and it is the divine essence is understood; 'tis the divine being that loves, and it is the divine being that is loved. The Father understands, the Son understands, and the Holy Ghost understands, because every one is the same understanding divine essence.[27]

However Edwards's use of the simplicity tradition was infrequent and idiosyncratic, and he did not hesitate to reject it outright when it conflicted with his notion of divine excellency. In his *Discourse on the Trinity*, Edwards explicitly rejected the 'maxim amongst divines' that required the identification of all of God's attributes with God:

> If a man should tell me that the immutability of God is God or that the omnipresence of God and authority of God, is God, I should not be able to think of any rational meaning of what he said. It hardly sounds to me proper to say that God's being without change is God, or that God's being everywhere is God, or that God's having a right of government over creatures is God.[28]

Here Edwards self-consciously departed from the scholastic and Puritan consensus regarding the identity of all of God's attributes with God.

In Edwards's own portrayal of the various attributes of God, the 'plurality' required by divine excellency was evident. He devoted considerable effort to showing the harmony and 'consent' of the various divine attributes, rather than arguing for their metaphysical identity. One of the grandest, most elaborate examples of this can be found in his well-known sermon 'The Excellency of Christ,' in which he presented the 'admirable conjunction of diverse excellencies in Christ,' distinguishing between those excellencies that are diverse primarily 'in our manner of conceiving' and those that are 'really diverse.'[29] Those in the second group are unique to Christ, being 'conjoined in no other person whatever, either divine, human, or angelical.'[30] These truly diverse attributes are presented in pairs, such as 'infinite glory and lowest humility,' 'infinite majesty and transcendent meekness,' and 'absolute sovereignty and perfect resignation.' There is no argument, common among defenders of divine simplicity, that these seemingly opposed attributes are simply different 'cognitive fixes' on the simple divine essence. Edwards nowhere claimed, for example, that majesty and meekness are diverse only according to our limited human conception. To the contrary, the excellency of Christ resides in the fact that, in him, these *truly* diverse attributes are perfectly conjoined.

Admittedly, the case of the incarnate Son is unique within the Trinity; neither the Father nor the Spirit exhibits such perfect humility and resignation. Still, Edwards made similar arguments concerning the first person of the Trinity, in discussing the 'Harmony of God's Attributes in the Work of Redemption.'[31]

> These attributes being thus united in the divine nature and not interfering one with another is what is a great part of their glory: God's awful and terrible attributes, and his mild and gentle attributes. They reflect glory one on the other; and 'tis the glory of God that those attributes should always be exercised and expressed in a consistence and harmony one with the other.[32]

For the Father as well, in 'this wonderful meeting of diverse excellencies,' the beauty of the whole is one of complex harmony, not simplicity.

The only sense that Edwards could make of the 'maxim amongst divines' that identified all of God's attributes with God's essence was a trinitarian one. 'God's understanding and love are God,' Edwards declared, 'for deity subsists in them distinctly.'[33] Throughout his *Discourse on the Trinity*, Edwards was careful to protect the genuine distinctness of these two attributes. He invoked divine simplicity to infer, for example, that in God's love there are no distinctions of 'faculty, habit, and act, between will, inclination, and love, but that it is all one simple act.'[34] But he never collapsed the 'real distinction' in God between his attributes of understanding and love, for, he asserted, 'they are distinct Divine persons.'[35] Moreover his understanding of these 'real distinctions' in God was in explicit contradiction with the doctrine of divine simplicity: 'If God has an idea of himself, there is really a duplicity ... And if God loves himself and delights in himself, there is really a triplicity, three that cannot be confounded.'[36] As Turretin noted, 'simplicity and triplicity are opposed to each other, and cannot subsist at the same time.'[37]

Edwards betrayed little of the longstanding Christian ambivalence toward the term *person* in trinitarian vocabulary. According to the rules of simplicity theory, the works of the Trinity are indivisible – all of them are the works of the entire Godhead. At most there was an 'economic' appropriation of certain acts to particular members of the Trinity; the incarnation, for example, was appropriated to the Son. But these appropriations did not imply the existence of distinct personal agency within the Trinity, for that would disturb the uncompoundedness of the Deity. The terminology of *relations* gradually developed within classical trinitarianism to express difference within the immanent Godhead in a way that accommodated the exigencies of divine simplicity. It showed how there could be true distinctions within the immanent Trinity, without suggesting any metaphysical 'parts' in God. The three in God are distinct relations of the one, undivided divine essence. In a manuscript fragment on the equality of the members of the Trinity, Edwards showed familiarity with the conceptuality of *relations* when he asserted that 'their personal glory is only a relative glory, or a glory of relation, and therefore may be entirely distinct ... to apply distinct attributes in this sense in no wise implies an applying of a distinct essence, for personal relations are not of the divine essence.'[38]

However, he more characteristically rejected the use of the terms *relation* and *mode* to signify the real distinctions within the Godhead. ''Tis evident,' he declared, 'that there are no more than these three really distinct in God: God, and his idea, and his love or delight.' It is the remaining divine attributes that are 'meer modes or relations' of God's essence. For example, God's goodness and mercy are simply 'his love with a relation.' Even in creatures, 'duration, extension, changeableness or unchangeableness' are not real distinctions but 'only mere modes and relations of existence.'[39] In a departure from the strictures of the simplicity tradition, Edwards expressed his confidence in the appropriateness of the term *person* to denote trinitarian distinctions:

> I believe that we have no word in the English language that does so naturally represent what the Scripture reveals of the distinction of the Eternal Three, – Father, Son, and Holy Ghost, – as to say they are one God but three persons.[40]

Edwards's use of *person* language for the Godhead was not always felicitous. His picturesque imagery of 'a consultation among the persons of the Trinity' in the eternal covenant of redemption risked falling into crude anthropomorphism.[41] But his most fundamental theological rationale for speaking of *persons* in God was the aptness of that vocabulary for expressing trinitarian love:

> That in John God is love shews that there are more persons than one in the deity, for it shews love to be essential and necessary to the deity so that His nature consists in it, and this supposes that there is an eternal and necessary object, because all love respects another that is the beloved.[42]

According to Edwards's understanding of divine perfection, the excellency of the Godhead required a plurality of persons united in loving consent.

Edwards's distance from the simplicity tradition is also reflected in his aesthetics. 'God is God, and distinguished from all other beings and exalted above 'em, chiefly by his divine beauty.' While divine beauty 'is infinitely diverse from all other beauty,'[43] yet 'the beauty of the world is a communication of God's beauty,'[44] and so reflects in a dim, partial way the divine excellency. The beauty of the created world derives from the fact 'that God does purposely make and order one thing to be in an agreeableness and harmony with another.'[45]

> That sort of beauty which is called 'natural,' as of vines, plants, trees, etc., consists of a very complicated harmony; and all the natural motions and tendencies and figures of bodies in the universe are done according to proportion, and therein is their beauty.[46]

In the creaturely realm as well, 'one alone' cannot be beautiful. Beauty is a matter of proportion and harmony, both within a creature's internal constitution and in its relations with other beings.

Beauty thus requires ontological complexity. Within the divine simplicity tradition, complexity was a mark of creaturely limitation. Edwards practically reversed this, finding creaturely limitation reflected in the incapacity for complexity. 'We see that the narrower the capacity, the more simple must be the beauty to please. Thus in the proportion of sounds, the birds and brute creatures are most delighted with simple music, and in the proportion confined to a few notes.' Human creatures already enjoy more complex beauties on earth than animals can; and the saints can hope for at least a partial overcoming of their creaturely limitations in heaven. 'Then perhaps we shall be able fully and easily to apprehend the beauty, where respect is to be had to thousands of different ratios at once to make up the harmony. Such kind of beauties,' Edwards insisted, 'when fully perceived, are far the sweetest.'[47]

Physical beauty, however complex, was for Edwards only 'secondary'; 'when we spake of excellence in bodies we were obliged to borrow the word "consent" from spiritual things.'[48] 'Much more ravishing' than the external beauties of heaven, he speculated, 'will the exquisite spiritual proportions be that shall be seen in minds, in their acts; between one spiritual act and another, between one disposition and another,' culminating in the saints' vision of the relations 'among the persons of the Trinity, the supreme harmony of all.'[49] Beauty more properly applies to 'perceiving and willing being' than to material things: even the 'notes of a tune or the strokes of an acute penman' are beautiful by appearing 'like a society of so many perceiving beings, sweetly agreeing together.'[50] God has made the 'mutual consent and agreement of [physical] things beautiful and grateful' to us, because 'there is in it some image of the true, spiritual original beauty, ... consisting in being's consent to being, or the union of minds or spiritual beings in a mutual propensity and affection of heart.'[51] The aesthetic dimensions of Edwards's theology derived from the more basic category of loving consent, because 'all the primary and original beauty or excellence that is among minds is love.'[52] More specifically, they derived from his understanding of divine excellency: because there is true 'plurality' in God, there can be consent and thus true beauty within the Godhead itself. ''Tis peculiar to God that he has beauty within himself, consisting in being's consenting with his own being, or the love of himself in his own Holy Spirit.'[53]

The enduring appeal of Edwards's philosophical reflections is not their narrow consistency or precision, but their imaginative, synthetic power. Convinced that God 'does purposely make and order one thing to be in an agreeableness and harmony with another,'[54] Edwards sought and found connections between physics and ethics, theology and ontology. As Daniel B. Shea, Jr, has affirmed, 'It is appropriate to consider Edwards's thought, not as a system, but as the expression of a profound experience of the interrelatedness of things.'[55] Edwards's well-known declaration of theological independence from the Calvinist tradition[56] meant that he felt free to wrestle with and often to depart from the tradition of divine simplicity. His vision of metaphysical excellency required that divine unity be measured 'by a scale of intensity of unifying power' rather than 'by a scale of degrees of absence of multiplicity.'[57] If Wolterstorff is right that the prospects are dim for 'finding a satisfactory non-trivial formulation of the doctrine of divine simplicity'[58] within a 'relentlessly relational' ontology, Edwards's alternative conception of divine perfection may deserve further exploration.

Notes

1. Edwards, Jonathan (1994), *The 'Miscellanies', a-500, The Works of Jonathan Edwards Volume 13*, ed. Thomas A. Schafer, New Haven: Yale University Press, p. 284 (No. 117). (After the first citation, subsequent references to the Yale edition of Edwards's works will be indicated by *Works*, followed by volume and page number.)
2. Fiering, Norman S. (1981), *Jonathan Edwards's Moral Thought and Its British Context*, Chapel Hill: University of North Carolina Press, p. 74. See also Thomas Schafer's discussion of excellency and its connection to the Trinity in *Works*, 13, pp. 53–8.
3. Portions of this essay are drawn from my larger study of Edwards's trinitarianism. See Plantinga Pauw, Amy (2002), *The Supreme Harmony of All: The Trinitarian Theology of Jonathan Edwards*, Grand Rapids: Eerdmans.
4. Wallace E. Anderson, in Edwards, Jonathan (1980), *Scientific and Philosophical Writings, The Works of Jonathan Edwards Volume 6*, ed. Wallace E. Anderson, New Haven: Yale University Press, p. 84.
5. *Works*, 6, p. 337.
6. Ibid., p. 363. See more generally Edwards's first entry on 'Excellency' in *Notes on the Mind, Works*, 6, pp. 332–8.
7. Leftow, Brian (1991), *Time and Eternity*, Ithaca: Cornell University Press, p. 67.
8. Wolterstorff, Nicholas (1992), 'Divine simplicity,' in Clark, Kelly James (ed.), *Our Knowledge of God: Essays on Natural and Philosophical Theology*, Dordrecht: Kluwer Academic Publishers, p. 142.
9. Anselm (1975), *Proslogion*, 18, in *Anselm of Canterbury*, 4 vols, ed. and trans. Jasper Hopkins and Herbert Richardson, Toronto and New York: Edwin Mellen Press, vol. 1, p. 106.
10. Wolterstorff, 'Divine simplicity,' p. 134.
11. Marshall, Bruce D. (1989), 'Aquinas as a Postliberal Theologian,' *The Thomist* **53**, July, 382. I think Marshall overstates the case when he claims that 'When applied to God, "simple" is not primarily a metaphysical description for Aquinas, but rather a metalinguistic stipulation rooted in the conviction of God's transcendence.' Aquinas's rules for speaking are rooted in his metaphysical convictions about the nature of God's transcendence.
12. Alston, William P. (1993), 'Aquinas on Theological Predication: A Look Backward and a Look Forward,' in Stump, Eleonore (ed.), *Reasoned Faith: Essays in Philosophical Theology in Honor of Norman Kretzmann*, Ithaca: Cornell University Press, p. 163.
13. Wolterstorff, 'Divine simplicity,' p. 147.
14. O'Hanlon, S.J., Gerard F. (1990), *The Immutability of God in the theology of Hans Urs von Balthasar* Cambridge: Cambridge University Press, p. 147.
15. For a contemporary defense of the doctrine's philosophical coherence, with attention to its theological dividends, see Stump, Eleonore and Kretzmann, Norman (1985), 'Absolute Simplicity,' *Faith and Philosophy* **2** (4), 353–82.

16. O'Hanlon, *The Immutability of God*, p. 147.
17. Wolterstorff, 'Divine simplicity,' p. 146.
18. *Works*, 6, p. 85.
19. Hyun Lee, Sang (1988), *The Philosophical Theology of Jonathan Edwards*, Princeton: Princeton University Press, p. 170.
20. Lee, Sang Hyun (1999), 'Jonathan Edwards's Dispositional Conception of the Trinity: A Resource for Contemporary Reformed Theology,' in David Willis and Michael Welker (eds), *Toward the Future of Reformed Theology: Tasks, Topics, Traditions*, Grand Rapids: Eerdmans, p. 452.
21. In a letter to Joseph Bellamy, Edwards praised van Mastricht's *Theoretico-pratica Theologia* as 'much better than Turretin or any other book in the world, excepting the Bible, in my opinion.' See Edwards, Jonathan (1998), *Letters and Personal Writings, The Works of Jonathan Edwards Volume 16*, ed. George S. Claghorn, New Haven: Yale University Press, p. 217. But Edwards's notebooks also reveal numerous appreciative appeals to Turretin.
22. Mastricht (1682), *Theoretico-pratica Theologia*, Amsterdam, II.vi.21.
23. Turretin (1688), *Institutio Theologiae Elencticae*, Geneva, III.xii.4.
24. Cotton, John (1656), *A Practical Commentary ... upon the first Epistle Generall of John*, London, p. 11.
25. Ibid., p. 317.
26. Edwards, Jonathan (1957), *Freedom of the Will, The Works of Jonathan Edwards Volume 1*, ed. Paul Ramsey, New Haven: Yale University Press, p. 377.
27. *Works*, 13, p. 392 (No. 308). Edwards concluded this unusually muddled entry with the disclaimer, 'But I would not be understood to pretend to give a full explication of the Trinity, for I think it still remains an incomprehensible mystery, the greatest and the most glorious of all mysteries.'
28. Edwards, Jonathan (1971), *Treatise on Grace*, ed. Paul Helm, Greenwood, South Carolina: Attic Press, p. 119.
29. Edwards, Jonathan (1829–30), *The Works of President Edwards with a Memoir of His Life*, 10 vols, ed. Sereno E. Dwight, New York: S. Converse, vol. 5, p. 537. See John B. Carmen's incisive analysis of this conjunction, in Carmen, John B. (1994), *Majesty and Meekness: A Comparative Study of Contrast and Harmony in the Concept of God*, Grand Rapids: Eerdmans, pp. 231–51.
30. Dwight, *Works of President Edwards*, 5, p. 539.
31. Title of 'Miscellanies,' No. 38 (*Works*, 13, p. 221). See also Edwards's sermon 'God's Excellencies' in Edwards, Jonathan (1992), *Sermons and Discourses 1720–1723, The Works of Jonathan Edwards Volume 10*, ed. Wilson H. Kimnach, New Haven: Yale University Press, pp. 415–35.
32. Edwards, Jonathan (1999), *Sermons and Discourses, 1703–1733, The Works of Jonathan Edwards Volume 17*, ed. Mark R. Valeri, New Haven: Yale University Press, p. 159.
33. Helm, *Treatise on Grace*, p. 119.
34. Ibid., p. 99.
35. Ibid., p. 119.
36. *Works*, 13, p. 262 (No. 94).
37. Turretin, *Institutio*, III.vii.9, my translation.
38. *Fragment on the Trinity*, Boston Public Library, c. early 1740s. Used by permission of The Works of Jonathan Edwards, Yale University.
39. *Works*, 13, p. 367 (No. 259).
40. Helm, *Treatise on Grace*, p. 57. 'The Scripture does sufficiently reveal the Holy Spirit as a proper Divine person, and thus we ought to look upon Him as a distinct personal agent.'

41. Edwards, Jonathan (1997), *Sermons and Discourses 1723–1729, The Works of Jonathan Edwards Volume 14*, ed. Kenneth P. Minkema, New Haven: Yale University Press, p. 378.
42. Helm, *Treatise on Grace*, p. 100.
43. Edwards, Jonathan (1959), *Religious Affections, The Works of Jonathan Edwards Volume 2*, ed. John E. Smith, New Haven: Yale University Press, p. 298.
44. *Works*, 13, p. 384 (No. 293).
45. Edwards, Jonathan (1993), *Typological Writings, The Works of Jonathan Edwards Volume 11*, eds Wallace E. Anderson, Mason I. Lowance and David H. Watters, New Haven: Yale University Press, p. 53.
46. *Works*, 6, p. 335.
47. *Works*, 13, p. 329 (No. 182).
48. *Works*, 6, p. 362. I am indebted here to Norman Fiering's analysis in *Jonathan Edwards's Moral Thought*, pp. 80–82.
49. *Works*, 13, pp. 328–9 (No. 182).
50. *Works*, 6, p. 382.
51. Edwards, Jonathan (1989), *Ethical Writings, The Works of Jonathan Edwards Volume 8*, ed. Paul Ramsey, New Haven: Yale University Press, p. 564.
52. *Works*, 6, p. 362.
53. Ibid., p. 365.
54. *Works*, 11, p. 53.
55. Shea, (1972), 'Jonathan Edwards: Historian of Consciousness,' in Emerson, Everett (ed.), *Major Writers of Early American Literature*, Madison: University of Wisconsin Press, p. 180.
56. *Works*, 1, p. 131: 'I should not take it at all amiss, to be called a Calvinist, for distinction's sake: though I utterly disclaim a dependence on Calvin, or believing the doctrines which I hold, because he believed and taught them; and cannot justly be charged with believing in everything just as he taught.'
57. Hodgson, Leonard (1944), *The Doctrine of the Trinity*, London: Nisbet, p. 94. Hodgson's contrast between 'mathematical' and 'organic' unity is cited in a helpful article by Christopher Stead (1989), 'Divine simplicity as a problem for orthodoxy,' in Rowan Williams, (ed.), *The Making of Orthodoxy: Essays in honour of Henry Chadwick*, Cambridge: Cambridge University Press, pp. 255–69.
58. Wolterstorff, 'Divine simplicity,' p. 136.

Chapter 9

Jonathan Edwards, John Henry Newman and non-Christian Religions

Gerald R. McDermott

Jonathan Edwards (1703–58) and John Henry Newman (1801–90) share at least two characteristics: both showed creative genius in their reshaping of Anglo-American religious thought, and neither is known for his interest in non-Christian religions. Yet both were stimulated by polemical challenges to investigate the religions, and each devoted considerable attention to the question of how Christian faith relates to other faiths. Each concluded that God is at work in all the world, both scattering truth among the religions and probably saving some of those outside Judaism and Christianity.

Edwards's interest in other religions seems to go back, at least in part, to deist attacks upon Christian particularity. Deists charged that a god who damns to hell five-sixths of the world because it fails to accept a gospel that it never heard (this was a popular form of Calvinist Christianity upon which deists pounced) was a monster unworthy of devotion. Whether for the purpose of answering this challenge or simply for curiosity's sake, Edwards scoured New England and old England for treatises and encyclopedias on other religions, and scores and scores of pages in his theological notebooks to the religions. If these notebook entries are any indication, Edwards became more and more fascinated with the religions the older he got.[1]

Edwards used three models to understand the role of the religions in the history of the work of redemption. The first was the *prisca theologia* (ancient theology), which was a tradition in apologetic theology, resting on misdated texts (such as the Hermetica, Chaldean oracles, Orpheia and Sybilline oracles) that attempted to prove that vestiges of true religion were taught by the Greeks and other non-Christian traditions. Typically it alleged that all human beings were originally given knowledge of true religion (monotheism, the Trinity, *creatio ex nihilo*) by Jews or by tradition going back to Noah's good sons (Shem and Japheth) or antediluvians such as Enoch or Adam. Then it passed down to Zoroaster, Hermes Trismegistus, Brahmins and Druids, Orpheus, Pythagoras, Plato and the Sybils.[2]

The *prisca theologia* was developed first by Clement of Alexandria, Origen, Lactantius and Eusebius to show that the greatest philosophers had stolen from the Chosen People, and then in the Renaissance by Marsilio Ficino and Pico Della Mirandola to synthesize Neoplatonism and Christian dogma.[3] In the seventeenth and

127

eighteenth centuries it was revived by the 'Jesuit Figurists,' who tried to win acceptance of their mission in China by claiming that China worshipped the true God two thousand years before Christ, and a number of other, mostly Protestant, thinkers.

In his own appropriation of the *prisca theologia*, Edwards said that the heathen learned Reformed truths by what could be called a trickle-down process of revelation. In the 'first ages' of the world the fathers of the nations received revelation of the great religious truths, directly or indirectly, from God himself.[4] These truths were then passed down, by tradition, from one generation to the next. Unfortunately, there is also a religious law of entropy at work. Human finitude and corruption inevitably cause the revelation to be distorted, resulting in superstition and idolatry.

Nevertheless selected heathen were apprised of extraordinary mysteries. From Hugo Grotius he learned that the Greeks said that the Spirit moved on the waters at the beginning and knew that one can commit adultery in the heart but must forgive and love one's enemies (*Misc.* 1012; *Misc.* 1023). Vergil, Seneca, Juvenal and Ovid, Edwards noted, confessed that our original nature was corrupt (*Misc.* 1073). Chevalier Ramsay taught him that the Hindu *Vedas* and the Chinese *I Ching* contain stories about a hero who expiates crimes by his own sufferings, and that many heathen from different traditions acknowledged a divine incarnation and realized that virtue comes only by an infusion of grace (*Misc.* 1351; *Misc.* 1355). Edwards noted in his Blank Bible[5] that heathen stories about gods and goddesses were actually distortions of Hebrew counterparts. Saturn, for example, is a transmutation of Adam, Noah and Abraham; Hercules is a Greek rendition of Joshua, Bacchus of Nimrod, Moses and the Hebrew deity; Apis and Serapis are Egyptian retellings of the Joseph story (pp. 6, 11, 39).

Edwards's second model for understanding non-Christian religion was typology. Against the deist allegation that God had not revealed himself in either history or the Bible, Edwards retorted that God constantly communicates Reformed truths wherever the eye can see and the ear can hear. Types, Edwards pronounced, 'are a certain sort of language, as it were, in which God is wont to speak to us.'[6] These types are words in persons, places and things – not only are they located in the Old Testament where traditional biblical typology had found them, but they are found in every part of the creation. Hence there are sermons in the stones, flowers and stars. God also speaks in history, both sacred and profane. He even speaks in the history of religions, heathen included. Indeed, every last atom of his creation pulsates with a divine melody. If the deists did not hear it, they were stopping their ears.

But if they opened their ears, they could hear the biblical God speaking even in religious systems that were finally false. God outwitted the devil, Edwards suggested, by using diabolically deceptive religion to teach what is true. In an early entry in the *Miscellanies*, Edwards suggested, for example, that the heathen practice of human sacrifice was the result of the devil's mimicry of the animal sacrifice which God had instituted after the Fall.

Sacrifice was taught not by the light of nature but by God's express commandment immediately after he revealed the covenant of grace in Genesis 3: 15 ('And I will put enmity between thee and the woman, and between thy seed and her seed; it shall bruise thy head, and thou shalt bruise his heel.' KJV). The skins with which God clothed the first couple in v. 21 were taken from animals sacrificed by God, who taught them thereby that only the righteousness of Christ won by his sacrifice could cover their sins (*History of the Work of Redemption*, 134–6).

Edwards insisted that animal sacrifice, the main type of Christ in the Old Testament but revealed to all the heathen, taught the necessity of propitiatory sacrifice to atone for sin. Imitating this divine type, the devil led the heathen to sacrifice human beings, even their own sons. Satan believed he had 'promote[d] his own interests,' outsmarting God; but God outflanked the devil. He permitted this diabolical deception because through it 'the devil prepared the Gentile world for receiving ... this human sacrifice, Jesus Christ' (*Misc.* 307).

Similarly, the devil induced human beings to worship idols and think that the heathen deities were united to their images. But God used this deception as well for his own purposes, to prepare the Gentile mind for the concept of incarnation, perfectly realized in Christ.

Twice, then, in the history of religions, God used false religion to teach the true. In each case the devil's machinations were overruled, ironically, by divine wisdom. Practices considered by all Jews and Christians to be abominable – human sacrifice and idol worship – were transposed by a divine stratagem into pedagogical devices to prepare the heathen for true religion. In both cases God used non-Christian religions typologically to point to Christian truths.

Edwards believed that far more than incarnation and propitiatory sacrifice, however, was taught by sacrifices. They also showed the heathen that God would not pardon without satisfaction being made, that sin 'must be suffered for.' They demonstrated God's jealousy and hatred for sin, indicated the need for fear of God and respect for the glory of his holiness, and suggested to sinners that they must trust in God's mercy (*Misc.* 326).

If typology and the *prisca theologia* enabled Edwards to show the deists that the biblical God had *not* limited his revelation to a minority of humankind, his dispositional soteriology (his third model) provided a way to understand how God might save those who never heard the Gospel. Drawing upon a tradition that originated with Aristotle's *hexis* and developed through Thomas's *habitus* and Reformed scholastic permutations, Edwards conceived of 'disposition' as an active and real tendency that has ontological reality even when it is not exercised. Early in his career Edwards defined a saving disposition, which is common to Christians, Old Testament Jews, and all other religionists *'from the beginning of the world'*: 'a sense of the dangerousness of sin, and of the dreadfulness of God's anger ... [such a conviction of] their wickedness, that they trusted to nothing but the mere mercy of God, and then bitterly lamented and mourned for their sins' (*Misc.* 39).

Just a short time earlier Edwards had written that it is this inner religious consciousness (disposition) that is the only prerequisite to salvation. No particular act, even the act of receiving Christ, is necessary: 'The disposition is all that can be said to be absolutely necessary. The act [of receiving Christ] cannot be proved to be absolutely necessary ... 'Tis the disposition or principle is the thing God looks at.' For an illustration of this point Edwards used the Old Testament Jews. They did not receive Christ in any conscious or explicit manner, but they had the proper disposition, which alone is necessary for salvation:

> It need not be doubted but that many of the ancient Jews before Christ were saved without the sensible exertions of those acts in that manner which is represented as necessary by some divines, because they had not those occasions nor were under circumstances that would draw them out; though without doubt *they had the disposition, which alone is absolutely necessary now, and at all times, and in all circumstances is equally necessary. (Misc. 27b;* emphasis added)

Edwards went on to stipulate that in some cases regeneration takes place before conversion, and that there are four types of persons without explicit knowledge of Christ who may nevertheless find salvation: infants who die, Old Testament saints, New Testament saints such as Cornelius who in some sense already believed in Christ before Peter told him about Jesus, and holy pagans such as Melchizedek and Job. In all these cases disposition, not explicit faith in Jesus as the Christ, is the critical determinant of eschatological destiny.[7]

Despite these remarkable theological concessions, Edwards rarely allowed more than the possibility of salvation for the heathen. While he made some cryptic remarks in the *Miscellanies* about how the heathen might use religious truth for the good of 'their own souls' (*Misc.* 1162), and the consequent 'possibility' of their 'reconciliation' (*Misc.* 1338), these concessions were largely limited to his private notebooks; in his published treatises and sermons, 'heathen' was usually a synonym for 'damned.' Yet the extensive use he made of the *prisca theologia*, the advances he made in typology, and his development of a dispositional soteriology prepared the theological way – for whatever use he or others might later have used them – for more expansive views of truth in the religions and salvation for religious others.

In John Henry Newman's day, roughly a century after Edwards's death, 'liberals'[8] in England objected that anything in Christian faith or practice that smacked of 'Platonism' or 'paganism' could never have been part of Christian revelation. Since ideas resembling the Trinity, the Incarnation and the atonement could be found in such sources, the very heart of Christian faith – at least as understood by Newman – was alleged to be without divine authority.

Newman, inspired by Justin Martyr's logos theology and Clement of Alexandria's notion of a separate divine dispensation for the Greeks, responded that the coincidence of the same truth found in both Christian and pagan sources only reinforced the divine origin of those truths:

for the Almighty scattered through the world, before His Son came, vestiges and gleams of His true Religion, and collected all the separated rays together, when He set Him on His holy hill to rule the day, and the Church, as the moon, to govern the night. In the sense in which the doctrine of the Trinity is Platonic, doubtless the doctrine of mysteries generally is Platonic also ... Unbelievers have accused Moses of borrowing his law from the Egyptians or other Pagans; and elaborate comparisons have been instituted, on the part of believers also, by way of proving it; though even if proved, and so far as proved, it would show nothing more than this, – that God, who gave His law to Israel absolutely and openly, had already given some portions of it to the heathen.[9]

In this brief quote Newman refers to what he called elsewhere 'universal revelation,' by which he meant a global diffusion of divine truth, scattered unequally around the world in all times and all places. The Church is the ordinary channel of this revelation, and has the fullest access to it through its Bible (which is the 'unadulterated and complete revelation'[10]) and sacraments. But by what Newman called 'traditionary religion'[11] God has spoken to human beings outside of Christianity and Judaism, never leaving himself without a witness but in every nation accepting those who feared and obeyed him.

The witness can be found in four places: philosophy, natural religion and conscience, the arts, and other religions. Newman was particularly influenced by Clement, who proposed that God taught the Greeks through a Gentile dispensation. Hence, for Newman, 'The Greek poets and sages were in a certain sense prophets; for "thoughts beyond their thought to those high bards were given."'[12] If Palestine had been the seat and foundation of supernatural truth, 'Attica was chosen by Providence as the home and center of intellectual excellence.'[13] Newman noted that, for Clement, God had inspired Plato, Aristotle, the Pythagoreans, Sophocles, Euripides and Homer, but had deemed the 'barbarians' more interested in truth for truth's sake than the Greeks, who loved doubting and fame (Strom. 8.1.490). By 'barbarians' he meant the Egyptians, Chaldeans among the Assyrians, the Druids, Celts, Magi and the 'Indian gymnosophists' (Strom. 1.15.398–9).

According to Newman, natural religion is a second channel through which God disseminates truth. Providing information about God and our responsibilities to God, natural religion speaks through the collective voice of humanity, the history of the world, and the human conscience, which is the most reliable source.[14] From conscience humans learn not only that God exists but also that their supreme judge is holy, just and powerful. In his second University Sermon, Newman said that conscience implies a relation between the soul and something external, and that something is superior to itself – hence an excellence which it does not possess, and a tribunal over which it has no power. 'The more closely this inward monitor is respected and followed, the clearer, the more exalted, and the more varied its dictates become.'[15] In his *Apologia* Newman added that obedience even to an erring conscience 'was the way to gain light.'[16]

The third and fourth channels for universal revelation are poetry, art and music, on the one hand, and world religions, on the other. 'There is nothing unreasonable in the notion,' Newman wrote in his *Arians of the Fourth Century*, 'that there may have been heathen poets and sages, or sybils again, in a certain extent divinely illuminated, and organs through whom religious and moral truth was conveyed to their countrymen; though their knowledge of the Power from whom the gift came, nay, and their perception of the gift as existing in themselves, may have been very faint or defective.'[17] In fact, he added, there is something 'true and divinely revealed' in every religion around the globe, though those truths and revelations are mixed and sometimes overwhelmed by 'impieties' inspired by the 'corrupt will and understanding of men.' Most teach 'the power and presence of an invisible God, of His moral law and governance, of the obligation of duty, and the certainty of a just judgment, and of reward and punishment, as eventually dispensed to individuals.'[18] Some of them also teach Christian doctrines, such as the Trinity, washing, Divine Word, Incarnation, angels, demons, new birth and sacramental virtue.[19]

For John Henry Newman, then, the relationship between Christianity and other religions is a matter of continuity rather than discontinuity. He referred to this as the principle of mediation, by which God always blesses human beings through the 'mediation of others.'[20] Parents are the 'instruments of God's bounties to their children,' and food, clothing, medicine are all gifts from providence, but none come immediately from God. Everything is mediated through the 'instrumentality of others.'[21]

Therefore the Incarnation was nothing new. As God always does and did, he was dispensing his gifts through others, this time through his own Son.[22] And at certain important points in the history of providence, God gave truth to his Church through paganism, and the Holy Spirit guided the Church to collect these truths as it assembled its own traditions.

> As Adam gave names to the animals around him, so the Church from the first looked around the earth noting and visiting the doctrines she found. She began in Chaldea, and then sojourned among the Canaanites, and went down into Egypt, and then passed into Arabia, till she rested in her own land. Then to the merchants of Tyre, the wisdom of the East, luxury of Sheba, Babylon, the schools of Greece, sitting in the midst of the doctors, both listening and asking questions, claiming to herself what they said rightly, supplying their defects, completing their beginnings, expanding their surmises, and gradually by means of them enlarging the range and refining the sense of her own teaching. In this way she has sucked the milk of the Gentiles and sucked the breasts of kings.[23]

Therefore by what Newman called the principle of 'addition' the Church's task when it comes to a foreign religion is not to destroy but to add to the foundation already laid. When divine providence reveals something, God 'does not begin anew but uses the existing system.'[24] God comes not to undo the past but to fulfill and perfect it.[25] Therefore a 'religious mind,' 'sincerely attached to some form of heathenism ... would be drawn off from error into truth, not by losing what it had, but by gaining what it had not, not by being unclothed, but by being "clothed upon" ... True conversion is ever of a positive, not a negative character.'[26] The missionary, then, should not assume that all pagan beliefs and practices are corrupt, or that all pagans are damned, but will aim to recover and purify rather than reverse 'the essential principles of [pagan] belief.'[27]

Christian faith could build upon and even learn from heathen religions because the essence of all true religion is faith. Aristotle showed this, Newman reasoned, by saying he would follow moral excellence without reference to the pleasure which may or may not attend it, because it is good and his best instincts prompted him to follow it. This was the same 'self-neglect and self-denial' and 'noble disinterestedness' that Abraham showed – 'trusting the voice of God without worrying about present enjoyment.' Many 'ungifted' heathen such as Rahab, Naaman and Cornelius had less light but were better and holier than those with much light.[28] This demonstrated that faith is 'substantially the same habit of mind' everywhere.[29] It is a 'principle of action' not to be identified with specific doctrines. Therefore pagans may have, but heretics cannot, the same principles as Catholics.[30] And for this reason, we can be confident that the sacrifice which availed for Christians also did for our pagan brethren who 'seek God with their whole heart.'[31]

Jonathan Edwards and John Henry Newman, for all their doctrinal differences on authority, sacraments, worship and ministry,[32] shared remarkably similar convictions about spirituality and the religions. The spirituality of both was forbiddingly rigorous: each said he was the greatest of sinners, and each was convinced that unwillingness to yield in even one area of life could derail one's journey to God.[33] While both were impressed by certain beliefs and practices of Muslims, both believed that Islam is an arm of Antichrist.[34] Neither believed that explicit confession of Christ was absolutely necessary for salvation; each stipulated that an underlying attitude of heart ('disposition' for Edwards, 'faith' for Newman) is the soul of true religion and transcends doctrine. Each was convinced that an original revelation of Christian doctrines was distributed to the founders of the nations, but was later forgotten or obscured; we have called this the *prisca theologia* for Edwards, while Newman called it the 'primeval tradition.'[35] Both marveled at the conversion of the (pagan) Roman empire and considered it the greatest miracle in Christian history.[36] Finally, each theologian regarded sympathetically religious law that teaches, on its face, salvation by obedience; both noted that law is often an outer covering meant to protect an inner treasure (grace) from being trampled by swine, and that the sincere attempt to follow law will drive the genuine seeker to grace.[37] This dialectical understanding of religious law helped both to see God at work in some religions where their theological predecessors had seen only the demonic.

Nevertheless, Edwards and Newman on the religions differed in some intriguing ways. First, Newman more than Edwards stressed the continuities between

Christian and other faiths. Newman used the Thomistic theme of grace perfecting nature, or, in this case, later Christian grace completing earlier pagan graces. For this reason Newman was more positive about pagan superstition. He remarked more than once that superstition is preferable to skepticism because the former believes in an admixture of human invention and divine truth while the latter denies both. So the Church should not harshly oppose, for example, polytheism, but moderate and purify it. Besides, he said, truth and error are so intimately interwoven in religion that they cannot be decisively separated, as in the parable of the wheat and the tares.[38]

While Edwards conceded that some pagan doctrines contained traces of truth, he believed they were usually demonic imitations of divine types. He never tired of telling of the numerous 'absurdities' he found elsewhere in the religions: for example, he poked fun at the Greek philosophers who made dangerous journeys by sea to visit the 'celebrated Prostitutes of their time,' let out their own wives 'for Hire,' kept mistresses and gave the world 'the strongest reasons to think them guilty of greater crimes, than it was possible to commit with the other sex.' Aristotle, Edwards dutifully recorded, was a fob, a debauchee, a traitor to Alexander his master. Xenophon kept a boy lover. Sometimes Edwards's comments bordered on the ridiculous: 'The most solemn act of worship performed to the Syrian Baal by his ordinary devotees, was to break wind and ease themselves at the Foot of his Image' (*Misc.* 1350).

While both believed in development of doctrine, Newman saw more pagan influence on Christian tradition. Edwards believed that Christian thought has evolved over time, just as God's work of redemption is a 'progression' making 'eternal progress,' even as God himself ontically self-enlarges.[39] To prove that Christian understanding must go beyond mere biblical statements, he boasted once that he was 'not afraid to say twenty things about the Trinity which the Scripture never said[!]' (*Misc.* 94). But while Edwards's God has placed typical truths among the religions, Edwards never gave any sign of believing that these truths were not already found within Christian revelation.

Newman, on the other hand, sees the development of the Christian tradition in somewhat Hegelian fashion, gathering from truths found both within and without the Church, and by the testing of theses against antitheses discovering newly nuanced truths if not syntheses. Just as God used heresies in the early Church to help the Fathers tease out in dialectical fashion the true implications of the raw deposit he had left with the apostles, so too the Church has learned in similar fashion from its engagement with pagan religions.

Third, Newman was more willing than Edwards to talk about saved pagans. Because Newman saw the religions teaching so much of what he considered to be the heart of true religion, and because he was convinced by Clement that there was a separate Dispensation of Paganism, he spoke with more certainty of pagans who rested in the bosom of Abraham. Edwards was more cautious and suspicious. What hope he left for the heathen was buried in cryptic terms deep within his private notebooks. He believed more than his favorite Reformed theologians that the heathen had access to truth that could save. But he was never as expansive in his hope as Newman, or for that matter Watts, Baxter or Wesley.[40]

Yet Edwards could be exuberant about cultures as foreign as China's. Chevalier Ramsey convinced him that the Chinese culture captured more religious truth than any other. He believed that the *I-Ching*, Laotze and Confucius all knew of a coming Messiah, and that they and others were given glimpses of the Trinity and the need for regeneration. When he assumed the presidency of Princeton, he seems to have been prepared to tell his students that the Chinese possessed all the essential truths of Reformed religion but in mythological form, and that they had received these truths from none other than Noah himself.[41]

In sum, ours is not the first age to have been dazzled by the world's astonishing religious diversity, or puzzled by the theological meaning of religious pluralism. In the midst of a profusion of glib comments about our unprecedented awareness of religious pluralism in recent decades, we might be reminded that the greatest Anglo-American theologians of the eighteenth and nineteenth centuries were similarly intrigued by religious pluralism and gave considerable and sophisticated attention to it.

Notes

1. For a fuller narrative of the story presented here, see McDermott, Gerald R. (2000), *Jonathan Edwards Confronts the Gods: Christian Theology, Enlightenment Religion, and Non-Christian Faiths*, New York: Oxford University Press, esp. pp. 1–54.
2. On the *prisca theologia*, see Walker, D. P. (1953), 'Orpheus the theologian and Renaissance Platonists,' *Journal of the Warburg and Courtauld Institutes* **16**, 100–120; idem (1972), *The Ancient Theology: Studies in Christian Platonism from the Fifteenth to the Eighteenth Centuries*, London: Duckworth; idem (1964), *The Decline of Hell: Seventeenth-Century Discussions of Eternal Torment*, London: Routledge; Yates, Frances A. (1964), *Giordano Bruno and the Hermetic Tradition*, Chicago: University of Chicago Press; Schmitt, Charles B. (1966), 'Perennial Philosophy: From Agostino Steuco to Leibniz,' *Journal of the History of Ideas* **XXVII**, Oct.–Dec, 505–32; Droze, Arthur J. (1989), *Homer or Moses? Early Christian Interpretations of the History of Culture*, Tübingen: J.C.B. Mohr; Seznec, Jean (1953), *The Survival of the Pagan Gods: The Mythological Tradition and Its Place in Renaissance Humanism and Art*, New York: Bollingen.
3. Even Augustine seems to have been influenced by this tradition. In his *Retractions* he wrote, 'What is now called Christian religion has existed among the ancients, and was not absent from the beginning of the human race, until Christ came in the flesh: from which time true religion, which existed already, began to be called Christian' (1.13).
4. *Misc.* 953; *Misc.* 986; *Misc.* 984. Usually Edwards was ambiguous about the location of the original deposit of revelation. Only occasionally did he pinpoint Adam; in *Misc.* 884 he said that Adam learned the moral law from God and taught it with great clarity to his descendants. In *Original Sin* he wrote that Adam 'continued alive near two thirds of the time that passed before the flood,' so that most people alive until the flood heard from

Adam what 'passed between him and his Creator in paradise.' Edwards, Jonathan (1970), *Original Sin, The Works of Jonathan Edwards Volume 3*, ed. Clyde A. Holbrook, New Haven: Yale University Press, p. 170. Most often, however, he simply referred to the fathers of the nations as identical to or descended from Noah's sons.

5. A small copy of the King James Version interleaved with quarto-sized sheets of paper and bound in a large volume; Edwards Papers.

6. Types, 150. 'Types' is one of three notebooks which Edwards devoted exclusively to elaboration of his typological scheme. The other two were 'Images of Divine Things' (hereafter referred to as 'Images') and 'Types of the Messiah' (hereafter referred to as TM). All three are published in Edwards, Jonathan (1993), *Typological Writings, The Works of Jonathan Edwards Volume 11* [*TW*], eds Wallace E. Anderson and Mason I. Lowance, Jr, with David H. Watters, New Haven: Yale University Press. Other notebooks, such as the 'Notes on Scripture,' the 'Blank Bible,' and the 'Book of Controversies' (Edwards Papers) contain numerous references to typology.

7. For this and the following paragraph, see *Jonathan Edwards Confronts the Gods*, ch. 7.

8. These were Anglicans like Thomas Arnold and Richard Whately, who, influenced by Locke's *An Essay Concerning Human Understanding* and certain deist lines of thinking, were suspicious of dogma, particularly traditional understandings of the Trinity and the Incarnation, and disapproved more generally of sacraments, religious mystery, creeds, catechisms and tradition. McGrath, Francis (1997), *John Henry Newman: Universal Revelation*, Macon: Mercer University Press, pp. 19, 51.

9. *Discussions and Arguments on Various Subjects*, pp. 210–11; quoted in McGrath, pp. 75–6.

10. (1968), *The Arians of the Fourth Century*, Westminster: Christian Classics, pp. 83–4.

11. Ibid., p. 79.

12. Newman, Henry (1956), *Apologia Pro Vita Sua*, Boston: Houghton Mifflin, p. 46.

13. Newman, John Henry (1973–7), *The Letters and Diaries of John Henry Newman*, ed. Charles Stephen Dessain et al., Oxford: Oxford University Press, xxxi, 25; cited in McGrath, p. 85.

14. McGrath, p. 19.

15. University Sermon, 'The Influence of Natural and Revealed Religion Respectively,' pp. 18–19; cited in McGrath, p. 69.

16. *Apologia*, p. 199.

17. *Arians of the Fourth Century*, p. 82.

18. Ibid., p. 80.

19. Newman, John Henry (1989), *An Essay on the Development of Christian Doctrine*, Notre Dame: University of Notre Dame Press, p. 380.

20. *Anglican Sermons* I, p. 213; cited in McGrath, pp. 41–2.

21. Ibid.

22. Ibid.

23. *Essay*, p. 380.

24. *Essays Critical and Historical* II, p. 194; cited in McGrath, p. 77.

25. *Essay*, pp. 356–7.

26. Ibid., pp. 200–201.

27. *Arians of the Fourth Century*, p. 84.

28. (August 1829), Birmingham Oratory Archives A.7.1., cited in McGrath, p. 42; *Anglican Sermons* II, p. 189, cited in McGrath, p. 42.

29. *Lectures on the Doctrine of Justification*, pp. 242–3; cited in McGrath, p. 75.

30. Lash, Nicholas (1975), *Newman on Development: The Search for an Explanation in History*, London: Sheed and Ward, p. 109; *Essay*, p. 181.

31. *Arians of the Fourth Century*, p. 82.

32. During his Roman period, Newman looked to church tradition for final authority, held to seven sacraments, saw liturgy and Eucharist as the best expressions of worship, and located authority for ministry in the apostolic succession. Edwards claimed Scripture for ultimate authority, held to an attenuated (by Roman standards) version of two sacraments, rejected most liturgy and the Roman Mass, and denied the legitimacy of apostolic succession.

33. On Newman, see Ker, Ian (1988), *John Henry Newman*, New York: Oxford, pp. 162, 95, 662; for Edwards, see 'Personal Narrative,' in Edwards, Jonathan (1998), *Letters and Personal Writings, The Works of Jonathan Edwards Volume 16*, ed. George S. Claghorn, New Haven: Yale University Press, p. 802; Edwards, Jonathan (1959), *Religious Affections, The Works of Jonathan Edwards Volume 2*, ed. John E. Smith, New Haven: Yale University Press, pp. 401–7.

34. Ker, 403; Edwards, Jonathan (1989), *History of the Work of Redemption, The Works of Jonathan Edwards Volume 9*, ed. John F. Wilson, pp. 410–11, 463.

35. *Letters and Diaries*, xxviii, p. 257; cited in Ker, Ian, *John Henry Newman*, pp. 646–7. Newman refers to this also in *Arians of the Fourth Century*, c 79, 82, *Essay*, p. 79.

36. Ker, p. 646; *History of the Work of Redemption*, p. 396.

37. *Jonathan Edwards Confronts the Gods*, pp. 157–9; *Arians of the Fourth Century*, pp. 50–78.

38. Ker, pp. 52, 706.

39. *Jonathan Edwards Confronts the Gods*, pp. 100–102.

40. Baxter forthrightly granted salvation to those (outside the 'Jewish church') who did not have 'knowledge of Christ *incarnate*,' and Wesley said pagans just need to live up to the light they are given. Baxter, Richard (1667), *The Reasons of the Christian Religion*, London, pp. 201–2; Wesley, John (1975–), Sermon LXVIII, 'The General Spread of the Gospel,' in *The Works of John Wesley, vol. IX*, ed. Frank Baker, Oxford: Oxford University Press, p. 234; see Pailin, David (1984), *Attitudes to Other Religions: Comparative Religion in Seventeenth- and Eighteenth-Century Britain*, Manchester: Manchester University Press, p. 48.

41. See *Jonathan Edwards Confronts the Gods*, ch. 12.

Chapter 10

Salvation as Divinization: Jonathan Edwards, Gregory Palamas and the Theological Uses of Neoplatonism

Michael J. McClymond

Scholars have long recognized that certain elements in Edwards's theology are in tension with classical Protestantism. Jaroslav Pelikan, a world authority on the history of Christian thought and a later-life convert to Eastern Orthodoxy, has made reference to the affinities between Edwards's theology and the Orthodox doctrine of divinization.[1] Traditional Calvinists, though typically delighted with Edwards's treatment of grace, predestination and the issue of free will, have often been troubled by his affirmations of continuity between the Creator and creatures. The nineteenth-century Presbyterian stalwart Charles Hodge wrote that Edwards's theology 'in its consequences is essentially pantheistic.'[2] Others have used softer terms, such as 'mysticism' or 'Platonism,' to describe an aspect of Edwards's thought that is allegedly alien to, and in tension with, his doctrinal Calvinism. Even Edwards's partisans and defenders have sometimes felt the need to explain or qualify his assertions regarding the depth and pervasiveness of God's union with creatures.

Paul Ramsey notes that Edwards uses three principal figures of speech in the *Religious Affections* to describe the relation of believers to God – the shining forth of light, the flowing of water from a fountain, and a branch that draws sap from a tree trunk. He adds that 'sometimes Edwards' enthusiasm leads him to use language that was easily misinterpreted.' As an example of such language, Ramsey cites Edwards's statement that believers are 'little suns, partaking of the nature of the fountain of their light.'[3] While Ramsey notes that Edwards does not teach 'monism,' it is clear from his analysis that Edwards sometimes speaks in a way that seems to be at odds with traditional Calvinism.

Thomas Schafer's 1951 article 'Jonathan Edwards and Justification by Faith' may have been the first to raise the question of Edwards's position *vis-à-vis* classical Protestantism. At first blush, the thesis of Edwards's treatise on justification is impeccably Protestant: 'We are justified only by faith in Christ, and not by any manner of virtue or goodness of our own.' Edwards goes on to state that justification is not merely a remission of sins, but a positive state of righteousness before God, based exclusively on Christ's merit, and imputed to the believer by faith. Yet Schafer finds that certain features of Edwards's argument 'cause the doctrine of justification to occupy an ambiguous and somewhat precarious place in his theology.' Edwards teaches that the soul becomes acceptable to God only in and through its union with God, which is the proper 'ground' of justification: 'What is *real* in the union between Christ and His people, is the foundation of what is *legal*.' Faith is related to justification only because it 'is the soul's active uniting with Christ, or is itself the very act of unition.' Moreover, Edwards argues that faith is not the only 'condition' of justification, in the ordinary meaning of 'condition' as 'that … without which … a thing shall not be.'[4] The 'agreeing or consenting disposition' toward God may be variously understood as faith, belief, hope, obedience, or love, and Edwards lays special emphasis on love. Schafer comments that 'the reader cannot help feeling that the conception of "faith alone" has been considerably enlarged – and hence practically eliminated.'[5] The stress on actual union rather than legal imputation, the relative de-emphasis on faith *per se*, and the presentation of love and obedience as intrinsic to faith, establish an affinity between Edwards's teaching on justification and what is generally found in Roman Catholic and Orthodox theologies.

Anri Morimoto's *Jonathan Edwards and the Catholic Vision of Salvation* offers an unexpected conclusion:

> Edwards learned much from the theology of the continental Roman Catholic tradition and allowed himself to be profoundly influenced by it … His vision of human salvation can therefore offer today's Protestant theology reliable help in reformulating and revitalizing its own understanding of salvation, without forcing it to surrender or compromise its genuine Protestant concerns.[6]

Morimoto notes that Edwards's nineteenth-century editors were well aware of the Catholic element in his theologizing, and sought to suppress it by fair means or foul. Tryon Edwards – a descendant of Jonathan – tampered with the text in his 1852 publication of *Charity and Its Fruits*. In no less than fourteen instances, he eliminated Edwards's word 'infusion,' which was too Catholic for his tastes.[7] For Morimoto, the Catholic aspect of Edwards needs to be acknowledged alongside the other elements of his thought. Moreover Edwards's theology hints at a possible reconciliation between the 'Protestant concern' that 'salvation is totally dependent on the sovereign activity of God' and rests on 'God's immediate and continual activity from above,' and the 'Catholic concern' that 'the transformative power of grace effectuates in human nature a real and qualitative change' so that 'regenerate persons enjoy an abiding reality of salvation within them.'[8]

While it is not clear to me that Roman Catholic writers directly influenced Jonathan Edwards, I share Morimoto's conviction that Edwards's theology represents a bridge between Protestant teachings on salvation, on the one hand, and Catholic or Orthodox modes of thought, on the other. What Morimoto calls the

'Catholic concern' is no extraneous addition to his theology, but is woven throughout his writings. In Edwards, the biblical and Calvinistic themes mesh closely with metaphysical and unitive images of God within humanity and humanity within God. In Edwards's first publication, the sermon 'God Glorified in Man's Dependence,' one finds clear expressions of both the 'Protestant concern' for dependence on God and the 'Catholic concern' for the abiding reality of salvation. Edwards speaks of the 'absolute and universal dependence of the redeemed on him [God],' and yet adds that the saints have 'spiritual excellency and joy by a kind of participation' and so are 'made partakers of God's holiness.'[9]

A. N. Williams identifies the defining features in the Orthodox teaching on divinization as follows:

> There is a firm core that distinguishes this doctrine from some other model of sanctification. First, we can safely say that where we find references to human participation in divine life, there we assuredly have a claim specifically of theosis. This kind of claim regarding participation in divine life is carefully to be distinguished, however, from the idea of divine indwelling in the human person. Both schemes of sanctification draw on the notion of union, but whereas the latter locates sanctification within the creature and *in via*, the former locates it at the level of the divine and insists on the inseparability of life *in via* and *in patria*. A second infallible marker of the doctrine, then, is the union of God and humanity, when this union is conceived as humanity's incorporation into God, rather than God's into humanity, and when conceived as the destiny of humanity generally rather than the extraordinary experience of the few.

In summary, Williams writes: 'Deification, then, focuses not on humanity, but on the God who invites humanity to share divine life.'[10] While Orthodoxy insists that creatures cannot share in the divine *essence*, the possibility of participation in the divine *nature* seems to be directly sanctioned in the New Testament: 'He has given us ... his precious and very great promises, so that through them you may ... become participants of the divine nature' (2 Peter 1: 4; New Revised Standard Version). This biblical text played a key role in the development of the doctrine of divinization in Eastern Christianity, and is frequently cited and commented on by Edwards as well.[11]

As I hope to show in this chapter, there is a wide area of overlap between Edwards's teaching on salvation and the Orthodox doctrine of divinization. To demonstrate this point, I will compare Edwards's writings with those of St Gregory Palamas (1296–1359), the definitive Orthodox writer on the subject of divinization. A further claim arises out of the parallels between Edwards and Palamas. I contend that Edwards and Palamas share a common Platonic or Neoplatonic philosophical heritage that they modified in analogous ways under the impact of their understanding of God's grace and the Christian experience of communion with God.[12] For Palamas, Neoplatonism was a part of his cultural environment, since he was educated in Constantinople in an era in which ancient Greek philosophy continued to be a living tradition.[13] For Edwards, Neoplatonism was mediated primarily by means of the seventeenth-century Cambridge Platonists, whose work has been called 'the first modern attempt to unite the essential spirit of Christianity with the essential spirit of Greek philosophy.'[14] Numbered among the Cambridge Platonists were Benjamin Whichcote (1609–83), Ralph Cudworth (1617–88), John Smith (1618–52) and Henry More (1614–87), of whom more will be said below.

To build my case, I will provide a brief sketch of some aspects of ancient and seventeenth-century English Neoplatonism, proceed to a point-by-point comparison of Edwards's texts with those of Palamas, and then examine Edwards's teaching on divinization more closely. At the conclusion of the chapter, I hope to show what bearing my discussion of Edwards and Palamas might have for an understanding of Orthodox–Reformed relations.

The Neoplatonic Background to Edwards

Edwards's teaching on divinization should be understood against the backdrop of Neoplatonism, and specifically the seventeenth-century Cambridge Platonists.[15] The English thinkers, beginning with their founding figure, Benjamin Whichcote, used and defended the term 'deification,' and made the idea central in their reflections.[16] John Smith captured the idea of divinization when he wrote that: 'God is the First Truth and Primitive Goodness: True Religion is a vigorous Efflux and Emanation of Both upon the Spirits of men, and therefore is called a participation of the divine Nature.'[17] Regarding the specific books that may have influenced Edwards, John Smith's *Select Discourses* (1660) and Ralph Cudworth's *True Intellectual System of the Universe* (1678) are both cited in his writings, and so he must have read these.[18] While it is hard to see any direct influence of Ralph Cudworth on Edwards, in John Smith's *Select Discourses* there are numerous passages that anticipate the later argument of Edwards's *End of Creation*.[19] Moreover, Edwards's notebooks make it clear that he read Henry More in his early years, and that he shared with him and the other Cambridge Platonists a deep aversion to materialistic philosophy. One of the very earliest entries into the 'Miscellanies' was directed against Thomas Hobbes: 'As we have shown and demonstrated (contrary to the opinion of Hobbes, that nothing is substance but matter) that no matter is substance but only God, who is a spirit.'[20] Edwards sought to turn the tables on materialistic philosophy with his assertion that 'spirit' is substance' and 'matter' is merely a 'shadow' in comparison. His idealism or immaterialism was an attempt to undermine the foundations of materialistic and mechanistic philosophy.[21]

Many Christian thinkers through the centuries have perceived an affinity between Neoplatonism and Christian teaching. Yet the Neoplatonic tradition carried conflicting tendencies in its way of conceiving the relationship of God and the world. Plato wrote that 'the framer of this universe of change was good, and what is good has no particle of envy in it; being therefore without envy he wished all things to be as like himself as possible.'[22] Thus there is a broad movement in Plato's thought toward some idea of divinization, so that the first principle seeks to make all other things 'like himself.' Yet, as Dockrill notes, 'often associated with this teaching is a doctrine of divine transcendence in which the governing principle of reality, the Good, is said to be so different from the realities it governs, that it cannot be accurately described in terms appropriate to mind at all.'[23] In the *Republic*, Socrates says that 'the Form of the Good' is 'the cause of knowledge and truth; and so, while you may think of it as an object of knowledge, you will do well to regard it as something beyond truth and knowledge.'[24] It is 'even beyond being, surpassing it in dignity and power.' Plotinus writes concerning the first principle: 'There is no name that suits it really. But, since name it we must, it may appropriately be called "one", on the understanding, however, that it is not a substance that possesses unity only as an attribute. So, the strictly nameless, it is difficult to know.'[25]

Some English Platonists, including Thomas Jackson (1579–1640), Robert Greville (1608–43) and Peter Sterry (1613–72), agreed with Plotinus in conceiving of 'the One' as transcending mind, thought and intellectual activity. On this point, the Cambridge Platonists Henry More and Ralph Cudworth dissented. Cudworth commented that he rejected this 'one *Peculiar Arcanum* of the *Platonick* and *Pythagorick* Theology.' For if the One transcends the realm of knowledge and intelligibility in all respects, then Neoplatonism becomes 'a certain kind of *Mysterious Atheism*.' The ultimate principle of all things would be as 'devoid of Mind and Understanding' as '*Sensless* [sic] *Matter*.'[26] Yet despite differences among the Neoplatonists, they showed a common tendency to assert God's metaphysical distance from the world, and this had ramifications for an understanding of religious experience.

Neoplatonists of all eras generally regarded the physical body as an impediment to soul. Henry More wrote that the '*Soul of every man … is his individual Person*,' and this means that 'the Body is not sensible of anything,' as was taught by the 'best sort of Philosophers.' Another author of the period, Henry Hallywell, commented that man has 'a double life within him, *Intellectual* and *Animal*, which the Sacred Writings call *Flesh* and *Spirit*.'[27] For Neoplatonists, it was the intellectual life, and not the animal, which formed the human point of contact with God. Henry More's account of bodily life laid emphasis on the soul's misery while in its terrestrial state. In the physical world, the soul is 'hoppled and fettered, clouded and obscured by her fatal residence in this prison of the Body,' and 'so deeply and muddily immersed into Matter, as to keep company with Beasts, by vitall union with gross flesh and bones.'[28] While denigrating the body, the English Neoplatonists extolled the soul and affirmed its spiritual and intellectual prerogatives. Henry More wrote that the soul is 'the *Image* of *God*, as the *Rays* of light are of the *Sun*.' More taught that the doctrine of the pre-existence of souls had 'plausible Reasons for it, and nothing considerable to be alleged against it.' Ralph Cudworth did not go quite so far in this respect, but said it was clear that God 'intended and designed' our souls 'for other *Bodies* and other *Regions*.'[29]

Dockrill observes that 'Orthodox Christian teaching is that the soul is a created entity; for Plato and Plotinus it belongs to the divine order.'[30] This disparity creates a theological tension within Platonized Christianity or Christianized Platonism. Among the critics of the Neoplatonists was Edward Stillingfleet (1635–99), who inveighed against those who thought of the soul as 'a Particle not of Matter, but of the Divine Nature it self, a little Deity in a Cottage, that stays here a-while, and returns to that upper Region from whence it came.'[31] For Christian thinkers, an inescapable issue posed by the Neoplatonic conception of God and the soul is that of nature and grace. Plato and Plotinus attributed far more to the human soul by nature than was taught in the Bible, namely, a divine or quasi-divine status. Yet in their stress on divine transcendence, Plato and Plotinus would seem to be denying to the soul what, according to Christian teaching, is possible in and through divine grace, namely, a direct participation in God. Furthermore, the Neoplatonic disparagement of the body would suggest that even if communion with God were somehow possible, this could only occur in and through the soul or reason, and not by means of the body and its affections. As will become evident, Edwards and Palamas modified the Neoplatonic tradition to accommodate the reality of a direct human participation in God that involved both soul and body.

Between Constantinople and Northampton: Comparing Palamas and Edwards

In Eastern Christianity, the doctrine of divinization is linked with a set of spiritual practices, devotional writings, monastic communities and intellectual arguments. Understanding the concept of divinization requires some attention to the larger social, institutional and intellectual contexts in which the concept developed.[32] The related term Hesychasm (Gk, *hesychia*, or 'quietness') refers to a tradition of prayer associated above all with the monks of Mount Athos. While the roots of this tradition extend back to the fourth and fifth century AD, and such writers as St Gregory of Nyssa, Evagrius Ponticus and Pseudo-Macarius, the focal point for the definition and defense of Hesychasm lies in the fourteenth-century debate between St Gregory Palamas (*c.* 1296–1359) and Barlaam of Calabria. The Hesychasts attached special importance to unceasing prayer, and to this end they advocated a particular bodily posture, with head bowed and eyes fixed on the place of the heart. The immediate aim of the Hesychasts was to achieve what they termed 'the union of the mind with the heart,' so that their prayer became the 'prayer of the heart.' This process involved a gradual refinement of a person's bodily faculties, so that they became spiritual in character. In time, such prayer led on to a visionary experience by which it became possible for select individuals, in this present life and with their bodily eyes, to see the divine light, which was taken to be identical with that light that surrounded Jesus at the moment of his Transfiguration. In the teaching of St Gregory Palamas, the light seen by Hesychasts was a manifestation of the 'energies' of God, which he took to be distinct from the divine 'essence,' and yet uncreated and eternal just like the 'essence.'

Beginning about 1337, a Greek living in Calabria, named Barlaam, attacked the practices of the Mount Athos monks as superstitious. He ridiculed the Hesychast claim to see the divine light with bodily eyes, and he argued that the distinction between the 'essence' and 'energies' of God impaired the divine unity and simplicity. St Gregory Palamas defended Hesychasm, and secured the acceptance of its key claims in the monks' *Hagioretic Tome* (1340–41), and the formal adoption of Hesychastic teaching in councils held at Constantinople in 1341, 1347 and 1351. Subsequently Hesychasm became an accepted part of Orthodox tradition. Palamas's major work is entitled *Triads in Defense of the Holy Hesychasts* (*c.* 1338). There he depicted human nature as an inseparable unity of body and soul, so that the bodily exercises of the Hesychasts as well as their claim to seeing the divine light with the bodily eyes could be considered as legitimate. Palamas argued that the essence of God remains unknowable and inaccessible to the human mind, while the uncreated energies – which are God himself – permeate all things and can be directly experienced by a person who has received deifying or divinizing grace.[33]

While some aspects of Palamas's teaching have nothing in common with Edwards's theology, there are a number of uncanny resemblances. Among them are the following, which will be discussed in the order mentioned: (1) a divine light that conforms human beings to God's character, together with optical language to describe spiritual experience; (2) an immediacy of contact and connection between God and humanity in the state of grace; (3) a concern to define the relationship between spiritual experience and the divine 'essence'; (4) a notion of unceasing spiritual development both in this life and the next; (5) an emphasis on the role of the body, and bodily affections, within the spiritual life; and (6) a teaching on divinization *per se*, that is, a human participation in the life of God.

Palamas describes the divine light in terms that are reminiscent of Edwards. He distinguishes 'knowledge about God and his doctrines' from 'the supernatural union with the more than resplendent light, which is the sole source of sure theology.'[34] The Transfiguration of Jesus involved a vision of uncreated light. 'That light is not a light apparent to the senses … thanks to another power which was not of the senses.' The vision occurred 'through a transformation of the activity of the senses, brought about in them by the Spirit.'[35] While the light on Mount Tabor (the Mount of Transfiguration) was 'from outside,' for the Hesychast it illumines 'from within.'[36] Palamas speaks of the vision of the divine light as a 'spiritual sensation,' and yet his discussion makes it clear that this 'sensation' is not to be identified with ordinary sense experience:

Though they have indeed seen, yet their organ of vision was, properly speaking, neither the senses nor the intellect … This is why their vision is not a sensation, since they do not receive it through the senses; nor is it intellection, since they do not find it through thought or the knowledge that comes thereby, but after the cessation of all mental activity.'[37]

Moreover, Palamas sees the divine light at Mount Tabor as an anticipation of future glory. 'The brilliance which blazed from the Saviour on the mountain is a prelude and a symbol of the glory of God which must be revealed in the future.'[38]

Edwards's teaching parallels that of Palamas. He uses the very term 'divine light' in the title of one of his best-known sermons. Moreover, the manner in which Edwards speaks of the divine light suggests that it is a particular mode of God's presence: 'There is no gift or benefit that is in itself so nearly related to the divine nature, there is nothing the creature receives that is so much of God, of his nature, so much a participation of the Deity: 'tis a kind of emanation of God's beauty, and is related to God as light is to the sun.'[39] The adjectives 'divine' and 'supernatural' in the phrase 'divine and supernatural light' also intimate that this 'light' is a direct manifestation of God. In many respects Edwards's 'divine light' recalls Palamas's 'divine energies.' Though logically distinct from God's essential being, it is not separable in practice or function. Edwards teaches that the divine light transforms the human self into conformity with itself: 'This light is such as effectually influences the inclination, and changes the nature of the soul. It assimilates the nature to the divine nature, and changes the soul into an image of the same glory that is beheld.' Edwards's sermon on the divine light makes reference to the Transfiguration of Jesus, and connects it with the coming Kingdom, in a fashion reminiscent of Palamas.[40]

Some of the Hesychast monks had visions of light that seemed to involve the physical senses, and Palamas both affirmed the operation of the physical senses in spiritual experience and yet insisted that the divine light transcended the physical senses. As already indicated, Palamas wrote that '[the] light is not a light apparent to the senses ... thanks to another power which was not of the senses,' and again, 'though they have indeed seen, yet their organ of vision was, properly speaking, neither the senses nor the intellect.' Similarly, Edwards writes of the divine light that, ''tis no impression upon the mind, as though one saw anything with the bodily eyes,' and yet he qualifies this by saying:

'Tis not intended that the natural faculties are not made use of in it [that is, the divine light]. The natural faculties are the subject of this light: and they are the subject in such a manner, that they are not merely passive, but active in it; the acts and exercises of man's understanding are concerned and made use of in it.[41]

So Palamas and Edwards not only share a teaching on the divine light, but an understanding of this light as something that both involves the natural faculties and yet transcends them. For Palamas and Edwards, faith in its very nature is a kind of vision, and this is true not only for a spiritual élite but for all genuine believers in Christ.

In his defense of the Hesychasts, Palamas insisted that human beings can enter into immediate contact or connection with God, and this was a key point in the debate with Barlaam. For Barlaam, as Meyendorff explains, the vision of God was only a 'created *habitus* and not a contact with the divine Being.' Barlaam posited an ultimately inscrutable and non-relational divine 'essence,' and, outside of that, a realm of created effects. On this assumption, no genuine communion of Creator and creatures was possible, and grace itself had to be construed as a kind of external effect caused by God.[42] Barlaam wrote that 'God is only known through the mediation of His creatures,'[43] and this meant that the knowledge of God was at second hand. Palamas by contrast stressed the immediacy of the human knowledge of God: 'God lets himself be seen face to face, and not through enigmas ... he unites himself to them to the extent of coming to dwell in his entirety in their entireties ... [and] the Spirit spreads in abundance over them.'[44] The purpose of the doctrine of the 'energies' was to provide a dogmatic basis for the Hesychast experience of direct and immediate communion with God.

Like Palamas, Edwards sought to uphold the immediacy of human communion with God. In the 'Divine Light' sermon, Edwards states that 'God is the author of all knowledge and understanding whatsoever,' and yet most forms of human knowledge are communicated through intermediary means. 'But this spiritual knowledge, spoken of in this text, is what God is the author of, and none else: he reveals it, and flesh and blood reveals it not. He imparts this knowledge immediately, not making use of any intermediate causes, as he does in other knowledge.' This statement is in effect an affirmation of Palamas's position and a rejection of Barlaam's. Edwards, like Palamas, affirms a knowledge that derives immediately from God and is not based on ordinary sense experience. Palamas describes the immediacy of God's presence primarily in terms of the divine 'energies,' and yet also sometimes in terms of the Holy Spirit. When not referring to this presence as a divine light, Edwards almost always speaks of the Spirit. For Edwards, the Spirit does not merely come alongside of believers, but is united to them in an especially intimate way: 'He [the Spirit] acts in the mind of a saint as an indwelling vital principle ... He unites himself with the mind of a saint, takes him for his temple, actuates and influences him as a new, supernatural principle of life and action.'[45]

One of the more interesting parallels between Palamas and Edwards relates to their teaching on the divine essence. Palamas's basic position is that 'the divine and deifying illumination and grace is not the essence but the energy of God.'[46] The essence of God and the energy of God are both uncreated, and yet the distinction between them does not involve complexity in God, since both belong to the one unique living God. Barlaam's objection was that the Hesychasts spoke as though they had a direct vision of, or communion with, the divine essence – something both he and Palamas held to be impossible. A fragmentary letter of Jonathan Edwards, published for the first time in 1989, embodies the same kind of objection and response.[47] Apparently Hesychast teaching and Edwards's *Religious Affections* were close enough to one another that they evoked the same objection, namely, that they were teaching that believers participate in the divine essence.

An unidentified clergyman was under the impression that Edwards's *Religious*

Affections taught that God communicated his very essence to the saints, and Edwards responded as follows:

> As to my saying that the Spirit of God in his saving operation communicates himself to the soul in his own proper nature, implying, as you suppose, God's communicating his essence. After all that is said, the objection is only about the use of language and propriety of expressions. It can't be anything else, for I have particularly explained my meaning and expressly declared what I do not mean, that by his proper nature I don't mean his essence; and have also declared particularly what I do mean, viz. that by the Spirit of God's communicating himself in his proper nature, I mean communicating something of his holiness ... A diamond or crystal that is held forth in the sun's beams may properly be said to have some of the sun's brightness communicated to it; for though it hasn't the same individual brightness with that which is inherent in the sun, and be immensely less in degree, yet it is something of the same nature.[48]

In the same context, Edwards discusses the term 'nature' at some length, and indicates that it carries a range of meanings, and need not be taken as synonymous with 'essence.'

Both Palamas and Edwards deny that believers participate in the divine essence,[49] and yet both speak of a direct and intimate communion with God. Palamas speaks of a sharing in the 'divine energy,' while Edwards writes that 'God communicates himself to the soul in his own proper nature.' Yet, as Ramsey summarizes the argument of Edwards's letter, 'his point is that God's power, light, and love have gone forth, not his essence,'[50] and this description seems to match in functional terms what Palamas had in mind when he spoke of the 'divine energy.'

Another area of concord between Palamas and Edwards is in their teaching on everlasting spiritual progress. In his *Triads*, Palamas posed the question: 'Will not the vision that the saints have of God develop infinitely in the age to be?' He answers his own question as follows:

> Clearly it will develop infinitely ... But we do not know and have never heard of anyone from the beginning of time who, having received this vision while on earth, has not desired a still more perfect vision ... since the grace already granted them gives them the power to receive greater vision ... how can the sons of the age to come not progress infinitely in this vision, acquiring grace after grace and joyfully ascending the ascent that never wearies? Thus, 'every perfect gift comes from above,' yet we never receive a gift that is most perfect, for the most perfect admits of no addition.[51]

This teaching was not unique to Palamas. Both Gregory Nyssa and Maximus Confessor taught that all created natures, even that of the angels, are susceptible to unceasing development in acquiring goodness.[52]

The conclusion to *End of Creation* is the most celebrated discussion of everlasting progress in Edwards's writings, but the idea crops up repeatedly in the 'Miscellanies' and in the sermons, and Paul Ramsey devoted an appendix to it in Edwards's *Ethical Writings*.[53] As early as 1730, Edward had written of the Church in heaven that 'much of their happiness has consisted in seeing the progressive wonderful doings of God with respect to his church here in this world.'[54] Because redemptive history progresses here on earth, Edwards reasoned that the Church in heaven must also progress as well, by means of a kind of 'beatific vision' of divine providence on earth. All creatures are changeable by nature, and while heaven 'is subject to no evil changes, yet 'tis subject to great changes and revolutions of a contrary nature ... 'Tis only God that is unchangeable. The whole universe consisting in upper and lower worlds is in a changing state.'[55] Palamas, as cited, wrote of the person who 'desired a still more perfect vision,' and this idea is prominent in Edwards's *Religious Affections*. It is characteristic of gracious experience, writes Edwards, that every new vision of God leads to a still greater desire for the vision of God.[56] Thus divinization in Edwards is a progressive reality, just as it is in the teaching of Palamas.

Yet another analogy between Palamas and Edwards lies in their respective teachings on the role of the affections and bodily exercises in the spiritual life. Unlike many of the Neoplatonic thinkers discussed above, Palamas did not typify the Christian life as that of a soul acting in independence of – or opposition to – the physical body. He writes: 'What pain or movement of the body is there, which is not shared by soul and body? ... There are blessed passions, activities common to soul and body, which do not attach the spirit to the flesh, but which draw up the flesh to a dignity nearer to that of the spirit, and make it turn toward the height.' The goal of the spiritual life is not the extinction of bodily desires but rather their correction and redirection by divine grace. 'Insensibility,' that is, dispassion toward temptation and evil, 'does not consist in making the passionate part die, but in moving it from evil to good, and in directing its very being toward divine things.' Palamas's opponent, Barlaam, adopted an opposing position on this point, and wrote that 'the fact of loving activities common to the passionate part of the soul and to the body, attaches the soul to the body and fills it with darkness.'[57]

Much like Palamas, Edwards in his *Religious Affections* argued that 'true religion' has a place for 'holy affections' and even 'in great part, consists in holy affections.'[58] He took issue with the anti-revivalists, like Charles Chauncy, who contended that the so-called revival of religion that Edwards defended was nothing but a 'Commotion in the Passions' among those who mistook 'the working of [their] own passion for divine communications.'[59] C. C. Goen writes that 'a veritable chasm separated Edwards and Chauncy with respect to the functions of "reason" and "passion" in religion.' In a manner reminiscent of Palamas's opponent Barlaam, Chauncy stressed that passion was an impediment to the spiritual life: 'Satan works upon the reason by the passion; the Spirit upon the passion by the reason.'[60] In Edwards's revival writings, he argued from scriptural texts that persons deeply affected by the Holy Spirit were sometimes so overcome as to exhibit bodily symptoms, such as falling to the ground. Bodily manifestations were therefore not a mark of religious inauthenticity. On the other hand, bodily manifestations also were not *ipso facto* a sign of the presence and work of the Holy Spirit.[61] While there were different issues at stake in the debates related to Greek Hesychasm and to the American 'Great Awakening,' the link between Palamas and Edwards lies in their understanding of the human self as body and soul together, and the spiritual life as an integrated experience involving the mind, will, affections or passions, and body.

Divinization in Edwards

Now we turn to consider divinization from two directions. First, in what ways does Edwards's discussion of human beings suggest that they become participants in the divine life? Second, how, in Edwards's view, does God incorporate human beings within the inner, divine life?

One way that humans share in divine life is through the knowledge of God. For Edwards, the human knowledge of God is part and parcel of his teaching on divinization. In one of Edwards's sermons on heaven, he notes that 'the Beatifical vision will be an act of love in God.' This act will involve the full participation of each person of the Trinity together along with each of the beatified saints, who

> enjoy God as *partaking* with Christ of his enjoy[ment] of God, for they are united with him and are Glorified and made happy in the enjoyment of God as his members ... They being in Christ shall *partake* of the love of God the Father to Christ, and as the Son knows the Father, so they shall *partake with him in his sight of God* as being as it were parts with him. As he is in the bosom of the Father, so are they in the bosom of the Father.

The saints share in intra-divine relationships within the Godhead in multiple ways. They '*partake* of the love of God the Father to Christ,' and yet also '*partake with him* [that is, Christ] *in his sight of God*.' Again Edwards writes: 'So we being members of the Son, are *partakers in our measure of the Father's love to the Son*.'[62] Thus the saints partake both in the Son's love of the Father and the Father's love of the Son. As Ramsey says: 'The participation is a partaking of the three persons' very own participation in one another within the divine life.'[63] What is true pre-eminently of saints in heaven is also true in a lesser degree of saints on earth. Their knowledge of God is also by means of a participation in God's inner life.

Paul Ramsey explains that, for Edwards, 'God's knowledge of himself is the only knowledge of God there is.' The creature knows God by sharing in God's self-knowledge. Ramsey continues:

> So if there is knowledge of God communicated to any human understanding, this is God's very own knowledge of himself, for that happens to be the only

knowledge of God there is in heaven or on earth. If there is any love to God enkindled in any human will, this must be God's own love spread abroad in human hearts. If there is in human affections any happiness, joy, and delight in God, this must be God's own felicity communicated by us.

The genitive expressions like 'love of God,' or 'knowledge of God,' can of course have two meanings – our love of God, or God's love for us. Yet according to Edwards these are 'but one and the same thing.'[64]

According to Edwards, human beings are incorporated into God's life through the power of the Holy Spirit. The Holy Spirit works in the saint differently than in others: 'He acts in the mind of a saint as an indwelling vital principle ... He unites himself with the mind of a saint, takes him for his temple, actuates and influences him as a new, supernatural principle of life and action.' Edwards speaks of the 'proper nature' of the Holy Spirit expressed in the thoughts and actions of the saints.

The Spirit of God, in acting in the soul of a godly man, exerts and communicates himself there in his own proper nature. Holiness is the proper nature of the Spirit of God. The Holy Spirit operates in the minds of the godly, by uniting himself to them, and living in them, and exerting his own nature in the exercise of their faculties.[65]

This in effect is divinization, seen from the human side. The life of the Holy Spirit is, so to speak, expanded to include the sanctified thoughts, affects and actions of the saints.[66]

In examining divinization from the divine side, the question becomes: how does God incorporate human beings within the inner, divine life? Edwards's briefer answer, puzzling as it seems, is that God draws creatures in by means of a pre-eminent self-regard. As early as 'The Mind' he wrote that God's 'love to the creature is ... according as they partake more or less of excellence and beauty ... that is, according as he communicates more or less of his Holy Spirit.'[67] What God loves in the creature is the creature's reflection of himself. In the argument of *End of Creation*, the reason that God's self-regard and his regard for creatures are not 'entirely distinct' is that the latter are, in some measure, an extension of God's own life and fullness.[68] So God's love for his own holiness and goodness is not separate from his love for the holiness and goodness of creatures, and we find again the logic of divinization, in which creatures become incorporated within the divine life.

Many statements in *End of Creation* imply that creatures enter into God's inner life. 'Elect creatures' are 'brought home to him, united with him, centering most perfectly in him, and as it were swallowed up in him: so that his respect to them finally coincides and becomes one and the same with respect to himself.'[69] Just before this quoted passage, Edwards cites John 17: 21, 23, a concise yet rich text on the mutual indwelling of God in Christ, Christ in God, believers in God, believers in Christ, and believers in one another: 'That they all may be *one*, as thou Father art in me, and I in thee, that they also may be one in us, I in them and thou in me, that they may be made perfect in *one*.' Edwards's theological reflections were often rooted in biblical exegesis, and his teaching on divinization closely follows this Johannine language of mutual indwelling (technically, perichoresis or circumincession).

In one of the most striking passages in *End of Creation*, Edwards states that God is not 'complete' apart from the world:

> This propensity in God to diffuse himself may be considered as a propensity to himself diffused, or to his own glory existing in its emanation ... Thus that nature in a tree, by which it puts forth buds, shoots out branches, and brings forth leaves and fruit, is a disposition that terminates in its own complete self. And so the disposition in the sun to shine, or abundantly to diffuse its fullness, warmth and brightness, is only a tendency to its own most glorious and complete state. So God looks on the communication of himself, and the emanation of infinite glory and good that are in himself to belong to the fullness and completeness of himself, as though he were not in his most complete and glorious state without it. Thus the church of Christ (toward whom and in whom are the emanations of his glory and communications of his fullness) is called the fullness of Christ: as though he were not in his complete state without her; as Adam was in a defective state without Eve.[70]

Here Edwards construes creation as an act that expands and enhances God's own being. Divinization is the category under which Edwards interprets God's work of creating – an event that both commences and terminates within God.[71]

Yet one more way in which God incorporates creatures into the inner divine life is through a kind of expanding family relationship, intimated already in the reference to Adam and Eve. In an early notebook entry Edwards wrote: 'God created the world for his Son, that he might prepare a spouse or bride for him to bestow his love upon; so that the mutual joys between this bride and bridegroom are the end of creation.'[72] Another entry speaks of Eve as a type of the Church, in which the Church is said to be the 'fullness or completeness' of Christ.[73] Edwards develops his theme of family relationship in a number of different images, and all these images reduce the chasm between the divine and the human realms:

> In heaven all shall be nearly related. They shall be nearly allied to God, the supreme object of their love; for they shall be his children. And all shall be nearly related to Christ; for he shall be the Head of the whole society, and husband of the whole church of saints. All together shall constitute his spouse, and they shall be related one to another as brethren. It will all be one society, yea, one family.[74]

Edwards speaks of the 'propriety' of God and the saints in heaven, citing Song of Songs 2: 16: 'My beloved is mine, and I am his,' and adding, 'in heaven all shall not only be related one to another, but they shall be each other's. The saints shall be

God's ... And on the other hand God shall be theirs.' In the final consummation 'Christ and the saints will have given themselves, the one to the other.'[75]

Reflections on Orthodox and Reformed Christianities

Edwards taught a doctrine of divinization. The only thing missing is the word itself, although, as shown above, Edwards employed a rich vocabulary of terms and phrases such as 'communication,' 'emanation,' 'participation,' 'partaking' and 'uniting' to describe the divine–human communion from either God's side or the creature's. Edwards referred to creatures as 'of,' 'in' and 'to' God, believers as 'swallowed up' in God, the Church as the 'fullness' or 'completeness' of Christ, and the world as God 'himself diffused' or the 'remanation' that reflects back God's 'emanation' in creating. Even more striking than these phrases are Edwards's frequent citations of 2 Peter 1: 4 – 'partakers of the divine nature' – which is the biblical *locus classicus* for the Orthodox teaching on divinization. Furthermore, Edwards in his letter to the unknown correspondent distinguishes God's 'essence' from God's 'nature' (or 'proper nature') and insists, as do Palamas and other Orthodox teachers, that salvation implies a sharing or participation in the 'nature' but not the 'essence' of God.

Edwards and Palamas concur in accepting religious experience as a starting point or basis for theological reflection. Edwards's teaching on divinization was rooted in his own experience of God and his observation of others' experiences, as attested by the 'Personal Narrative' and the writings on revivalism. Similarly, Palamas's theologizing was grounded in the religious experiences of the monks of Mount Athos, and it is helpful to remember that the work commonly known as *The Triads* was actually named *For the Defense of Those Who Practice Sacred Quietude* or *In Defense of the Holy Hesychasts* (Gk *hyper ton hieros hesychazonton*). Palamas wrote to defend the legitimacy of the religious experiences claimed by members of his own monastic community. Palamas and Edwards were both, on some level, personally engaged with divinization as a practice rather than simply as a theory. For Barlaam God was *inaccessible*. No direct relationship to God is possible in human experience. Yet for Palamas God was not so much inaccessible as *inexhaustible*. The experience of the Hesychasts was a genuine participation in God or the divine 'energies.' God is truly tasted, and though the taste is but a single swallow from the river of divine goodness, the taste is truly a taste nonetheless.

The openness to grace-filled experience in Palamas and Edwards forced them to refashion the Neoplatonic tradition. Far from being remote, God is truly known by human persons. In one sense, Palamas and Edwards uphold the Neoplatonic dictum that like is known by like. Yet, in another sense, Palamas and Edwards transformed Neoplatonism by laying emphasis on the priority of divine grace. It is not that we know God, but rather that God knows us, and so assimilates us to his own character. The Christian experience of divinization is not fundamentally an exercise in self-purification, as it tended to be among non-Christian Neoplatonists. Rather it is an ever-deepening and ultimately limitless process of receiving the divine light and being transformed by light and into light. The resplendent light of God is not merely for the reason or mind, but also affects the will, heart, affections and body. Every dimension and aspect of human nature receives the benefit and blessing of God's illuminating and divinizing grace.

While Palamas is not an end-all or be-all of the Orthodox tradition in theology, nor Edwards of the Reformed tradition, the parallels between these two thinkers on divinization suggest that the two traditions may not be as far apart in their understanding of salvation as is commonly assumed.[76] If one examines Orthodox–Reformed relations from the standpoint of creedal or confessional documents, the encounter between the two traditions appears to be an unhappy and unfruitful one, and generally less promising than that between the Orthodox and the Lutherans.[77] The defining moment was the career of Cyril Lucar (1572–1638), Archbishop of Constantinople, and the reaction to Cyril's Calvinistically influenced *Confessio Fidei* (1629). His views were condemned at synods held at Constantinople (1638, 1642), at Jassy (1642), and at Jerusalem (1672). The official statement issued in Jerusalem, under the Patriarch of Jerusalem, Dositheus, did not mince words:

> For the Calvinists … gratuitously indulging in wickedness, say that our Apostolic and Holy Church … thinketh concerning God and divine things as they themselves do wrongly think … And not only by their words, but also by their writings, do these heretics … endeavour to malign us.[78]

Particularly troubling to the Orthodox leaders and teachers was Cyril Lucar's teaching that

> the most good God … before the foundation of the world, predestinated unto glory those whom He hath chosen, without having in any wise regard to their works, and having, forsooth, no actuating cause for this election, except His good pleasure, the Divine mercy.[79]

The Fathers assembled at Jerusalem responded that those holding these views are 'maligners not only of men but of God Himself,' that 'God is not the author of evils, nor a respecter of persons, so as to love one, and hate another without cause; but desireth and willeth the salvation of all,' and that 'the thesis of free-will is certain.' Cyril's Orthodox opponents understood predestination as conditional, much like the seventeenth-century Dutch Arminians and eighteenth-century Wesleyans.[80] Cyril Lucar came to an unhappy end, executed by the Sultan after being accused of inciting the Cossacks against the Turks, and with him ended the effort to interpret the Orthodox tradition in terms of Reformed categories.

To see the possibilities for a mutually fruitful relationship between Orthodoxy and Reformed Christianity, one must move beyond the 1672 Synod of Jerusalem and its doctrinal antitheses to Calvinism on predestination and free will. Broadly speaking, the history of the creeds and confessions in modern Christendom is a story of increasing exclusivity. Especially since the sixteenth century, the churches have given formal expression to their faith in terms and concepts that are ever more specific to one theological tradition and ever more insulated from all others. A recent comparative study on Orthodoxy and heresy in four religions – Neo-Confucianism, Islam, Judaism and Christianity – found that all four religions exhibit what the author calls a 'progressive constriction of orthodoxy.' As various opinions compete over time, the general trend is toward 'the survival of the most exclusionary.'[81] This finding suggests that a new theological engagement between Orthodoxy and Reformed Christianity would do well to return to the creative thinkers within each tradition. The commonalities between Edwards and Palamas can serve as a stimulus for revisiting the question of Orthodox–Reformed relations.

Edwards's distinctive notion of God as a 'communicating' being, and his correlative conception of the creature's 'participation' in God, can be seen as a continuation of John Calvin's view of God as the source of all goodness to be found anywhere in the universe.[82] The God who acts in every action of every agent is not only powerful, but is also a God of infinite goodness, desiring to share himself with creatures. God is self-imparting by nature, according to Calvin. Alexandre Ganoczy notes that Calvin's discussions of God's grace are typically 'found in a Trinitarian context,' and he explains that 'the mystery of the activity of the triune God constitutes the comprehensive systematic framework of what Calvin says about God's will for salvation.' This indicates, says Ganoczy, that for Calvin 'the eternal community of the three persons with one another is the condition for the possibility of, and the creative support for, all the human community in Christ which constitutes the essence of the relationship of grace.'[83] This remarkable conclusion, coming from one of the world's leading Calvin scholars, suggests that trinitarian theology is integral and indispensable to Calvin's teaching on salvation. And it suggests that Calvin, together with Edwards and perhaps also Karl Barth, may represent a strand of Reformed theology that shares the Orthodox conception of Father, Son and Spirit as abundant in goodness and overflowing toward creatures in divinizing grace.

Notes

1. Pelikan writes: 'The definition of salvation as deification was not confined during this period – any more than it had been in earlier periods – to Eastern Orthodox theologians … Jonathan Edwards repeatedly quoted 2 Peter 1:4 to prove that "the grace which is in the hearts of the saints is of the same nature with the divine holiness," adding the proviso that this would be only "as much as 'tis possible for that holiness to be, which is infinitely less in degree"' (1989), *The Christian Tradition vol. 5: Christian Doctrine and Modern Culture*, Chicago: University of Chicago Press, p. 161.

2. Hodge, Charles (1873), *Systematic Theology*, 2 vols, New York: Scribner, Armstrong & Co., vol. 2, p. 219. Specifically Hodge is addressing Edwards's *Original Sin*, which he says makes 'God ... the only substance in the universe.'

3. Ramsey, Paul in Edwards, Jonathan (1989), *Ethical Writings, The Works of Jonathan Edwards Volume 8*, ed. Paul Ramsey, New Haven: Yale University Press, p. 633; for the passages cited by Edwards, Jonathan (1959), *Religious Affections, The Works of Jonathan Edwards Volume 2*, ed. John E. Smith, New Haven: Yale University Press, pp. 200–201, 343, 347.

4. Schafer, Thomas (1951), 'Jonathan Edwards and Justification By Faith,' *Church History* **20**, 56–63, citing Edwards, Jonathan (1830), 'Justification By Faith Alone,' in Dwight, Sereno (ed.), *The Works of President Edwards*, 10 vols, New York, 5: 354–5, 394ff, 370–74, 361, 364.

5. Schafer, 'Justification,' p. 60; citing Misc. 218.

6. Morimoto, Anri (1995), *Jonathan Edwards and the Catholic Vision of Salvation*, University Park: Pennsylvania State University Press, p. 2.

7. Morimoto, *Jonathan Edwards*, p. 8; see also Ramsey, 'Editor's Introduction,' in *Ethical Writings*, 59–60, n. 5, and Ramsey's 'Appendix IV: Infused Virtues in Edwardsean and Calvinistic Context,' in *Ethical Writings*, pp. 739–50.

8. Morimoto, *Jonathan Edwards*, pp. 7–8.

9. Edwards, Jonathan (1984 [1834]), 'God Glorified in Man's Dependence,' in Hickman, Edward (ed.), *The Works of President Edwards*, 2 vols, Edinburgh: Banner of Truth, 2: 3.

10. Williams, A. N. (1999), *The Ground of Union: Deification in Aquinas and Palamas*, New York: Oxford University Press, pp. 32, 36.

11. In *Charity and Its Fruits*, the first verse quoted after the statement of 'doctrine' is 2 Peter 1: 4, and so this text occupies a prominent place (*Ethical Writings*, p. 132). In the *Treatise on Grace*, Edwards cites the same biblical text and comments: 'Being made "partakers of the divine nature" is spoken of as the peculiar privilege of true saints.' See Edwards, Jonathan (1971), *Treatise on Grace and Other Posthumously Published Writings by Jonathan Edwards*, ed. Paul Helm, Cambridge: James Clarke, p. 28, cf. p. 72. In the 'Unpublished Letter on Assurance and Participation in the Divine Nature,' Edwards cites both 2 Peter 1: 4 and Hebrews 12: 10, which refers to believers as 'partakers of his [that is, God's] holiness' (*Ethical Writings*, pp. 639–40). Paul Ramsey, in an editorial note, indicates that Edwards is relying on 2 Peter 1: 4 in his distinctive use of the term 'nature,' as for example when he writes that the Spirit communicates his 'proper nature' to the saints (*Ethical Writings*, p. 133, n. 1).

12. I will generally use the rubric 'Neoplatonism' rather than 'Platonism' to emphasize the ways in which Plato was customarily read in light of Plotinus. Samuel Taylor Coleridge, in reference to the seventeenth-century English 'Platonists,' commented that that were not 'Platonists' but 'more truly Plotinists' (Patrides, C. A. (1970), ' "The High and Aiery Hills of Platonisme": An Introduction to the Cambridge Platonists,' in Patrides, C. A. ed., *The Cambridge Platonists*, Cambridge: Harvard University Press, p. 3; citing Brinkley, Roberta F., ed. (1955), *Coleridge on the Seventeenth Century*, Durham, North Carolina: Duke University Press, p. 366). In fact, the intellectual lineage involves more than Plato and Plotinus, since the 'Platonism' of seventeenth-century England was mostly filtered through the Florentine School of Marsilio Ficino and Pico della Mirandola.

13. To be sure, Plato and Plotinus were not the only philosophers known in fourteenth-century Constantinople, and we know that the young Gregory Palamas both read and excelled in the study of Aristotle's *Logics*. See John Meyendorff, 'Introduction,' in Palamas, Gregory (1983), *The Triads*, ed. John Meyendorff, trans. Nicholas Gendle, preface by Jaroslav Pelikan, New York: Paulist Press, p. 5. Yet Platonism, as John Peter Kenney has argued, was central to the evolution of philosophical monotheism in the pre-

modern world and 'dominated this process of conceptual articulation'. See Kenney, Peter (1991), *Mystical Monotheism: A Study in Ancient Platonic Theology*, Hanover: Brown University Press / University Press of New England, p. x.

14. John H. Muirhead, quoted in Pawson, G. P. H. (1930), *The Cambridge Platonists and Their Place in Religious Thought*, London: SPCK, p. 92; the original has redundant quotation marks before the work 'essential.'
15. On the Cambridge Platonists, see Cassirer, Ernst (1953), *The Platonic Renaissance in England*, trans. James E. Pettegrove, Austin: University of Texas Press; Dockrill, D. W. (1997), 'The Heritage of Patristic Platonism in Seventeenth Century English Philosophical Theology,' in Rogers, G. A. J., Vienne, J. M. and Zarka, Y. C. (eds), *The Cambridge Platonists in Philosophical Context*, Dordrecht: Kluwer Academic Publishers, pp. 55–77; Patrides, '"The High and Aiery Hills of Platonisme",' pp. 1–41; Pawson, *The Cambridge Platonists*; and Powicke, Frederick J. (1926), *The Cambridge Platonists: A Study*, Cambridge: Harvard University Press. Patricia Wilson-Kastner (1978), in 'God's Infinity and His Relationship to Creation in the Theologies of Gregory of Nyssa and Jonathan Edwards,' *Foundations* [American Baptist Historical Society] **21**, 305–21, discusses Gregory of Nyssa's *On the Soul and Resurrection* as a backdrop to Edwards's *End of Creation*, but admits that we have 'no reason to believe' that Edwards ever read Gregory of Nyssa (pp. 310–11), and ultimately falls back on the Cambridge Platonists as the connecting link between Edwards and early Christian thought (p. 317).
16. Patrides writes: 'The deification of man is one of the most thoroughly Greek ideas espoused by the Cambridge Platonists' ('Introduction,' in Patrides, ed., *Cambridge Platonists*, p. 19). When Benjamin Whichcote used the term 'deification,' he added: 'Do not stumble at the use of *the Word*. For, we have Authority for the use of it, in Scripture. *2 Pet. 1.4. Being made Partakers of the Divine Nature*; which is in effect our *Deification*' (in Patrides, ed., *Cambridge Platonists*, p. 70).
17. Patrides, ed., *Cambridge Platonists*, p. 148; citing Smith, John (1660), *Select Discourses* IX, 'The Excellency and Nobleness of True Religion.' Regarding divinization in seventeenth-century English thought, see the new study by Newey, Edmund (2002), 'Form of Reason: Participation in the Work of Richard Hooker, Benjamin Whichcote, Ralph Cudworth, and Jeremy Taylor,' *Modern Theology* **18**, 1–26.
18. Johnson, Thomas H. (1931), 'Jonathan Edwards's Background of Reading,' *Publications of the Colonial Society of Massachusetts*, **28**, pp. 193–222, esp. pp. 197, 207–8.
19. Consider the following passages from Smith, John (1979 [1660]), *Select Discourses*, introduction by C. A. Patrides, Delmar: Scholars' Facsimiles & Reprints. 'God does most *glorifie* and exalt himself in the most triumphant way that may be *ad extra* or out of himself ... when he most of all communicates himself ... And we then most of all *glorifie* him when we partake most of him' (p. 142). 'All true Happiness consists in a participation of God arising out of the assimilation and conformity of our souls to him' (p. 147). 'The Divinity could propound nothing to it self in the making of the World but the *Communication* of its own *Love* and *Goodness*' (p. 155).
20. Edwards, Jonathan (1994), *The 'Miscellanies', Nos a-500, The Works of Jonathan Edwards Volume 13*, ed. Thomas A. Schafer, New Haven: Yale University Press, p. 166 (Misc. f).
21. See the discussion in McClymond, Michael (1998), *Encounters with God, An Approach to the Theology of Jonathan Edwards*, Oxford: Oxford University Press, pp. 32–4.
22. Dockrill, 'Heritage,' p. 56.
23. Dockrill, 'Heritage,' p. 56; and citing Plato (1965), *The Timaeus*, trans. H.D.P. Lee, Harmondsworth: Penguin Books, 29e (p. 42).
24. Dockrill, 'Heritage,' p. 56; and citing Plato (1951), *The Republic*, trans. F. M. Cornford, Oxford: Clarendon Press, 508e, 509b (p. 215).

25. Dockrill, 'Heritage,' p. 56; and citing Plotinus (1964), *Enneads* 6.9.5, in *The Essential Plotinus*, trans. E. O'Brien, New York: New American Library, p. 80.
26. Dockrill, 'Heritage,' p. 58; citing Cudworth, Ralph (1678), *The True Intellectual System of the Universe*, London, pp. 584, 587.
27. Dockrill, 'Heritage,' p. 60; citing More, Henry (1660), *An Explanation of the Grand Mystery of Godliness* (London), p. 223, and Hallywell, Henry (1668), *Deus Justificatus*, London: W. Kettilby, p. 260.
28. Dockrill, 'Heritage,' p. 62; citing More, Henry (1659), *The Immortality of the Soul*, London: W. Morden, pp. 332, 309, 488, 330.
29. Dockrill, 'Heritage,' pp. 64, 67, 68; citing More, *An Explanation*, London, p. 22, Cudworth, *True Intellectual System*, p. 798, cf. pp. 43–4, 66; and More, Henry (1662), 'The Preface General,' and *Conjectura Cabbalistica*, in *A Collection of Several Philosophical Writings* 1: v, 2: 3.
30. Dockrill, 'Heritage,' p. 56.
31. Dockrill, 'Heritage,' p. 61; citing More, *Immortality of the Soul*, p. 500, and Stillingfleet, Edward (1709 [1662]), *Origines Sacrae*, London: H. & G. Mortlock, p. 263. Among the other critiques of the Cambridge Platonists were Samuel Parker's two-part work, *A Free and Impartial Censure of the Platonick Philosophie* and *An Account of the Nature and Extent of the Divine Dominion and Goodness* (1666), and Warren, Edward (1667), *No Praeexistence*.
32. There is an abridged English translation of Palamas's most important work, *The Triads*, in (1983), *The Triads*, ed. John Meyendorff, trans. Nicholas Gendle, preface by Jaroslav Pelikan. See also Lossky, Vladimir (1957), *The Mystical Theology of the Eastern Church*, London: James Clarke; Meyendorff, John (1998), *A Study of Gregory Palamas*, trans. George Lawrence, Crestwood: St Vladimir's Seminary Press; Williams, *Ground of Union*; and Mantzaridis, Georgios I. (1984), *The Deification of Man: St. Gregory Palamas and the Orthodox Tradition*, trans. Liadain Sherrard, Crestwood: St Vladimir's Seminary Press.
33. (1983), 'Gregory Palamas,' 'Hesychasm,' in F. L. Cross and E. A. Livingstone (eds), *The Oxford Dictionary of the Christian Church*, 2nd edn, Oxford: Oxford University Press, pp. 600, 644.
34. Meyendorff, *Study*, p. 120, citing Palamas, *Triads*, 1.3.15.
35. Meyendorff, *Study*, p. 173, citing Palamas, *Triads*, 1.3.28, 2.3.22.
36. Meyendorff, *Study*, p. 151, citing Palamas, *Triads*, 1.3.38.
37. Palamas, *The Triads*, ed. Meyendoff, 1.3.21 (p. 37), 1.3.17–18 (p. 35).
38. Meyendorff, *Study*, p. 196, citing Palamas, *Against Akindynos*, 5. 8.
39. Edwards, Jonathan (1995), 'A Divine and Supernatural Light, Immediately Imparted to the Soul by the Spirit of God, Shown to be Both a Scriptural and Rational Doctrine,' in *A Jonathan Edwards Reader*, eds John E. Smith, Harry S. Stout, and Kenneth P. Minkema, New Haven and London: Yale University Press, p. 121.
40. 'If Christ should now appear to anyone as he did on the Mount at his transfiguration; or if he should appear to the world in the glory that he now appears in in heaven, as he will do at the day of judgment; without doubt, the glory and majesty that he would appear in, would be such as would satisfy everyone, that he was a divine person' (Edwards, 'Divine Light,' in *Edwards Reader*, p. 119).
41. Ibid., pp. 109, 114.
42. Vladimir Lossky writes that Western theology sees 'grace' as 'an effect of the divine Cause, exactly as in the act of creation.' By contrast, Orthodoxy teaches that God's presence is not 'a causal one, such as the divine omnipotence in creation; no more is it a presence according to the very essence – which is by definition incommunicable.' Rather it is by 'deifying energies which the Holy Spirit communicates to us' (*The Mystical Theology of the Eastern Church*, pp. 86, 88).

43. Barlaam, in Palamas, *Triads*, 1.1, cited in Meyendorff, 'Introduction,' to Palamas, *Triads*, 12.
44. Meyendorff, *Study*, p. 213, citing Palamas, *Triads*, 3.1.29, cf. 2.3.36, 2.3.37. The word 'spirit' is not capitalized in Meyendorff's rendering of Palamas, but the context seems to require a capital letter.
45. Edwards, 'Divine Light,' pp. 106, 108–9.
46. Lossky, *Mystical Theology*, p. 70, citing Palamas, *Capita physica, theologica, moralia, et practica*, p. 69.
47. The letter is printed in Edwards, *Ethical Writings*, ed. Paul Ramsey, pp. 636–40, as 'Unpublished Letter on Assurance and Participation in the Divine Nature,' with an 'Introduction' by Paul Ramsey, pp. 631–5.
48. Ibid., pp. 638, 640. The statements that evoked the objection may be found in *Religious Affections*, pp. 201, 233, 236–7.
49. 'Not that the saints are made partakers of the essence of God, and so are "Godded" with God, and "Christed" with Christ, according to the abominable and blasphemous language and notions of some heretics.' Instead, they are 'made partakers of ... God's spiritual beauty and happiness, according to the measure and capacity of a creature'. *Religious Affections*, p. 203.
50. Ramsey, 'Introduction,' in *Ethical Writings*, p. 632.
51. Mantzaridis, *Deification*, pp. 124–5, citing Palamas, *Triads*, 2.2.11.
52. Lossky, *Mystical Theology*, p. 103.
53. Ramsey, 'Appendix III: Heaven is a Progressive State,' in *Ethical Writings*, pp. 706–38.
54. Edwards, Misc. 421; cited in Ramsey, 'Appendix III: Heaven is a Progressive State,' in *Ethical Writings*, p. 706.
55. Edwards, Misc. 940, cited in Ramsey, 'Appendix III: Heaven is a Progressive State,' in *Ethical Writings*, pp. 711–12.
56. 'Another great and very distinguishing difference between gracious affections and others is, that gracious affections, the higher they are raised, the more is a spiritual appetite and longing of soul after spiritual attainments, increased. On the contrary, false affections rest satisfied in themselves' (*Religious Affections*, pp. 376–83, citing p. 376).
57. Meyendorff, *Study*, pp. 143, 169, citing Palamas, *Triads*, 2.2.12, 2.2.19; Barlaam cited in Meyendorff, *Study*, p. 142.
58. Edwards, *Religious Affections*, p. 95.
59. Charles Chauncy, cited in Lambert, Frank (1999), *Inventing the 'Great Awakening'*, Princeton: Princeton University Press, pp. 190, 211.
60. C. C. Goen, 'Editor's Introduction,' in Edwards, Jonathan (1972), *The Great Awakening, The Works of Jonathan Edwards Volume 4*, ed. C. C. Goen, New Haven: Yale University Press, p. 83, and citing Chauncy, Charles (1743), *Seasonable Thoughts on the State of Religion in New England*, Boston, p. 111.
61. Edwards, *The Great Awakening*, pp. 233–4, 263–70, 303–6, 399–400, 533.
62. Ramsey, 'Appendix III,' in *Ethical Writings*, pp. 725, 736.
63. Ibid., p. 735.
64. Ramsey, 'Editor's Introduction,' in *Ethical Writings*, pp. 19–20.
65. Edwards, 'Divine Light,' in *Edwards Reader*, pp. 108–9.
66. In his introduction to the *Treatise on Grace*, Helm explains that Edwards thought that traditional theology did not do justice to the role of the Holy Spirit in salvation. If the role of the Spirit is merely to 'apply' the work achieved by the Son sent from the Father, then the Spirit's role is entirely a subordinate one. So Edwards suggests that 'the Holy Spirit is not the agent of application, He is what is given to the Church' (p. 7). The Spirit, as he writes in the *Treatise on Grace*, is 'the *summum* of all good ... the fulness of God' (p. 66).

67. Edwards, 'The Mind,' in (1980) *Scientific and Philosophical Writings, The Works of Jonathan Edwards Volume 6*, ed. Wallace E. Anderson, New Haven: Yale University Press, p. 364.

68. For a more thorough discussion of *End of Creation*, see McClymond, *Encounters*, pp. 50–64.

69. Edwards, *End of Creation*, in *Ethical Writings*, p. 443.

70. Edwards, *End of Creation*, in *Ethical Writings*, pp. 439–40. Ramsey notes that *pleroma* or 'fulness' or 'partaking of the divine nature' are the ideas that 'clinch the argument of *End of Creation*' ('Editor's Introduction,' in *Ethical Writings*, p. 70).

71. Many statements in *End of Creation* stress the continuity between the Creator and creatures. 'God's external glory is only the emanation of his internal glory' (p. 529). In discussing the image of the 'fountain,' he writes: 'The communication itself ... is something divine, something of God, something of his internal fullness; as the water in the stream is something of the fountain; and as the beams are of the sun' (p. 531).

72. Edwards, *Ethical Writings*, p. 460, n. 2, citing Misc. 271.

73. Edwards, *Ethical Writings*, p. 508, n. 6, citing Misc. 770.

74. Edwards, *Charity and Its Fruits, in Ethical Writings*, p. 380.

75. Ibid., pp. 380–81.

76. The sacraments and sacramental grace are key issues in any attempt at an Orthodox–Reformed rapprochement on soteriology, but the present essay cannot begin to address these questions.

77. In the 1570s there was an Orthodox–Lutheran exchange of letters, which, though broken off because the apparent disinterest of Jeremiah II, Patriarch of Constantinople, still involved substantive theological exchange. See Schaff, Philip (1877), *The Creeds of Christendom*, 3 vols, New York: Harper and Brothers, 1: 50–52; and the full discussion and translation of the letters in Mastrantonis, George (1982), *Augsburg and Constantinople: The Correspondence Between the Tuebingen Theologians and Patriarch Jeremiah II of Constantinople on the Augsburg Confession*, Brookline, MA: Holy Cross Orthodox Press. The recent Lutheran–Orthodox dialogue on salvation is embodied in John Meyendorff and Robert Tobias (eds), (1992), *Salvation in Christ: A Lutheran–Orthodox Dialogue*, Minneapolis: Augsburg Press.

78. (1969 [1899]), *The Acts and Decrees of the Synod of Jerusalem*, trans. with notes by J. N. W. B. Robertson, New York: AMS Press, pp. 10–11. As an appendix, this work includes 'The Eastern Confession of the Christian Faith' (pp. 185–215) by Cyril Lucar.

79. 'The Eastern Confession of the Christian Faith,' in *Acts and Decrees*, pp. 187–8.

80. *Acts and Decrees*, pp. 10–11. 'Since He foreknew the one would make a right use of their free-will, and the other a wrong, He predestinated the one, or condemned the other' (p. 114).

81. Henderson, John B. (1998), *The Construction of Orthodoxy and Heresy: Neo-Confucian, Islamic, Jewish, and Early Christian Patterns*, Albany, New York: State University of New York Press, pp. 47, 83. See my review of this book in (2000), *Journal of the American Academy of Religion* **68**, 182–5.

82. Calvin writes: 'Wherever you cast your eyes, there is no spot in the universe wherein you cannot discern at least some sparks of his glory' (1960), *Institutes of the Christian Religion*, 2 vols, ed. John T. McNeill, trans. Ford Lewis Battles; Philadelphia: Westminster, 1.5.1 (p. 52).

83. Ganoczy, Alexandre (1989), 'Observations on Calvin's Trinitarian Doctrine of Grace,' in McKee, Elsie Anne and Armstrong, Brian G. (eds), *Probing the Reformed Tradition; Historical Studies in Honor of Edward A. Dowey, Jr.*, Louisville, KY: Westminster John Knox, pp. 96–107, citing p. 96.

Index

actions
  regress of 34–5
acts of will 33, 41
Adam 51f. 56f.

aesthetics xiv, 122
affections 149f.
Agapeistic ethics 96
agency 35
Agent causation 37
Anderson, W. xi
annihilation 17
Anselm 116
Aquinas, T. 79, 192
archangels 19
Arianism 107
Arians of the Fourth Century 132
Aristotelianism 102
Aristotle 81, 133, 134
Arminian 17, 29–30 33, 36
Arminianism xii, 32
Atoms 102

Barlaam 153f.
Barth, K. 155
Baxter, R. 135
beauty 81, 83, 85, 87, 91
being
  general 5, 7, 85, 95
  simply considered 89, 94, 95
benevolence
  absolute 88
  of God 5, 18, 86
  to Being in general 4, 7, 88–9, 93,
    94, 95
  virtuous 90, 93
benevolent love 91
Berkeleian idealism 107

Berkeley, G 50
Boethius 30–1
Brown, J. H. 82

Calvin, J. 21, 155
Calvinism 79, 139
Calvinist 27, 32
Calvinist tradition 122
Cambridge Platonists xiv, 100, 105,
  142, 143
Carr, E.H. x
Catholicism 140f.
causation 39, 70
Charity and its Fruits, 140
Chauncy, C. 149
Christ
  excellency of 119
  human flesh of 102
Christian ethics 96
Christianity and other faiths 134f.
circularity 86f.
Clement of Alexandria xiv
compatibilism 40
  Lockean 36
complacent love 86
concrete individual 66
Condillac 45
conscience 131
consciousness 46f.
consent 84, 85, 91, 115
conservation 61, 71
  divine 9
  immediate 62
constitutent ontology 116
constraint 36
conversion 45,133
Cotton, J. 118
Creatio ex nihilo 53, 106

creation
    continuous 8–9, 54, 64, 67
    free 106
    human 41
    re-creation 64
creator 152
creaturely freedom 31
Crisp, O. xiii
Cudworth, R. 142f.

damned 29
death 3
decisions 37, 42
deificatio 141
deism 50, 58, 62, 101
Deists 105
delight 88
Descartes, R. 53–5, 63
desire 37–8
    predominant 38
    and decision 38, 40
determinism 28, 34, 35
devil 128, 129
Diderot, D. 45
Discourse on the Trinity 119, 120
dispositional ontology 99, 108
dispositions 104
    divine 106
divine
    beauty 121
    dynamism 109–110
    energies 146
    essence 147, 121
    eternity 30
    immediacy 50, 53
    light 146
    perfection 119
    simplicity 108
    sovereignty 31, 54
divinization 139, 144, 149, 150f.
Dockrill, D.W. 144

ecosystems 86
Edwards, T. 140
election 37
Emanation 108

End of Creation 142, 151f.
endurantism 51, 67–8
ethics of belief 82
Eusebius 127
evidence 32
excellency 115
existence
    degrees of 90
    maximal 115
existential quantifier 89–90

faith 140
faith and reason 45
fallibility 47
Fiering, N. 115
Filioque 103, 105
foreknowledge 30
Form of the Good 143
freedom 27, 36, 40, 90
Freedom of the Will 27f., 45, 70, 119
free will xii

Ganoczy, A. 155
Genidentity 56–7
Gettier E. 87
God
    as author 41
    as dispositional 107
    doctrine of 101
    glory of 15
    hatred of 24
    holiness of 13
    justice of 13
    knowledge of 14
    knowledge of himself 150
    love of 1, 14
    presence of 16
    pure activity of 104
    relationships of 23
    self-enlarging 107f.
    self-existence of 117
    sin against 3f, 11, 21–2
    sovereignty of 41
    unity of 115
    vision of 149
God the Son 105f.

Goen C.C. 149
grace 22
gratitude 88
greater good 7
Gregory Palamas 141, 144–5, 146, 148, 153,
Grotius H. 128

habit 99f.
Hallywell, H. 143
hatred of sin 17
heathen 133f.
    salvation of 130
hell xi-xii
Helm, P. xiii
Hesychasm 144, 145, 150
Hobbes, T. 142
Hodge, C. 139
Holmes. S.R. xiii
Holy Spirit 132, 151
Homoousion 105, 106
Hopkins, S. 45
human freedom 40
Hume, D. 100
Hutcheson, F. 82
Hypostases 105

identity xii, 45
if-clauses 39–40
    conditions of 48
    over time 8
immediacy 54–6
incarnation 132
inclination 33f.
indifference, liberty of 33
infinite punishment 3–4, 16, 18
intention 37
Islam 133

Johnson, S. 101
Justification 139–40
Justin Martyr 130

Kvanvig, J. xi–xii, 19f., 62, 63

Lactantius 122

laws of nature 72
Lee, S. xi, xiii, 61, 71–2, 75, 99f., 117
Lewis, David 51
Lewis, Delmas 57
libertarian action 29, 34
libertarian freedom 28, 33, 42, 58
Locke, J. 32, 45f, 49, 52, 99, 100, 101, 103
love
    of benevolence 85f.
    of complacence 85f.
Lucar, C. 154
Lucretius 102

McCann, H. xii
McClymond, M. xiv–xv
McDermott, G. xiv, 101
McGinn, C. 84f.
Malebranche, N. 50, 65, 66
Maximus Confessor 148
medieval theology 116
memory 46, 58
middle knowledge 31
Miller, P. ix, x, 101
mind
    beauty of 82
Miscellanies 71f., 128, 130
Molina, L. de 31
moment 51
moral necessity 35
moral responsibility 29
morality 5f.
More, H. 143
Morimoto, A. 140
Mothersill, M. 82

Nasar, S. 83
Nash, J. 83
Native Americans xiv
natural religion 131
Nature 148
Nature of True Virtue 4, 79f., 86, 92
Neoplatonism 141, 142, 153–4
Newman, J.H. xiv, 127f.
Newton, I. 99, 100f., 103
Newtonian physics x

Nichomachean Ethics 79f
numerical
  distinctness 52
  identity 56

obligations 6
occasionalism xiii, 64, 66, 67, 69, 73
omniscience 32
ontological kinds 19
Origen 102
original sin 49f., 51
Orthodox-Reformed relations 153f.
Orthodox tradition xiv, 140f.
Owen, J. 103

Paganism 134
partiality 24
parts 116
passion 149
Pauw A. P. xiv
perdurantism 51, 67, 68
perfect being 116
personal identity 47f., 52–3, 69
persons 19
physical beauty 122
physical laws 71, 73
Plantinga, A. xi
Plato 142, 144
Platonism 130
Plotinus 143f.
Princeton xi
Prisca Theologia 127f.
process thought 100
punishment 16
  infinite 3–4
  retributive 24
Puritanism 45, 103

quantification logic 90
Quinn, P. xiii, 9, 57, 64f.

Ramsey, P. 80, 94, 139, 149, 150
reason 149
Reformed Orthodoxy 109
Reformed scholasticism 118, 129
Reformed theology ix

Reformed tradition 154
  and Orthodoxy 153f.
Reformed truth 128
regeneration 130
Religious Affections ix, 149
remanation 153
reprobate 29
restraint 36
retribution 2
revelation 131
Romanticism 102

sacrifice 129
Schafer, T. xi, 139
self-determination 33f.
self-perpetuation 33f. 48
self-sustenance 9–10, 62f
Shea D. B. 122
Shoemaker, S. 48
simplicity xiv, 115
Sircello, G. 82
Smith, J. 142
Smith J.E. xi
soul 49
spontaneity 41
status principle 19–20
Stillingfleet, E. 144
sufficient reason 35

temporal parts 56
theism, classical 104f.
trinitarian grammar 105
Trinity xiv, 100, 117, 120, 134
Turretin, F. 118, 120

uncreated light 145
union of heart 84, 85, 91
unity, maximal 115

Van Inwagen, P. 55
Van Mastricht, P. 118
vice 15
virtue 4, 18, 81
  a disposition 92
  intellectual 83
  theory xiii

For Product Safety Concerns and Information please contact our EU
representative GPSR@taylorandfrancis.com Taylor & Francis Verlag GmbH
Kaufingerstraße 24, 80331 München, Germany

Printed and bound by CPI Group (UK) Ltd, Croydon, CR0 4YY
01/05/2025
01858342-0014

wicked, the 13, 17
will and desire 32
Williams A.N. 141
willings 42
Wolterstorff, N. 116, 123

Xenophon 134